B   BC 14364
Len
Rice, Christopher
Lenin : portrait of a professional
      revolutionary.

B   BC 14364
Len
Rice, Christopher
Lenin : portrait of a professional
      revolutionary.

Lenin

portrait of a professional revolutionary

Lenin

portrait of a professional revolutionary

Christopher Rice

CASSELL

For Melanie.
Thank you for all your help.

First published in the UK 1990 by Cassell Publishers Ltd,
Villiers House, 41/47 Strand, London WC2N 5JE

Copyright © 1990 Christopher Rice

Distributed in Australia by
Capricorn Link (Australia) Pty Ltd,
PO Box 665, Lane Cove, NSW 2066

British Library Cataloguing in Publication Data
Rice, Christopher
    Lenin: portrait of a professional revolutionary.
    1. Soviet Union. Lenin, V. I. (Vladimir Ilyich), 1870–1924
    I. Title
    947.0841092

ISBN 0–304–31814–0

Typeset by Nene Phototypesetters Ltd, Northampton

Printed and bound in Great Britain by Mackays of Chatham Ltd.

Picture acknowledgements

The publishers would like to thank the following for permission to reproduce their
pictures: Hulton Picture Company (1, 2, 14, 20, 21, 22, 23, 24, 25, 26, 32, 34, 37,
38, 39, 40, 41, 44, 45, 46); David King Collection (27); Private Collection (8, 9, 12,
16, 18, 19, 28, 30, 31, 33, 35, 36); Society for Cultural Relations with the USSR (3,
4, 5, 6, 7, 10, 11, 13, 15, 17, 29, 42, 43).

Contents

Lenin's family

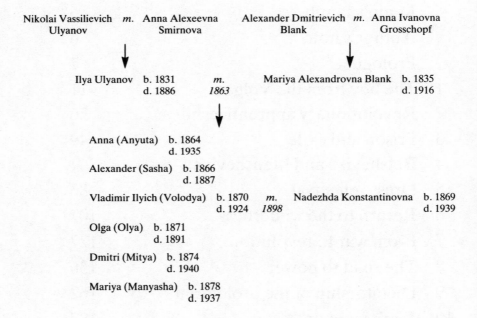

Nikolai Vassilievich *m.* Anna Alexeevna Alexander Dmitrievich *m.* Anna Ivanovna
Ulyanov   Smirnova   Blank   Grosschopf

Ilya Ulyanov b. 1831 *m.* Mariya Alexandrovna Blank b. 1835
    d. 1886 *1863*   d. 1916

Anna (Anyuta) b. 1864
     d. 1935

Alexander (Sasha) b. 1866
      d. 1887

Vladimir Ilyich (Volodya) b. 1870 *m.* Nadezhda Konstantinovna b. 1869
        d. 1924 *1898*   d. 1939

Olga (Olya) b. 1871
    d. 1891

Dmitri (Mitya) b. 1874
     d. 1940

Mariya (Manyasha) b. 1878
      d. 1937

Author's note

Dates are given according to the Western or Gregorian calendar, which in the nineteenth century was twelve and in the twentieth century thirteen days ahead of the Julian calendar, used in Russia until 1 February 1918.

Prologue[1]

There had been talk of recovery, of a possible return to work within months. 'Ilyich is on his feet again', the reports had said. 'He is steadily regaining his strength'. But now he was dead and, in the words of the nation's new leaders, Russia was fatherless. Vladimir Ilyich Ulyanov, known to the world as Lenin, was no more.

Even as the awesome news was tapped out on the telegraph, reaching the furthest outposts within 48 hours, a special commission, headed by J. V. Stalin and Grigori Zinoviev was already occupied with the funeral arrangements. Lenin had died at 6.50 p.m. on Monday 21 January 1924. At 11 o'clock the following morning the Head of State, Mikhail Kalinin, read, between sobs, an official statement to delegates of the eleventh All-Russian Congress of Soviets. Also at 11 a.m., a team of physicians led by Professor A. I. Abrikosov and the German, Otfrid Foerster, and accompanied by the Commissar for Health, N. A. Semashko, arrived at Lenin's Gorki retreat outside Moscow to conduct the *post mortem*; they completed their work later the same afternoon. A film crew was also on its way to Gorki to record the valedictory ceremonies.

By 9 p.m. on the 23rd, delegates from the Communist Party Central Committee, the Moscow party organization, the trade unions and the soviets began to assemble at the Paveletsky Station in the southern suburbs of the capital. About two hours later, 40 or 50 shadowy figures, shrouded in fur and astrakhan, filled the carriages of the special train. They passed the half-hour journey in silence, staring at the floor, each immersed in his own thoughts.

At Gorki an unusually bright moon gave the sky a bluish tinge and there was no wind, only intense cold. There were not enough sledges on hand so most of the mourners had to trudge the 4 miles (6 km) to the *dacha* on foot. From time to time the silence of the frozen forest was broken by the scraping of shovels as groups of peasants worked to clear the road. One of the delegates, Education Commissar Lunacharsky, fell behind, suffering from chest pains. He became lost and had to ask the way to the house. Eventually, he too came upon the elegant avenue of spruce trees which led directly to the Empire-style residence. Entering through the classical portico, Lunacharsky climbed the broad central staircase and was reunited with his comrades, spread out on chairs and sofas – even on the floor. At the appointed time they began to file into Lenin's room. The upper, visible part of the corpse had been dressed in a brown service jacket; the face, not contorted by illness as some had feared, bore a calm, somnolent expression. The hands rested on the chest, one clenched tight, the other relaxed, fingers slightly bent. From time to time Lenin's wife appeared at the doorway, exchanging a few words with people she knew well. Nadezhda Konstantinovna – Nadya, comrade-in-arms of 30 years standing – bore the heavy burden of her grief with exemplary calm and dignity.

The body was taken out of the house at about 10 a.m. the next day. The red coffin, protected from the elements of a tasselled curtain, rested on the shoulders of six old Bolsheviks: Kamenev, Zinoviev, Stalin, Bukharin, Bubnov and Krasin. A growing throng of peasants milled about the cortège and flanked the route to the station. More organized groups of workers and peasants gathered at train halts *en route* to Moscow. By the time the train reached the capital, a great crowd had formed at the Paveletsky terminus. Contingents of soldiers in green greatcoats, their distinctive pointed hats carrying the red star, formed a barrier between platform and station forecourt. An orchestra played the Chopin 'Funeral March'.

At about one o'clock, the long procession of dignitaries, preceded by members of Lenin's family, set out on the 5-mile (8-km) journey across the city to the House of Trade Unions, where the body was to lie in state. Red flags flapped vigorously from public buildings and black-trimmed sashes hung from windows overlooking the route. Banners proclaimed: 'Ilyich is dead but alive in the hearts of workers', 'The grave of Lenin is a cradle for the freedom of humanity'. The cortège was frequently hidden from view by gusts of swirling snow blowing aimlessly about the streets. As the procession crossed the bridge over the Moscow River, planes flew in formation overhead, scattering thousands of leaflets.

When the cortège finally arrived at the House of Trade Unions, the coffin was taken inside and placed on a dais in the splendid Hall of Columns, once a part of the Nobles' Club and later scene of Stalin's show trials. The light from the gleaming chandeliers was augmented by thousands of small electric lamps trained on the catafalque. Tropical palms formed a lush green canopy overhead, while the coffin itself was swathed in scarlet crêpe and surrounded by flowers and wreaths, forming a sea of red and white roses, narcissi, lilies, lilacs, azaleas, white and yellow chrysanthemums, oak, palm and laurel leaves, ivy and aster. The wreaths were wrapped in ribbons of black, red and gold. There were portraits of Lenin, plaques, hammers and sickles, arrangements of anchors and compasses, guns and cartridges – even motor parts. And, of course, messages of farewell: 'Sleep, dear Ilyich, your precepts will be steadfastly implemented', 'To our most loved leader, Ilyich', 'To V. I. Lenin, leader and liberator of the working class and the oppressed peoples of the East', 'To the leader of the world proletariat', 'You are dead but your teachings are immortal'.

The scene was filmed for posterity; then an official honour guard was posted and members of the public were allowed to pay their final respects. In the course of the next three days perhaps a million people filed past the bier. They came not only from Moscow but from all over the Soviet Union, many camping out in railway stations or in vacated army barracks. Doctors and ambulances were on hand for those who fainted while queuing in the freezing conditions.

On the day before the funeral, Saturday 26 January, the eleventh All-Union Congress of Soviets met to pay formal tribute to the dead leader. Kalinin, Zinoviev (head of the Leningrad party organization) and General Secretary Stalin were among those making speeches. There was one notable absentee: Leon Trotsky, hero of the civil war and, in some people's eyes, Lenin's natural successor. Trotsky was convalescing in the Caucasus at the time of Lenin's death. He would later allege that he had been deliberately misinformed about the date of the funeral.

Sunday 27 January 1924, 9 a.m.: Lenin's body is lifted from the catafalque in the Hall of Columns and carried on to the street. On this, the last journey, the pallbearers include party officials, members of the government, workers, peasants, delegates to the Congress of Soviets and trade-union officials. They are followed by Lenin's widow, his two sisters Anyuta and Manyasha, his brother Mitya and other relatives and close friends. The procession makes its way through Sverdlov Square, past the Historical Museum and into Red Square. Martial music can be heard throughout. The coffin is placed on a platform directly before a wooden mausoleum, hastily erected by the Kremlin wall. Military units file past with standards lowered. Gradually the square fills. There are no children present as the temperature has fallen to around −35°C (−31°F). The crowd tolerates an interminable succession of speakers; workers move among its ranks distributing biographies, portraits and leaflets. At 4 p.m. a message is transmitted to the people of the Soviet Union: 'Rise up comrades, Ilyich is being lowered into his grave.' Silence descends as Stalin, Kamenev, Zinoviev, Molotov, Bukharin, Tomsky, Dzerzhinsky and Rudzutak carry the coffin down a staircase into the vault. Above ground the square resounds to a salvo of rifle and artillery fire, followed by the concerted wail of sirens, hooters and whistles from factories and railway locomotives. As the pallbearers emerge, everyone breaks into the revolutionary hymn 'You fell in sacrifice'. Then official cars whisk the dignitaries off to the Kremlin, while the crowd slowly disperses.

A few days after the funeral, *Pravda* published a message from Lenin's widow:

> Comrades, workers and peasants, men and women – I have a great request to make. Do not let your grief for Ilyich spend itself in an outward honouring of his person. Do not raise monuments and palaces to his name. Do not organize splendid celebrations in his memory. In his life he attached little importance to such things. Such things oppressed him.[2]

It was too late. The funeral itself – and the attendant ceremonial – had taken place with a great deal more pomp and circumstance than Lenin would have wished. Much more shocking to many old Bolsheviks, however, was the decision to embalm the body in the manner of a religious relic and place it in a vulgar and ostentatious mausoleum. But the tide, part spontaneous, part generated, was now in full flood. The anniversary of Lenin's death was declared a national day of mourning. Petrograd, city of the Revolution, was renamed Leningrad and Lenin's birthplace became Ulyanovsk. Monuments to Lenin were erected in every major town and city. A Lenin Museum was projected; while his writings were not only collected and preserved as historical artefacts, but promulgated with the force of Holy Writ. Whatever their motive, the perpetrators could not have dealt a more calculated insult to his memory.

1

The boy from the Volga

Passengers crowded the deck rails as the river steamer approached the landing-stage. A man in his late thirties, full-bearded but already bald on top, was holding his little girl aloft to show her the view. His wife sat behind them, cradling her son in her arms; mercifully he had fallen asleep. The Ulyanovs had come from Nizhni-Novgorod, 250 miles (400 km) down river. They had grown fond of the old town and were sorry to leave it behind, but Ilya's promotion had decided the matter for them.

The view from the steamer was a gift for any landscape painter. The slopes rose steeply above the banks of the majestic Volga River to a height of more than 300 ft (90 m). Sandy, yellowish stretches merged with lush, green gardens and hazily outlined forest. Houses, some built of stone, some of wood, clung precariously to the hillsides, each with its own arrangement of balconies, mezzanines and belvederes, arbours and orchards; perched high above, the whitened outline of the town itself, seeking its reflection in the shimmering waters beneath.

If nature had painted Simbirsk in terms of broken contours and untidy splashes of colour, its inhabitants replied with a design based on order, conformity and precise social division. Down along the river bank, in the vicinity of the landing-stage, where peasants in bast shoes, greasy surcoats and hats resembling inverted plant pots manned the barges, was the slum quarter, a shambles of shacks and huts, its alley-ways reeking with the stench of putrefying fish heads and offal. On the higher slopes were the homes of merchants – expansive, vulgar, showy. Along the summit, flanking the town itself, were two districts known as the New Crown and the Old Crown. The former, protected by high walls and shrouded in trees, was the gentry quarter. Its privileged residents emerged on sunny afternoons to stroll along the promenade and take in the view. The Old Crown, on the other hand, though perfectly respectable, was the ugly sister: dusty, undistinguished and dull; home to junior Civil Servants, clerks and superior tradesmen. It was to this part of town, more precisely to a house on Streletskaya Street, that the Ulyanov family was heading on that September day in 1869. And it was here, seven months later, on 22 April 1870, that Mariya Alexandrovna Ulyanov gave birth to her third child, Vladimir Ilyich (Volodya).

Mariya was the daughter of Alexander Dmitrievich Blank, a physician of German or possibly Jewish stock who graduated in Petersburg before going on to practise in a number of provincial towns, including Riga, Perm and Smolensk. Blank's wife, Anna Ivanovna Grosschopf, was indisputably German. Her father, Johann Grosschopf, was a prosperous and cultivated merchant from Lübeck who emigrated to Petersburg in 1790. He married the daughter of a Swedish goldsmith from Uppsala. On Grosschopf's death, some of his not inconsiderable wealth was inherited first by his daughter and then, on her early death, by Dr Blank, who used the money to purchase an estate of about 1,000 acres (400 hectares) near the village of Kokushkino, about 30 miles (48 km) from the Volga city of Kazan. He retired there at the rather early age of 45. Mariya Blank, together with her brother and four sisters, was brought up strictly by Blank's German-speaking sister-in-law, Katerina Ivanovna Essen.

Dr Blank was a man of strong, uncompromising views which sometimes bordered on the eccentric. No tea or coffee was allowed in the house and the children were obliged to drink cold water (Blank had written a booklet on the beneficial effects of water on the system). Their diet was carefully controlled. They were permitted to wear only light clothing – even in winter – and were forced to endure cold compresses. Fortunately, there was a more conventional side to the Blank regimen. All the children received a good education. Mariya learned English and French from a tutor (German and Russian were spoken at home). She was an accomplished pianist and was thoroughly versed in Russian and foreign literature. Presumably, she also picked up some scientific knowledge from her father.

The family background of the Ulyanovs was quite different. Lenin's paternal grandfather, Nikolai Vassilievich Ulyanov, was a former serf of possibly Kalmyk or Tatar descent. The Kalmyks were semi-nomadic tribesmen from the shores of the Caspian Sea. They were Buddhists and spoke a Mongolian dialect. The Tatars came from an area of the Middle Volga around Kazan which remained independent from Russia until it was annexed by Ivan IV in 1552. They were descendants of the Mongol Golden Horde which, under Genghis Khan and his successors, had swept across Russia from Asia during the thirteenth century.

Whatever the racial origins of Nikolai Ulyanov – and he may after all have been Russian – it is known that he married an illiterate Kalmyk girl, many years his junior, called Anna Alexeevna Smirnova. They had four children, of whom the youngest, Ilya, was Lenin's future father. By the time he was 70, in 1835, Nikolai had scrimped together enough money to buy a small house in a poor quarter of Astrakhan, where he worked as a tailor. Acquiring this modest piece of property gave him the right to be registered as 'townsman' (*meshchanin*) rather than 'serf', but this made little difference to the family which was left destitute when he died several years later.

At that time, Nikolai's youngest son was still a small boy of 6 or 7 and had it not been for his teenage brother, Vassili, who took him under his wing and saved enough money to pay for his education, Ilya's future would have been very different. As it was, academic success snatched him from the clutches of grinding poverty. In 1850 he was awarded the silver medal on leaving Astrakhan secondary school and, exceptionally for a person of humble birth, was eventually admitted to the University of Kazan, where he enrolled in the faculty of mathematics and physics. His application for a scholarship, however, was rejected.

The former head of Ilya's chosen faculty at Kazan was the great mathematician, N. I. Lobachevsky, who had only recently retired. When Ilya graduated – with distinction – in 1854, Lobachevsky supported his appointment as senior master in maths and physics at the Penza Institute for the Nobility (the local high school). Ilya also took charge of the meteorological office – for no additional remuneration.

A little to the west of Simbirsk and the broad sweep of the Volga River, Penza was the epitomy of dull provincialism. The school too was undistinguished. But Ilya was much too conscientious and determined to succumb to the prevailing torpor and his work was praised by visiting inspectors on more than one occasion. And he was to have a more powerful reason for looking back on his stay in Penza with satisfaction. One day, a friend of his, I. D. Veretennikov, introduced him to his sister-in-law, Mariya Blank. They fell in love and were married in the summer of 1863. Ilya was then 32, Mariya 28.

Later the same year, Ilya obtained a new teaching post in Nizhni-Novgorod. A much more congenial place to live than Penza, Nizhni stood at the confluence of the Volga and Oka Rivers. Contemporary photographs reveal a town vibrant with mercantile activity: river traffic cluttered every available jetty; masts poked up from every angle; the quaysides were awash with the catches of fishermen – quantities of sturgeon and sterlet wriggling and twisting on boards or slithering around the rims of wheelbarrows before being swept into huge vats to be processed. The waterfront was the domain of workers in well-worn peaked caps, smocks and thigh boots, women in brightly coloured scarves and broad aprons, leathery-skinned peasants cadging a few copecks 'for tea' and, of course, the Volga boatmen, squatting on crates and boxes waiting to depart with the next consignment of timber, furs and leather.

Nizhni was also a town of historic interest and beauty, of gleaming cupolas and onion domes. The massive bastions and walls of the old kremlin still dominated the medieval quarter, little more than a stone's throw from Ilya's school on Tikhonovskaya Street. There were elegant hotels and restaurants, a sprinkling of modish shops and a theatre. The annual fair was the largest in Russia. The Ulyanovs were undoubtedly happy here and enjoyed a full social life. They stayed six years before, again, promotion intervened.

This time, Ilya had been appointed inspector of primary schools for the district of Simbirsk; five years later he was to receive one more promotion, to Director of Public Schools for Simbirsk Province. The post of director brought with it the Civil Service rank of Actual State Councillor, the equivalent of major-general in the army. Ilya was also awarded the Order of St Vladimir and raised to the status of hereditary nobleman. People now addressed him as 'Your Excellency'. It was the summit of his career.

Simbirsk was a vast region bordering three other provinces and incorporating a lengthy stretch of the Volga's west bank. There were the children of a million peasants to educate but Ilya soon discovered that many of the 'schools' existed only on paper, while even those with more substance fell well short of the required standard. Many buildings were unsuitable for one reason or another; there was no concept of regular attendance or of a fixed curriculum and the majority of teachers were either ignorant or demoralized, or both. In short, the task confronting Ilya at the time of his second son's birth was enormous.

When the Ulyanovs first moved to Simbirsk, they rented part of a large, two-storey house overlooking a gaol. Over the next few years they moved several times, settling permanently into more comfortable premises in Moscow Street in 1878. By this time the Ulyanov household had grown. Anna (Anyuta, born 1864), Alexander (Sasha, born 1866) and Volodya had been joined by Olga (Olya, born 1871), Dmitri (Mitya, born 1874) and Mariya (Manyasha, born 1878).

The house in Moscow Street was spacious. The ground floor of the long wooden structure included a study for Ilya, a dining-room, a living-room and a kitchen; upstairs were the children's bedrooms, with windows overlooking the yard. Volodya's room was next to Sasha's, while Anyuta and the younger children occupied the other end of the building; a balcony linking all the rooms was opened up in the summer. To the rear of the house was an extensive garden, the preserve of Mariya Alexandrovna. It was planted with cherry and apple trees, raspberry bushes and strawberry rows. There were flowers in profusion. The summer-house at the far end was a favourite family retreat.

Inside the house, order prevailed. The tea-table was never without a fresh white cloth. The mahogany furniture was kept well dusted and every- thing – grand piano, crystal mirrors, candelabras, palms and aspidistras – was spotlessly clean. A peasant woman, Varvara Sarabatova, helped Mariya with the housework and the children.

Mariya was the dominant figure at home, if only because her husband was frequently away on tours of inspection. The burdens imposed on her were considerable but she was quite equal to them. A quiet but strong- willed woman, she was loved and respected by her children: 'She had her children's love and obedience . . . she never raised her voice and almost never resorted to punishment.' Something of an introvert, Mariya disliked formal social gatherings and seems to have made few friends in Simbirsk (a notoriously conservative, not to say small-minded community), but if she was bored or restless, she kept these feelings to herself. She remains an enigmatic figure; one feels that there are hidden reaches of her life and personality which have successfully evaded the prying eyes of the biographer.

Ilya is rather more accessible. Industrious, energetic, enthusiastic – he was a man with a strong sense of duty and purpose. Conventional in many respects – sincerely religious, a firm upholder of tsarism and a believer in evolutionary political development – he was also kind, generous and humane, and much more open-minded and tolerant than many Civil Servants of his rank and generation. When at home, Ilya was accessible to his children, playing chess and other games with them, taking them fishing and so on. At the same time, he was a hard taskmaster. Strict silence was observed during homework time and a special daily reading hour was assigned. Offenders were dispatched to Ilya's study – specifically to the 'black armchair' – for a spell of silent reflection. Once young Volodya fell asleep there. There is, though, no mention of corporal punishment ever being administered.

Were there disagreements between husband and wife? It would be unusual if there were not. However, at this point a wall of silence descends in the memoir literature. The parents of Vladimir Ilyich Lenin must be seen to serve as perfect role models for young communists. Certainly, there is no evidence that the couple were not happy in each other's company, but there were sources of incompatibility which may have surfaced from time to time. The Ulyanovs were from sharply contrasting social backgrounds. Ilya was much less quiet, less retiring than his wife. He professed strong political views and was quick to enunciate them, whereas virtually nothing is known of Mariya's opinions on the subject. They differed seriously on religion. Ilya was a loyal son of the Orthodox Church and attended regularly. His children too were baptized into the Orthodox faith (Volodya's baptismal certificate, issued by the little church of St Nicholas in Simbirsk is still extant). Mariya went occasionally to church, sometimes to Orthodox, sometimes to Lutheran services but for her, observance was largely perfunctory. Her indifference may have contributed to her children's subsequent abandonment of the faith. (Sasha announced his defection during his father's lifetime; Volodya followed suit at the age of 16, probably shortly after Ilya's death). Religion is usually a sensitive issue within families and there may have been arguments on the subject.

On a more trivial level, one might speculate that Ilya's regular and some-times prolonged absences may have required some adjustment on Mariya's part and it would not be surprising if there was occasional friction as her husband attempted to settle back into the well-oiled domestic routine.

A child of angelic, almost cloying sweetness, his roundish face graced by rings of fair, curly hair sits contentedly in the company of a younger sister. The child is Volodya Ulyanov, captured by the camera at the age of 4. Colour photography would have revealed hazel eyes and hair of a reddish hue. But film can be a discreet medium; in this instance it conceals young Volodya's reputation for noise and boisterousness and the fact that his physical appearance caused merriment among the younger members of the household on account of his large head, which seemed disproportionate to his short trunk and legs. Perhaps this explains why Volodya was slow to walk.

A destructive streak soon manifested itself. Whenever Volodya was given a toy, he immediately began taking it apart. One of his sisters recalls an occasion when his nurse gave him a present of a papier-mâché troika, complete with horses, and he disappeared: 'We began to look for him and found him behind a door. He stood there in deep concentration, twisting the legs of the horses until one by one they came off.'[3]

The Ulyanov children tended to pair off according to their ages. Volodya was closest to Olya who was just a year his junior. He liked to boss her about and their noisy games usually ended with Olya being chased under the table. All the children were fond of Volodya and he of them, but it was his elder brother, Sasha, whom he most admired:

> Whatever Vladimir was asked – what game he wanted to play, whether he would go for a walk, or wanted milk or butter with his porridge – he would invariably look at Sasha before answering. The latter would purposely take his time and look at his brother, a twinkle in his eyes. 'I'll do as Sasha does.'[4]

Yet despite the adulation, the two never became close. Sibling rivalry was undoubtedly part of the explanation and was probably exacerbated by Volodya's extremely competitive nature. Perhaps the disparity in age (four years) contributed to the distancing between them. Temperamentally they were poles apart. Though both brothers were studious, Sasha was drawn to the natural sciences, especially to biology. He liked nothing better than exploring the waters of the neighbouring Sviaga River in search of specimens. Such amusements left Volodya cold and he never accompanied his brother on these nature-study trips. Nor was he interested in the laboratory which his brother had set up in one of the outbuildings. While Sasha was quiet, thoughtful and reserved, much like his mother, Volodya was exuberant, outgoing and inclined to mischief. He had a cruel streak, not apparent in his brother, and he was quick to notice weaknesses and comic traits in others. On one occasion his brother Mitya was being read a story which frightened him. Volodya waited for the words 'and the bad wolves ate the little goat' before making a fierce grimace calculated to provoke tears. Of course, this is hardly exceptional behaviour and it was

not long before he was teaching Mitya to swim so that he could join in the
high jinks along the river bank.

Volodya loved the outdoors with a passion and was a first-rate sports-
man. Childish games like hide-and-seek soon gave way to tree-climbing
and swimming in the summer, toboganning and skating in winter. Croquet
was popular with the whole family and he was among its most enthusiastic
advocates. He liked indoor games too. His father taught him to play chess
with wooden pieces he had carved himself; subsequently, to Ilya's amusement, Volodya learned to beat him and took to playing Sasha instead. The
two spent hours together in this cerebral pastime, huddled over the board
with the menace and determination of sumo wrestlers; both became
formidable players.

In the Ulyanov household, of course, recreation always took second
place to study. Volodya was taught by his mother at home before starting
school formally at the age of nine and a half. By then he was able to read
and write, knew some arithmetic and probably a little French and German
as well. He had also learned to play the piano, though he soon lost interest
and eventually gave up. Volodya had a great deal of perserverance, but he
was not accustomed to drawing on it. From his first day he excelled at
school, consistently and in all subjects. '*Otlichno*' (excellent), was un-
erringly applied to everything he did. Breezing through the house at the
end of each day, he would call out his marks as he passed his father's study:
'Greek – five' [top marks], German – five, Latin – five, Algebra – five . . .'.
His sister Anyuta recalled:

> I can still see the scene clearly: I am sitting in father's study and I catch
> the contented smile which father and mother exchange as their eyes
> follow the bulky little figure in uniform, with the reddish hair sticking out
> from under the school cap.[5]

Always first to finish his homework, the ease with which he coasted
through school actually caused his parents some concern. Would it not
have a detrimental effect on his character, they wondered. Yet there is
precious little evidence of bad behaviour at school – a single episode
involving the ribbing of a French master appears in the memoirs. All in all,
young Ulyanov's record was as near perfect as one could wish. He was the
boy for whom everyone waited each morning to help them complete their
homework – he was even obliging enough to arrive early for precisely that
purpose. When he was in his teens he took on one or two pupils of his own.
He coached his elder sister in Latin, his favourite subject. He also gave
private tuition to a member of the Chuvash minority who was hoping to
qualify as a teacher. He passed – in record time and without having to pay
Volodya a copeck. Ilya's educational philosophy was encapsulated in this
generous gesture; how he must have glowed with pride at his son's example.

Like most gentry families, every summer the Ulyanovs put up the shutters in Moscow Street and made for their country estate near Kokushkino,

the property acquired by Mariya Alexandrovna's father many years previously. They shared their holidays with their Veretennikov cousins. Mariya's enthusiasm for the place was infectious and the children waited for the annual moment of departure with bated breath. Their love for the place did not diminish with their advancing years.

The journey took more than a day. The river steamer went as far as Kazan, where the family stayed overnight with an aunt before completing the trip on horseback. The Kokushkino estate consisted of a manor house and a large outbuilding surrounded by a garden, a pond and extensive grounds. It was situated near the River Ushna. The setting was idyllic. For young Volodya, Kokushkino was synonymous with the outdoor life. Besides fishing, swimming, climbing and hiking there were picnics and expeditions of various kinds. If the weather was poor, there was always chess or billiards to fall back on. As childhood gave way to adolescence, he could be found sprawled on the lawn, absent-mindedly chewing sunflower seeds while immersed in a book – Turgenev perhaps: an author he had come to know almost by heart.

But unaccustomed storm clouds were threatening the peaceful tranquility of the Ulyanov household. On an otherwise unexceptional day in 1884, when Volodya was 14, his father received a piece of devastating news: he was informed that he would be retired from the Civil Service within 12 months, several years earlier than he might have expected.

The decision reflected a major shift in government policy. Hitherto, Ilya had benefited from the reforming policies of Tsar Alexander II, introduced back in the 1860s. These amounted to a cautious but fundamental strategy aimed at modernizing Russia to enable her to compete more effectively with her European rivals. The corner-stone of the reforming programme was the decision to emancipate the serfs in 1861, but the judiciary, the army, local government and education were all affected. The statute on elementary schools (1864) gave the newly created *zemstvos* (elected local councils dominated by the gentry) powers to establish primary schools throughout Russia. These were a great improvement on the existing parish schools. Ilya Ulyanov was as successful as anyone in implementing the new policy. In the course of 15 years he founded more than 450 new schools in Simbirsk Province, introduced a proper curriculum and organized the training of local teachers, including those from the Chuvash and Mordov minorities.

Despite the scope of Alexander's reforms, however, large sections of society remained dissatisfied. The major focus of their discontent was the failure of the administration to move away sufficiently from autocracy towards constitutional government. At the same time, opposition group-ings were assisted by a more relaxed attitude to censorship. Radicals like Alexander Herzen, who published the journal *Kolokol* (*The Bell*) abroad and Nikolai Chernyshevsky, who wrote for *Sovremennik* (*The Contempor-*

ary) aroused the wrath of the government – Chernyshevsky was eventually arrested and imprisoned. Alexander's advisers were particularly concerned about the impact such thinkers were having on the nation's students, some of whom favoured revolution rather than piecemeal reform. These anxieties were exacerbated in 1863 when rebellion broke out in Russian Poland. The final straw came three years later when an unbalanced student, Dmitri Karakozov, fired several shots at Alexander II. Karakozov failed to find the target but his attempt was enough to set alarm bells ringing furiously in official circles.

Thus the tide of reform was already on the ebb by the time Ilya Ulyanov arrived in Simbirsk in 1869. Fortunately for him, the government's anxieties remained focused on the universities and he was able to continue his work largely unimpeded for another decade. Then, on 12 March 1881, Alexander II was assassinated in Petersburg by members of the People's Freedom terrorist faction. Ilya Ulyanov was as shocked and angered by the news as most Russians and he underlined his loyalty by attending the memorial service in the local cathedral dressed in his blue Civil Servant's uniform. He also gave his family the benefit of his views on the Tsar's assassins in no uncertain terms. Ilya may have sensed that Alexander's death would herald a return to the stifling repression which had darkened the reign of his predecessor, Nicholas I. His anger would have been exacerbated had he known that on the very morning of the assassination, Alexander had been making arrangements for the implementation of modest constitutional changes.

After hesitating for a few weeks, the new Tsar, Alexander III, turned his back resolutely on reform. His decision was to have fateful consequences for the future of Russia. It was also to destroy the life's work of a loyal inspector of education in Simbirsk who had given his best 30 years to the service of his country. The decision to retire him from the inspectorate was eventually rescinded, but this was small comfort. The moderately progressive views of Ilya Ulyanov, and his passionate commitment to popular enlightenment, were no longer what was required.

On 13 January 1886, exhausted from working on his annual educational report, Ilya stood at the door of the dining-room and told the family he would not be joining them for their midday meal. He had latterly been suffering from insomnia and only the previous day had been brought home unwell. 'He looked at us,' his wife later recalled, 'just as if he had come to say goodbye.' A few hours later, Mariya discovered him lying convulsed on the sofa. He had suffered a brain haemorrhage.

Ilya Ulyanov may have been forgotten by the government, but he was remembered with love and affection by the people he had served. The local paper spoke fulsomely of his services to education and the funeral was a major event. His elder son Sasha was unable to get back in time, so it was Volodya who led the coffin out of the house. He was in his sixteenth year.

His brother had now embarked on a degree course at Petersburg

University. A dutiful son, he wrote home regularly, often enclosing parcels of books and music for members of the family. Sasha lived frugally, returning any unspent money on his periodic visits home. In 1885 he had delighted his parents by being awarded the university's gold medal for a dissertation on 'The Segmentation and Sexual Organs of Freshwater Annulula'. He seemed destined for a brilliant academic career. However, this was not to be. Like his sister Anyuta, who was also living in the imperial capital, he was becoming increasingly drawn to social and political questions. Both had already read a number of subversive authors outlawed by the government: Pisarev, Dobrolyubov, Chernyshevsky. By the summer of 1886 Sasha, while holidaying at Kokushkino, was making translations from the works of a new political influence very much in vogue among radical circles – Karl Marx.

In September, Sasha returned to Petersburg. The atmosphere at the university was tense and there was much dissatisfaction. After the assassination of Alexander II, the government had identified the student intelligentsia as potentially the most dangerous source of opposition to the State and had taken appropriately draconian measures to stem the tide of radicalism. The universities were deprived of their recently won autonomy. Curators monitored all aspects of student life. Efforts were made to reduce the proportion of students from non-noble backgrounds by increasing tuition fees. Undergraduates were compelled to go back into uniform. Organized meetings and most societies (even the more innocuous ones) were outlawed. Lecturers suspected of the least deviation from the approved curricula were dismissed. It appeared that the government was quarantining the universities as the source of a most virulent form of contagious disease, freedom of thought, and was treating each student as potentially infected. Naturally, an increasing number of young intellectuals came to view this interpretation as an inversion of the truth: it was the government, not the flower of Russia's youth, which was the source of infection and equally drastic action would be needed to halt its progress.

Throughout the 1860s and 1870s the main course of the opposition movement had been peaceful in nature, though unequivocally radical in its aims. The Populists (*narodniki*), as they came to be called, focused their attention on the peasantry as the most promising source of potential opposition to the autocracy. Peasants represented about 80 per cent of the population and the emancipation of 1861 had done little to assuage their grievances. True, they were now free citizens, not serfs: free to marry, to own property and to resort to law in defence of their interests; but their livelihood was as precarious as ever. The land they were left with after 1861 was less than they had cultivated before and was often of inferior quality. This fundamental injustice caused a profound and lasting resentment, reinforced by a deep-seated belief that the land – *all* the land – belonged to the people as a whole, not to the individual proprietors cultivating it: 'We are yours, the land is ours' was how the peasants conceived their relationship with their former owners. To add salt to the wound, the newly liberated peasants had to pay for the land they were allocated – and these redemption payments, as they were called, though scheduled over a period of many years, were beyond the resources of most peasants. Debts soon began to accumulate. The situation was aggravated by a huge increase in the birth-rate, perversely concentrated in areas of 'land hunger'.

It was this smouldering resentment that the Russian intelligentsia hoped to exploit. The Populists believed in social revolution and that Russia could pass directly to the new socialist order without undergoing the traumas of industrial capitalism. The basis of this new order was to be the village commune, an institution which had survived the emancipation decree; indeed it had been strengthened by it. The commune's traditional practice of periodically redistributing the land in accordance with the size and needs of individual families had, it was believed, embedded notions of egalitarianism and democracy deep within the peasant's consciousness.

Propagandizing among the peasants themselves to alert them to their unique historical mission now became the order of the day. In 1874 students from the major cities dressed up in peasant garb and literally 'went to the people' in the hope of arousing them from their slumbers. The response was not encouraging. The students were met with bewilderment, even downright hostility; many were reported to the police and arrested. The heavy-handed response of the authorities forced the movement underground and in 1876 the Populists formed a clandestine organization called Land and Freedom (*Zemlya i Volya*). The political climate, generally, was becoming more confrontational. In January 1878 the Governor of Petersburg, F. F. Trepov, ordered the flogging of a prisoner for refusing to remove his hat during an inspection. Shortly afterwards, a young woman named Vera Zasulich made an attempt on his life. The governor was wounded but, to the consternation of the authorities, Zasulich was acquitted by a jury. Her action sparked off a spate of assassination attempts. The police chief, General Mezentsev, was the first victim, followed by the Governor of Kharkov. There were also six unsuccessful attempts on the life of Alexander II in the space of a year.

The trend towards terrorism eventually caused a split in the Land and Freedom movement. At a congress held in Voronezh during the summer of 1879, the terrorist wing, led by Lev Tikhomirov and known as the Executive Committee, won the day, causing Georgi Plekhanov to form his own group, called the Black Repartition. This organization (he was joined by Vera Zasulich and other *émigrés*, including Lev Deutsch and Pavel Axelrod) stood for social revolution and the communal repartitioning of the land. Killing the Tsar and a handful of ministers would, it believed, change nothing.

Meanwhile, the Executive Committee had transformed itself into a new party, called *Narodnaya Volya* (People's Freedom). It was this organization which successfully carried out the assassination of Alexander II in

March 1881. But, as Plekhanov and his associates predicted, the act failed either to provoke political change or even to destabilize the autocracy. Furthermore, there was little sympathy for the assassins in society at large. The perpetrators of the deed were captured and executed and the People's Freedom party obliterated. Everyone, it seemed, breathed a sigh of relief.

When Alexander Ulyanov arrived at Petersburg in 1884, terrorism was temporarily off the agenda. The most radical grouping at the university was the Petersburg Student Corporation: 70 students in a total population of about 2,700, existing mainly to assist its poorer brethren who had been adversely affected by the politically inspired hiking of tuition fees. But the Corporation had also assembled a library which included outlawed works on social theory and political economy, and a tiny minority of its members saw it as a possible springboard for revolutionary activity. At that time, even the more respectable aims of the Corporation were bound to arouse police suspicions (any gathering of students was suspect) and arrests in the autumn of 1884 heralded its eventual demise.

Most students from outside the capital (about 70 per cent of the total) joined *zemlyachestva* on their arrival. These were associations of under-graduates from the same province or region. Sasha Ulyanov duly joined the *zemlyachestvo* for the Volga region. By the end of 1885, however, repression at the university had become so stifling that these groups too were becoming potential sources of protest. In December of that year, Sasha was one of three hundred signatories demanding the reinstatement of a popular history lecturer, V. I. Semevsky, dismissed for his supposedly radical views. The following February, 400 students attended a meeting at the Volkovo Cemetery to commemorate the emancipation of the serfs. The event went ahead, but under the close scrutiny of the police. One of the organizers was Sasha Ulyanov. During the spring, the leader of the Don–Kuban *zemlyachestvo*, Peter Shevyrev, set up an illegal union of *zemlyachestva* which began to produce an underground newspaper. Sasha represented the Volga students in this organization. Nothing is known about his political views at this juncture, but Shevyrev's aims were undoubtedly revolutionary and the union had been infiltrated by several would-be terrorists.

The *zemlyachestvo* groups were now under suspicion and the leading radicals, led by Shevyrev, searched for a more innocuous front for their increasingly subversive activities. They found it in the university's Scientific–Literary Society. Alexander Ulyanov had been elected to this entirely respectable body after being awarded the gold medal for his zoological treatise. By October 1886 he was a member of the ruling council and served as secretary of the scientific section. Shevyrev was highly successful in his attempts to infiltrate the organization. By early 1887 its membership had swollen to 287, one-third of whom were new recruits.

Meanwhile, the students had arranged another demonstration. On 17 November 1886 about 1,000 of them returned to the Volkovo Cemetery, this time to commemorate one of their own radical heroes, Nikolai Dobrolyubov. The police closed off the cemetery gates but eventually allowed the students to enter in small groups. The demonstration was not, however, allowed to complete its programme by marching to Kazan Cathedral in the city centre. There were a number of arrests. Sasha Ulyanov retaliated with a leaflet addressed 'To Society'. Printed on an illegal press, it called for a renewed commitment to revolution.

While most of the students on the November demonstration were hostile to the government, a minority were coalescing into a unit bent on regicide. Their leader was Shevyrev. Numbered among his co-conspirators were Vasili Osipanov and Pakhomi Andreyushkin (both of whom had long-standing ambitions to assassinate the Tsar), Yosif Lukashevich (a Pole studying in Petersburg), Vasili Generalov of the Don–Kuban *zemlyachestvo* and four others. Shevyrev's second-in-command was Sasha Ulyanov, whose scientific background qualified him to prepare the explosives.

The plotters obtained their materials from fellow-students in Vilna, a town in Russian Poland. Among their contacts there were Boleslaw Pilsudski and his brother Joseph, the future leader of independent Poland. By mid-February 1887 Sasha had finished work on the explosives and Lukashevich had manufactured the bombs. Shevyrev, who was seriously ill with consumption, now brought the conspirators together for the first time before departing, as agreed, for a cure in the Crimea. In his absence Sasha, valued for his intelligence, quiet authority and determination, assumed the leadership of the conspiracy and set to work on its manifesto. This turned out to be a carefully balanced mixture of Populist and Marxist ideas, representing the widely differing philosophies of the conspirators.

Several times the bombers took up their positions along Petersburg's main street, the Nevsky Prospekt, but the Tsar failed to make his expected appearance. Finally, on 1 March 1887, they assembled once more, confident this time that they had chosen the right moment. They were arrested almost at once. Purely fortuitously, the police had intercepted a letter sent by Andreyushkin to a group of sympathizers in Kharkov and then had him followed. He, in turn, inadvertently led them to some of his comrades. The bombers were taken to police headquarters, where one of their number, Osipanov, tried to hurl a book containing a bomb at the chief of police, but it failed to detonate. The remaining conspirators were soon brought in. Sasha Ulyanov was arrested on the street; his sister Anyuta, who was only marginally involved in the affair, was picked up at his apartment. Shevyrev was taken at Yalta, in the Crimea, about a week later.

On hearing news of the plot, a relative urgently contacted a friend of Mariya's in Simbirsk. This was a local schoolteacher named Kashkadanova. 'When I received the letter,' she later recalled, 'I sent to the school for Vladimir and let him read it. He knitted his brows, stood silent for a long time in deep thought . . . "This may be very serious for Sasha," he said.'[6] Mariya immediately set out for Petersburg. There was no railway link to

Simbirsk in those days so she had to go as far as Syzran by coach. It is said that Volodya tried to find a neighbour to accompany his heartbroken mother, but in vain. The shutters were up. The Ulyanovs had been ostracized.

As soon as she reached the capital, Mariya threw herself assiduously, desperately, into writing letters and petitions. She had had no inkling of her elder son's terrorist background and was plunged into a state of shock. She was allowed to see him for the first time only on 30 March, a full month after the assassination attempt. The Tsar scribbled on the petition:

> It seems to me that it is desirable to give her permission to see her son, so that she can convince herself what sort of a person her dear little son is, and to show her his testimony, so that she can see what kind of convictions he has.[7]

During this meeting Sasha broke down and begged his mother's forgiveness. When she asked him why he had felt it necessary to resort to terrorism, he replied: 'What can one do, mother, when there are no other means available?'[8]

The trial began on 15 April and was over in a few days. It was held in camera. From the outset Sasha not only admitted his own guilt but tried to assume responsibility for his fellow-defendants. Even the chief prosecutor (by a curious twist of fate a former student of Ilya Ulyanov at Penza) conceded as much: 'Ulyanov is probably accepting guilt for what he did not do.' On the penultimate day of the trial, Sasha was allowed to read to the court a prepared statement in which he attempted to justify terror.

> Terror is a road which particular individuals take spontaneously only when their discontent becomes extreme . . . You will always find in the Russian nation a dozen people who are so devoted to their ideals and who feel so deeply their country's misfortune, that for them to die for their cause means no sacrifice. Such people cannot be intimidated.[9]

The outcome, of course, was never in doubt. Sentence was passed on 25 April; all 15 defendants were condemned to death, but ten subsequently had their sentences commuted. Sasha's mother begged him to plea for a pardon. At first he refused outright: 'I cannot do this after everything I have admitted at the trial. You see, that would be insincere.'[10] Moved by his mother's distress, he eventually wrote out a petition; but it was already too late.

Sasha lived out his last days in the grim Shlisselburg Fortress on Lake Ladoga. The end came early in the morning of 8 May 1887. Generalov, Andreyushkin and Osipanov were the first to be brought out for execution. On the way they managed one final act of defiance, shouting 'Long live the People's Freedom' into the eerie silence. Shevyrev and Sasha followed without comment or gesture. Sasha was just 21 years old.

When Mariya returned home to Simbirsk, her hair was completely white. Little wonder: twice she had been bereaved in the space of little more than a year, once in the most harrowing circumstances imaginable.

The future of her eldest daughter was also uncertain, though she was eventually allowed to return home, subject to police surveillance. Meanwhile, two of her other children, Volodya and Olya, were in the middle of their school-leaving exams. Both of them did their mother proud. They remained aloof from the whispers, nudges and knowing glances of their neighbours, ignored the sensational reports of the terrorist conspiracy in the Press and showed masterful composure and self-control throughout the arduous schedule of written papers and vivas. Like their brother and sister before them, both were awarded a gold medal for their performance.

Volodya now wanted to enter Kazan University to study law. But the scandal which had enveloped the family meant that this ambition might not be fulfilled (the police had already raised objections). In their hour of need, one person at least stood by the family. This was Volodya's headmaster, F. M. Kerensky, the father of Alexander Kerensky who was to lead the Provisional Government in 1917. Kerensky dutifully wrote out for Volodya the testimonial he so richly deserved:

> Exceptionally talented, constantly diligent and accurate Ulyanov was the first pupil in all forms; at matriculation he was awarded a Gold Medal as being the most deserving of it by his achievement, development, and behaviour. Neither within the gymnasium nor outside it has any single instance ever been noticed in which Ulyanov has either by word or deed given ground for . . . disapproval.

There was a single caveat:

> Watching more closely Ulyanov's private life and his character I could not fail to notice in him an excessive preference for seclusion and . . . a certain unsociability.[11]

What impact the events of the last two years had on the 17-year-old can only be a matter for speculation. After the death of his father, Volodya's behaviour displayed some of the sharper edges of adolescence. Though outwardly grown up and self-assured, he was showing increasing signs of insecurity and unhappiness. He was rude and occasionally insolent even to his mother and seems to have missed his father's restraining influence; but Sasha's death was a much deeper wound. The full nature and extent of its impact are difficult to determine, as Volodya rarely spoke about his brother and his terrible fate to anyone, even after the Revolution. In life, their personalities had diverged to such an extent that their relationship had become almost cold: 'Undoubtedly a very gifted person,' Sasha had said of Volodya on one occasion, 'but we don't get along.'[12] Now, perhaps, Volodya regretted the distance that had opened up between them. He became noticeably more sombre and taciturn; his zest for life temporarily deserted him. Why had his brother died? What had he been trying to achieve? These were the questions which haunted him during that bereavement-clouded summer in Kokushkino.

2
Revolutionary apprenticeship

Volodya finally received permission to enrol in the Juridical Faculty of Kazan University and took up residence there in August 1887. His mother had already decided to rent out the house in Simbirsk and in November the family joined him in Kazan. They rented a two-storey apartment on the Pervaya Gora, a street close to the university.

The eighth most populous city in Russia, with more than 130,000 inhabitants, Kazan provided a welcome contrast to sleepy Simbirsk. Founded by the Tatars in the second half of the twelfth century, it had been captured by the Russians in 1469. Three centuries later, the town was razed to the ground by the rebel peasant leader, Emelyan Pugachev: the kremlin walls still bore the scars in Volodya's day.

Kazan retained its oriental flavour, despite the Russian conquest. The Tatar minority, with its distinctive clothing, head-dress and customs, still numbered over 25,000 and this predominantly Muslim population was served by 14 mosques.

The university was an imposing building with an elongated classical façade. There were 900 students in all, 250 of whom were studying law. It seemed the perfect setting for Ilya Ulyanov's second son to follow in his father's footsteps, carving out a successful career for himself and a respectable place in society. Sadly, it was not to be.

Even before his arrival at the university, Volodya had been taking an interest in radical ideas. He had spent the summer browsing through his brother's book-shelves at Kokushkino and had discovered Nikolai Chernyshevsky's novel *What Is To Be Done?* – the revolutionary handbook of more than one generation of Russian students, including Volodya's own brother.

Of course, the Kazan undergraduates were already familiar with the name Ulyanov when Volodya came up in the autumn of 1887 and one can imagine him carrying it with pride. Kazan too had its radical student circles. The city was a government-designated place of exile for convicted revolutionaries, some of whom managed to make contact with disaffected individuals inside the university. In Kazan, as in Petersburg in the early 1880s, the focus of resistance to the government's repressive educational measures in particular, and its policies in general, was the student *zemlyachestvo* associations. Broken up in the spring of 1887 in the wake of the attempt on Alexander III's life, they continued to exist illegally. Volodya joined the Samara–Simbirsk association on his arrival and soon afterwards was elected as its representative on a university-wide secret council of *zemlyachestvo* organizations. He had also begun to associate with a much more extreme group intent on reviving the People's Freedom party and possibly launching a new terrorist campaign. Fortunately for Volodya, these plans came to nothing; otherwise his revolutionary career might have been as short-lived as his brother's.

Shortly after his family arrived in Kazan, his mother doubtless looking forward to turning a happier page in their history, he attended a council meeting which decided to call a demonstration to show solidarity with Moscow students involved in recent disturbances. On 4 December the student body assembled in the auditorium of the university to demand, among other things, the abolition of the repressive statute of 1884 and the restoration of the right to form student societies. The authorities reacted predictably. Lectures were suspended for two months and up to 100 of the participants, including Volodya, were arrested. The official investigation into the incident alleged that he had 'rushed to the front of the group in the auditorium' and that he had been 'one of the most active participants at the meeting', standing 'at the front, very excited, his fists clenched'.[13] The testimony may have been fanciful or exaggerated, possibly Volodya was already under surveillance. It matters little. He had willingly, not to say recklessly, allowed himself to be drawn into radical politics and had been caught. We have no record of his mother's feelings; but Volodya, anticipating the authorities' reaction, submitted his 'resignation' on the following day:

> Not considering it possible to continue my education at the University under the present conditions of university life, I have the honour humbly to request Your Excellency to issue the appropriate instruction withdrawing me from the student body of the Imperial Kazan University.[14]

His expulsion followed. On the order of the Ministry of Internal Affairs, he was 'exiled' to the family estate at Kokushkino and placed, like his sister before him, under police surveillance.

The atmosphere at Kokushkino was now very different. It was tainted by the still-fresh memory of Sasha's presence which seemed to pervade every corner. No longer did it have the appeal for his mother that it once had, as she was plunged again into worry and fretfulness over the future of her surviving children. As autumn retreated before winter's relentless advance, Kokushkino surrendered to a cold, damp and eerie silence. At times the estate was cut off entirely by snow; even when it was not, Kazan was all of five or six hours' journey away. Volodya's room was almost bare. There was a wooden bed, a dresser, one or two chairs, a table, a book-shelf and an old work-bench piled high with books. Every day, it seemed, the postman would arrive with a fresh supply of reading matter which he left in a basket outside the front door. For the first few months, Volodya shut himself away in his room, emerging only for meals. During the summer he established himself on a bench in the garden and worked several hours at a stretch, poring over the latest text or making copious notes in his small, neat handwriting. After dinner he would break for a walk in the woods, either alone or in the company of his sisters. Sometimes he would go sailing or swimming and then back to the books until bedtime. His cousins paid the occasional call; he treated them good-humouredly, providing they did not interrupt his work. Otherwise he would resort to a favourite phrase of Sasha: 'Kindly honour us with your absence'. His spirits improved as time progressed. He seemed to have found a new purpose which softened the rougher edges of his personality. He was not so harsh and ill-mannered as he had been when Sasha was still alive. What was inspiring him? The secret lay in the books shuttling back and forth from Kazan to Kokushkino with clockwork regularity – bound copies of *The Contemporary*, *Annals of the Fatherland*, *The European Herald* and other intellectual journals and periodicals dating back to the 1850s. The authors Volodya was seeking out read like a *Who's Who* of Russian radicalism: Belinsky, Nekrasov, Bakunin, Dobrolyubov, Herzen, Pisarev, Chernyshevsky . . .

Lenin would say of this period:

> Never, I think, later on in my life, even in prison in Petersburg and in Siberia, did I read so much as in the year after my exile to the countryside from Kazan. This was avid reading, from early morning to late at night.

And none of these illustrious writers made more of an impression on Volodya than Nikolai Gavrilovich Chernyshevsky. 'This author,' he said later, 'ploughed me over and over'.[15] He simply devoured the political novel *What Is To Be Done?*, reading it five times during that liberating summer of 1888.

Chernyshevsky was, on the face of it, an unlikely candidate to inspire a revolutionary movement. He was born in 1828 in Saratov, the son of a parish priest. Like his father he was educated in a seminary and was apparently an outstanding student. In 1846 he began several years' study at Petersburg University. He emerged a radical, acquainted with progressive Western thinkers like Fourier and Feuerbach, and Russian ones like Herzen and Bakunin. After a miserable period spent teaching, Chernyshevsky became a journalist and was soon contributing regularly to the prestigious journal *The Contemporary*. Eventually he became one of its editors. He was a controversial character, with views and manner calculated to give offence to those of a different persuasion. Two other contributors to *The Contemporary*, the novelists Tolstoy and Turgenev, thoroughly disliked him, Tolstoy referring to him as 'this gentleman who smells of bugs'.[16]

Chernyshevsky's importance as a social thinker became apparent at the end of the 1850s as the Russian intelligentsia hotly debated the imminent emancipation of the serfs. At first, like Herzen, he believed in the government's sincerity and supported what he thought would be a generous land settlement. He believed that this might become the basis for the transition to a socialist society founded on the commune. When the actual limitations of the proposed reform became apparent, both Herzen and Chernyshevsky went on the offensive. However, while Chernyshevsky and his supporters called for 'the axe', Herzen was unwilling to countenance violence. This disagreement turned out to be a final parting of the ways, opening up a rift between the men of the 1840s, typified by Herzen, and the 'new men' (and women) of the 1860s led by their prophet Chernyshevsky. The latter was content to see the gulf grow wider, treating Herzen and his 'armchair liberal' followers with increasing contempt. Chernyshevsky's message quickly gathered support in intellectual circles but it threw him into an unequal confrontation with the government. In the summer of 1862 he was arrested and imprisoned in the Peter–Paul Fortress, later serving a sentence of hard labour in Siberia where he acquired the aura of a martyr. He returned to Saratov and died there in 1889.

Chernyshevsky's best-known and most influential work is undoubtedly *What Is To Be Done?*. Written while in prison, this didactic novel was an attempt to crystallize his thinking in a form immediately accessible to his youthful audience. In this he was notably successful, a fact which would come as a surprise to many modern readers. However, Chernyshevsky was not setting out to write a great novel, as he makes clear in his preface:

> I don't have the shadow of an artistic talent. I even use the language badly. But that's not important . . . This reading will be useful to you, and you will experience no deception, since I have warned you that you will find in my novel neither talent nor art, only the truth.[17]

The main protagonists in *What Is To Be Done?* are role models for the men and women of the coming generation whose task will be to build a better world along socialist lines. Images of this Utopia are conveyed to the reader through the dreams of one of the characters. It is a world in which the oppressed have been released into the light, where poverty has ceased to exist and where everyone does as he or she pleases. Chernyshevsky highlights the qualities of his 'new people' by contrasting them with the venal, grasping and unprincipled types who represent the corrupt society of the old world. Vera Pavlovna, the novel's heroine, is contrasted with her selfish, scheming mother whose natural habitat is the *demi-monde*. Vera is saved from a sordid, arranged marriage only through the intervention of a 'new man', the medical student Lopukhov who agrees to marry her himself. The marriage is far from conventional. Vera's husband is thoroughly committed to female emancipation and is the first to applaud her desire for independence: 'Perfect Verochka! Let every woman maintain, with all her strength, her independence of every man, however great her love for and confidence in him'.[18] The couple share an apartment, but have separate bedrooms where their individual privacy is strictly observed. They meet only on neutral territory – a parlour adjoining the two rooms – and draw up (semi-seriously, it must be said) a highly elaborate code of rules and regulations which are to govern their behaviour in each other's presence.

Vera Pavlovna does not intend to live off her husband. She takes in sewing and laundry and eventually sets up a seamstresses' co-operative, where everything is communally ordered and the profits are shared. In this way she is able to release more females from exploitation on the streets. Her relationship with Lopukhov, however, deteriorates. Vera gradually comes to the painful realization that, for all his good qualities, Lopukhov is unable to love her with the warmth and physical tenderness she craves. Through the mediation of his mysterious young friend and mentor, Rakhmetov, Lopukhov comes to see that he is getting in the way of his wife's happiness.

Rakhmetov is a scion of the gentry but a most unusual one. He disposes of his ample private income, partly by maintaining impoverished students at his own expense. He builds his strength and stamina by eating raw beef-steak, practising gymnastics and taking up physically demanding work wherever he can find it – boat-hauling on the Volga, for instance. He neither drinks nor allows himself to become involved with women. Rakhmetov has an unquenchable thirst for knowledge, once reading continuously for 82 hours. However, he reads only what is necessary and original; for Rakhmetov there is no time to waste: each quarter of an hour has its pre-assigned function. Like Lopukhov and Kirsanov, he is unswerving in purpose, brutally honest and coldly rational.

After Rakhmetov's intervention, Lopukhov does not hesitate to make way for Vera's would-be lover, his best friend Kirsanov. Lopukhov feigns suicide to leave the field clear but reappears at the end of the book as the 'American' Beaumont who has taken up with Vera's friend, herself saved from a potentially disastrous marriage by Kirsanov! By this time, not only is Vera's co-operative venture flourishing, but she is studying medicine under the guidance of her now-famous doctor-husband.

Lenin later pronounced this verdict on Chernyshevsky:

> [He] not only showed that every right-thinking and really honest man must be a revolutionary, but he also showed – and this is his greatest merit – what a revolutionary must be like, what his principles must be, how he must approach his aim, and what methods he must use to achieve it.[19]

Volodya's commitment to study was doubtless encouraging to his mother, but she must have been concerned that a disproportionate share of his reading comprised radical (and therefore dangerous) literature rather than legal textbooks. If her son was to have any hope of establishing himself in a profession, then it was essential that he complete his formal studies. Therefore, in September 1888 she persuaded him to write to the Ministry of the Interior requesting permission to study abroad 'in order to support my family and acquire a higher education'. The rejection came discouragingly quickly; neither was he allowed to return to Kazan University. An official of the local education department appended a note on the application, querying: 'Isn't this the brother of that other Ulyanov? Wasn't he also from the Simbirsk gymnasium? . . . On no account should his request be granted'.[20] There was one small chink of light: Volodya was allowed to move back to Kazan. He returned in September, accompanied by his mother and younger brother Dmitri.

Once again the Ulyanovs found themselves on the Pervaya Gora. They rented a two-storey house with a balcony and two kitchens (one of which Volodya requisitioned as a study). There was also a garden with an orchard backing on to the hillside. Volodya was now 18 years old. He had of necessity discarded his student's uniform and taken to wearing a suit and soft-collared shirt. His brushed-back, reddish hair was already showing signs of receding at the hair-line, thus accentuating a broad, powerful forehead. He was neat, tidy and meticulous – there was nothing of the drop-out about him. His only notable bad habit was to take up smoking, a passion which did not last long. One day his mother, in a moment of irritation, pointed out that someone who was not yet contributing to the family finances had no right to indulge himself in this way. He never smoked again.

Volodya resumed his studies with a vengeance, surrounding himself with books and papers and scribbling away day and night. In the autumn he made contact with M. P. Chetvergova, a former member of the People's Freedom movement who had formed an illegal discussion circle in Kazan. She was to make a strong impression on him: he took the trouble to visit her on his return from exile in 1900.

Very little is known about Chetvergova's group. However, there were one or two other radical societies operating in Kazan towards the end of 1888 and their activities, probably similar to Chetvergova's, are better documented. Most of the membership (no more than 30 or 40 all told) was drawn from the university, but meetings were held in private houses. Political discussion was usually followed by supper and more relaxed conviviality. A collection might be taken for the support of political prisoners and their families or to purchase illicit books and materials for the group's secret library. From time to time the more daring members would risk duplicating and distributing leaflets and other forbidden literature. Propaganda activity of this type was especially dangerous and usually led to arrests: on account of this, and also because most groups contained at least one *agent provocateur*, the average lifespan of a discussion circle was measured in months.

The whole gamut of revolutionary views was represented in these discussion groups. Some were fierce supporters of terrorism who wished to revive People's Freedom; others, like the advocates of Black Repartition, rejected terror with equal vehemence and argued for peaceful political propaganda among the peasantry. There were those who put more faith in the revolutionary potential of urban workers. Advocates of a new strategy just coming into vogue envisaged an alliance of all democratic forces (including liberals) in an attempt to wrest essential political and civil freedoms from the government. This approach, heresy to some for implying that social revolution was not immediately attainable, would, its supporters argued, at least create more favourable conditions for its ultimate realization.

It was perhaps as a direct result of his participation in the Chetvergova circle that Vladimir Ulyanov began studying volume one of Karl Marx's *Das Kapital* during the winter of 1888; a study which, in a sense, was to last a lifetime. It would be some time before he could be described as a fully committed Marxist, but the comprehensiveness, intellectual cohesion and scientific rationale of Marxism quickly fired the young man's enthusiasm. His elder sister Anyuta retained this memory of him during the Kazan period: 'I can see him as if it were yesterday, sitting on a kitchen stove covered with newspapers and making violent gestures as he spoke of the new horizons which opened out to anyone who followed Marx's theories'.

Marx's work was already familiar in Russian intellectual circles by the late 1880s; the first volume of *Das Kapital* had been translated into Russian by the Populist N. F. Danielson in 1872, only five years after its original appearance. It remained something of a bibliographical rarity but not because it was banned – the censor approved publication on the grounds that the work was too dry and technical to exert any harmful influence. At first, Marx's researches were considered to have more relevance for Western Europe than for Russia; after all, Russia as yet had very little industry, still less capitalism and only an embryonic proletariat and bourgeoisie. It was Russia's very backwardness, the Populists argued, that would enable her to make a direct transition to socialism, avoiding the capitalist stage altogether. Marx himself, on being drawn briefly into the debate on two occasions – once in 1877, a second time in 1881 – conceded that Russia might take a different route to socialism than that imposed on Western Europe. But there was a significant rider: once capitalism was under way, the process could not be reversed.

By the time Volodya became acquainted with Marxism, evidence was growing that Russia had indeed embarked irrevocably on the capitalist road. But there were still those who contended that capitalism could never take root, because the necessary foreign markets had already been divided up by the advanced Western states, while a healthy domestic market could not be created because of the impoverished living standards of the peasantry. The question, in short, remained an open one.

Volodya's mother must have been aware of the dangerous company he was keeping and of the consequences of another brush with the authorities – in this case quite possibly a prison sentence. She was determined to get him away from Kazan in particular and from cities in general, at least for a time. Mariya purchased an estate at Alakaevka, a village about 150 miles (240 km) south of Kazan and 30 miles (48 km) east of Samara. The move (in May 1889) was timely: Chetvergova's group, together with other socialist circles in Kazan, was broken up shortly afterwards.

The Alakaevka property – consisting of 225 acres (90 hectares) of good farmland, a house, a mill, a pond, stables and other farm buildings – cost 7,500 roubles: 'for those times [according to Trotsky] a tidy sum of money'.[21] Mariya found the cash by selling the house in Simbirsk as well as her share of the Kokushkino estate. A bargain at the price, Alakaevka was chosen by Anyuta's husband, Mark Elizarov, who came from the Samara area and whose brother was himself a wealthy peasant farmer. The idea seems to have been that Volodya would learn the rudiments of farm management with a view to running the estate himself. His reaction has not been recorded; presumably he was none too pleased to be spirited away from his revolutionary comrades, albeit for the best of motives. On the other hand, the career of a professional revolutionary hardly offered prospects and a steady income. In the end he agreed to give it a go. There was the possibility that the situation might be turned to his advantage for, unlike many members of the intelligentsia who preached the virtues of the peasants and their innate socialism without actually ever meeting a representative of that class, Volodya now had the opportunity to encounter them and their problems at first hand. He could observe the difference in well-being between peasants who owned their own plough, horse or cow and those who had to hire them from richer neighbours. He could observe the impact of new machinery on the productivity of an estate. He could observe the misery of the poorest peasants – landless, overburdened with debt, unable to feed their families, forced to accept any work at any wage anywhere. These impressions, though perhaps casually encountered, would in time implant themselves firmly in Vladimir Ulyanov's consciousness.

As for estate management, he later told his wife: 'My mother would have liked me to have taken up farming. I started, but soon realized that things were not going right. Relations with the peasants were abnormal'.[22] What he meant by this we do not know, but his career as a landowner was short-lived. He placed an advertisement in a Samara newspaper: 'Former student wishes to give lessons. Willing to travel'.

This was a temporary measure: he had already decided to complete his legal studies. In September the Ulyanovs moved to Samara for the winter. Samara was a frontier town. Life here, according to Trotsky, 'was shaped by powerful cattlemen, wheat farmers, grain merchants, millers and pioneers of agrarian capitalism'.[23] And, as Mariya Ulyanov must have noted with satisfaction, there was no university to attract the radicals. Volodya brought his books, including heavy tomes on Roman law, Russian law, criminal law, and the philosophy of law, but he was also pursuing his more illicit interests. For poor Mariya had overlooked the fact that Samara, like Kazan, was a place of exile for political dissidents. Volodya immediately made contact with a number of revolutionaries who had formerly belonged to People's Freedom, including N. S. Dolgov, one-time associate of the arch-conspirator Sergei Nechaev, the model for Peter Verkhovensky in Dostoevsky's novel *The Possessed*. Most of them, though now retired, continued to advocate terrorism. By the end of 1889 Volodya had joined the discussion circle of A. P. Sklyarenko, a man of his own age who had been involved with Populist organizations for about three years. Their association was to last until Volodya moved to Petersburg in 1893; the following year Sklyarenko was arrested. Both of them were already moving towards Marxism and Volodya at least was becoming sceptical of the value of terrorism. In December 1889 he felt sufficiently confident in his views to take on M. V. Sabunaev in debate. Sabunaev was visiting Samara with the aim of reviving support for People's Freedom. According to M. I. Semenov, a member of Sklyarenko's circle, Volodya gave a good account of himself. In March 1891 he repeated the performance, and again in the autumn.

Though immersed in his legal studies, Volodya was also devouring any political literature he could lay his hands on. He read Friedrich Engels's *Condition of the Working Class in England*, abstracted Marx's *Poverty of Philosophy* and translated *The Communist Manifesto* into Russian for the benefit of Sklyarenko and his friends. He was also becoming acquainted with the writings of Georgi Plekhanov. Since leaving People's Freedom to form the break-away organization, Black Repartition, Plekhanov had become a convert to Marxism. By the mid-1880s he was the leading proponent of the view that the triumph of capitalism was inevitable in Russia and that consequently Marx's analysis was of supreme relevance there. Plekhanov's powerful arguments would provide the foundation-stone for Vladimir Ulyanov's Marxist convictions.

Meanwhile, Mariya Ulyanov was pulling strings to allow her son to sit his law exams as an external student. In October 1889, his own petition, in which he argued that he needed a university degree in order 'to support a family consisting of an aged mother and a brother and sister, both minors', was rejected. The following May his mother submitted a petition in her own name, emphasizing her husband's loyal service to the state and her own difficult circumstances. She also lamented the ill-effects which inactivity was having on her son: 'It is a grievous pain, to look at my son and see his best years being wasted away . . . Further disappointment', she added, 'would almost inevitably drive him to thoughts of suicide.'[24] This time her appeal did not fall on deaf ears. Her son was permitted to sit his exams externally at a university of his choice. He chose Petersburg.

He made a preliminary visit to the Russian capital in September and stayed for two months. His main aim was to familiarize himself with the university's syllabus and examination requirements for the law degree and to raid various legal libraries.

His physical appearance had altered dramatically. A photograph taken in Samara in 1891 reveals a mature-looking young man with a receding hair-line, thin, slightly drooping moustache and short, whispy beard. His Kalmyk features, particularly the rather slanted eyes, are never more in evidence. The son of a Samara magistrate close to radical circles remembers the young Ulyanov at one of Sklyarenko's meetings. He was struck by a 'mocking expression' in the eyes and observed how, in the middle of the conversation,

> while summing up some conclusion that evidently seemed to him particularly apt, he suddenly burst out laughing, with a gusty, short, distinctly Russian laugh . . . That laugh, healthy but not without cunning, accentuated by crafty wrinkles in the corners of his eyes, remains in my memory.[25]

In April 1891 Volodya was in Petersburg again, this time to submit an essay on criminal law. Immediately afterwards, he took the first half of his degree examination: five papers in a total of seven subjects. His mother, worried that he might be overworking, was reassured by his younger sister Olya who was also studying in Petersburg. She wrote:

> I think, darling Mamochka, that you have no reason to worry that he is over-exerting himself. Firstly, Volodya is reason personified and secondly, the examinations were very easy. He has already completed two subjects and received a 5 in both. He rested on Saturday (the examination was on Friday). He went early in the morning to the river Neva and in the afternoon he visited me and then both of us went walking along the Neva and watched the movement of the ice.[26]

Exactly a month after this letter was written, tragedy again visited the Ulyanov family. Olya was struck down with typhoid, a perennial hazard in Petersburg where public notices warned of the dangers of drinking tap-water. She died shortly afterwards in the arms of her mother, who had rushed to her bedside. It was four years to the day since the death of her adored brother, Sasha.

Volodya spent the summer with his mother in Alakaevka. By mid-September he was back in the capital to complete his examinations. Eight more papers in eleven subjects followed. Astonishingly, given that he had completed his course without a tutor and in just over twelve months rather than the customary four years, he obtained the equivalent of first-class honours with excellent marks in all subjects. Once again however, personal triumph had been marred by family tragedy.

Volodya was now entitled to practise law. In January 1892 he was authorized by the Samara regional court to act in the capacity of legal assistant; the following month he was taken on by a local lawyer, A. N. Khardin. Khardin had become chairman of the provincial *zemstvo* administration at the age of 28, but he had been dismissed for political unreliability. He was known to Volodya's brother-in-law, Elizarov. Khardin and his young assistant shared a passion for chess but, for once, Volodya was outgunned: Khardin was acknowledged to be a skilful player even by a Russian grandmaster of the day, Chigorin.

Volodya's work in the law office was satisfactory; by the summer he was conducting his own cases, mostly disputes among local peasants and artisans. However, it is unlikely that he regarded his legal calling as anything more than a useful cover for his real passion, revolutionary politics, for he was now wholly committed (at least in spirit) to political opposition. He was still one of the most active members of Sklyarenko's circle, which was by now (1892–3) tilting decidedly towards Marxism. Like most proto-Marxists in Russia, their convictions were shaped to a considerable extent by two works of Plekhanov: *Socialism and the Political Struggle* (1883) and *Our Differences* (1885).

Plekhanov challenged the notion that the peasantry was essentially a progressive social force. On the contrary, he asserted, peasants were motivated primarily by a desire to conserve and extend their private property. They were individualists, not socialists. The commune, Plekhanov argued, had been artificially preserved by the State for its administrative convenience; as a social institution, it was doomed. The inevitable spread of capitalism in the countryside would, in time, split the peasantry into a class of individual farmer–proprietors, on the one hand, and a property-less rural proletariat on the other. Russia was therefore fated to travel the well-trodden road already taken by the more advanced Western nations. However, Russia's backwardness presented certain advantages denied to other countries. Imported technology could speed up the process of capitalist industrialization. The Russian bourgeoisie was weak and would be unable to divert the revolution for its own ends. There was already a committed radical intelligentsia. And there was a sharply defined enemy in the form of the reactionary tsarist autocracy. The conclusion to be drawn therefore was that, while Russia was destined to undergo the full traumas of capitalism, it could foreshorten the period of its occupation.

Plekhanov went on to outline a strategy for Russian Marxists. All forces hostile to tsarism must unite to sweep away autocracy and force the introduction of political and civil freedoms. When this had been achieved, the revolutionary intelligentsia would sever its marriage of convenience with the bourgeoisie and build a party of the industrial proletariat. Russia's urban working class was still at an embryonic stage, but in time it would grow in strength and numbers just as in other Western capitalist societies. When it reached maturity and a sufficiently advanced revolutionary consciousness, it would carry out its pre-ordained task of establishing democratic socialism. Thus, to Russian Marxists the industrial proletariat, and not the peasantry, was the main harbinger of social change: the battle-lines between Populists and Marxists had finally been drawn.

In the summer of 1891 Volodya's Volga homeland was devastated by famine. The streets of Samara were filled with peasants from the outlying districts searching for food and work. The spectacle touched the hearts of Russia's educated classes. Everywhere, students, doctors, teachers and sympathetic local-government officials sprang into action. Relief committees were set up, soup-kitchens organized in the villages, and charity events held to raise money. Well-known figures like Lev Tolstoy and Anton Chekhov gave their active support. Everyone, it seemed, was involved – everyone, that is, but Vladimir Ulyanov and his confrères. On the contrary, rather than joining the local famine committee, Volodya, according to Trotsky, 'conducted systematic and outspoken propaganda against the committee'. Inspired by the arguments of Plekhanov, he was disdainful of the 'sentimentality' which implied that a 'sea of need could be emptied with the teaspoon of philanthropy'.[27] He wished to expose the bureaucracy's supposed incompetence and the Populists' hopeless illusions of a Russia in which capitalism could be held in check. In the context of the times, his behaviour and that of his friends could only be construed as fanatical callousness and blind obedience to dogma. How could one stand aside and do nothing? Was Marxism totally incompatible with humanitarian concern?

The burden of proof rested with Volodya and his associates. Evidence was required to demonstrate that Russia was firmly embarked on the road of capitalist development. The necessary materials were just being made available in the form of statistical surveys conducted by local-government officials in the countryside. Volodya and Sklyarenko set to work on these with a vengeance. From now on Volodya's own notes were frequently interspersed with statistical tables itemizing the proportion of land under cultivation in a given province and the crops grown, the economic position of hired labourers and their families, the distribution of draft animals according to household, the proportion of landowners renting additional land and their economic status. No aspect of agricultural life and practice was too trivial for investigation. Data on the percentage of farms using manure in Perm Province is cited by Volodya on occasion, while Sklyarenko went into print with an article entitled 'On the influence of bad harvests upon the distribution of horned cattle in peasant farming in Samara district'. The knowledge of contemporary economic developments in the countryside, which he acquired by undertaking this kind of detailed research, was to give him virtually unparalleled authority in Marxist circles in the years to come. He was helped in his quest by Mark Elizarov and by other Samara acquaintances with rural connections, including A. A. Preobrazhensky. These people introduced him to local peasants and provided him with useful information about current agricultural practices.

Volodya was anxious to carry his investigations to a wider audience. In the spring of 1893 he submitted an article entitled 'New economic developments in Russian peasant life' for publication in the liberal journal *Russian Thought*. Effectively little more than an extended review of V. I. Postnikov's book, *The Peasant Economy of Southern Russia*, it was turned down.

This must have come as a bitter blow to a 23-year-old used to being taken seriously in intellectual circles. It made him more conscious than ever of the need to escape the stifling dullness of provincial Samara. Volodya was keenly aware of the need to broaden his intellectual horizons and experiences. But for the death of his sister and dutiful feelings towards his mother, he would probably have eased himself away much earlier. In the autumn of 1893 the longed-for opportunity presented itself. His younger brother Mitya had enrolled at Moscow University and now Mariya decided to move in order to be near her son. Volodya too packed his bags, but his destination was Petersburg, not Moscow. On the way he stopped off in Nizhni-Novgorod to visit local Marxists. They provided him with contacts in the capital, mainly students at the Technological Institute.

The face of Petersburg, like the face of Russia, was undergoing a transformation during the 1890s. At the start of the decade the State had decided to accelerate industrialization by spearheading the drive itself. By 1900, thanks to a massive injection of capital in the form of foreign and domestic loans, revenue from indirect taxation and income from substantial increases in grain exports, Russia was well on the way to becoming an industrialized nation. Staggering annual growth rates of 7 to 8 per cent were recorded throughout the decade. Production of iron, coal and petroleum trebled. The railway network almost doubled in length. New industrial regions were opened up in the Caucasus and the Donbass. Foreign investors and entrepreneurs (mainly French, German and British) became heavily involved in Russian merchant banks and came to control large slices of Russian industry.

Those who had argued that capitalism would wither away because of a lack of markets were daily being confounded. The State was itself the greatest consumer; railway construction alone swallowed up huge quantities of pig-iron, steel, bricks, cement, lumber and fuel; while other industries provided an insatiable demand for new plant and factories. At the same time, higher domestic consumption accounted for an increase in the production of textiles, agricultural equipment and household appliances.

Petersburg, with a population of around one and a half million in 1900, encapsulated all these changes. Factory chimneys were already encroaching on the splendid vistas and landmarks of the city; industrial effluent was darkening and corrupting the canals; layers of soot blackened the façades of the palaces. Migrants poured in from the countryside in their thousands, finding jobs not only in industry but in transport, commerce and domestic service. After a time they began to abandon their peasant ways, adopting the attitudes and behaviour of a Western-style working class.

Volodya arrived in Petersburg on 31 August 1893. His first home was a room in an apartment block on Sergievsky Street in the Liteiny district. Shortly afterwards he moved to 7 Kazachy Alley, near the Haymarket (the setting of Dostoevsky's *Crime and Punishment*). He occupied a small room on the third floor. It was a typical student's room, as a fellow student, Michael Silvin remembers:

> The entrance led through a gateway to a gloomy, rather dirty staircase with decrepit-looking steps . . . In the left-hand corner [of the room] by the window was a table – I think the only one in the room – where Vladimir Ilyich worked. On the edge of the table was a tea service with a plate and bread, when needed.

Silvin also recalled a small bookcase sandwiched between a chest of drawers and an iron bedstead, which was covered with a cotton blanket. There was a couch along one wall and two or three chairs. The room was lit by a single kerosene lamp. There was little in the way of decoration or ornaments.[28]

Writing after the Lenin cult had been established, Silvin was anxious to make the hero's surroundings seem as poor and simple as possible. There may well have been photographs and one or two homely items in the room and the surroundings may not have been quite so gloomy as they are made to sound. Volodya was, however, extremely modest in his personal habits. He ate sparingly and drank only the occasional glass of beer; his only extravagance was books. Perhaps it was this weakness which, as early as October 1893, compelled him to ask his mother for money. While attempting to assure her of his thriftiness by quoting from a notebook itemizing his expenses, he had to confess that 'he had not been living carefully'.[29] Somehow or other Mariya, who was living on her pension of 1,200 roubles a year plus the income from her estate, always found the money to help him out.

He did, in fact, already have a job as assistant to the lawyer M. F. Volkenstein, but there was little time to practise. His contacts had put him in touch with an experienced revolutionary, S. I. Radchenko, who for over a year now had been running a discussion circle of a dozen or so students, mainly from the city's Technological Institute. Its members included G. B. Krasin, G. M. Krzhizhanovsky (future head of the Soviet State Planning Commission), M. Silvin, A. A. Vaneev and P. K. Zaporozhets. They called themselves Social Democrats, following the German Social Democratic Party which also had a Marxist orientation. Radchenko told Krasin about Volodya and they agreed to meet him. They already knew, of course, that he was the brother of Alexander Ulyanov, and for that very reason were a little wary of him; none of them wanted a People's Freedom sympathizer in the group. After questioning him, however, they were satisfied with his political credentials and he was allowed to join.

He soon had a chance to prove himself. At one of the meetings held in Radchenko's apartment in October 1893, Krasin presented a paper 'On Markets'. Volodya came well-prepared and, speaking with a quiet confidence and authority, offered substantial corrections and amendments to Krasin's work. He impressed them all with his erudition, especially his knowledge of Marx: 'Many of us knew nothing of Marx's work except for the first volume of *Capital* and had not even seen the text of *The Communist Manifesto*.'[30] Members of the circle were even more impressed by the wealth of statistical evidence the newcomer had at his fingertips. He was emerging as a leader.

Spurred on by this reception, Volodya intensified his studies, haunting the Petersburg libraries and honing the material he had collected in Samara. He was not too busy, however, to tend the grave of his dead sister. He told his mother: 'I went to the Volkovo cemetery shortly after my arrival: everything there is intact – both the cross and the wreath'.[31]

The Christmas holidays were spent with the family in Moscow. In January 1894 he and his sister Anyuta attended an illegal meeting at which the guest speaker was V. P. Vorontsov, better known by his literary pseudonym 'V. V.'. Vorontsov was an influential 'legal', or moderate Populist, whose book *The Fate of Capitalism in Russia* had caused considerable excitement when it first appeared in 1882. A portly, bespectacled, red-bearded figure, he still commanded respect – and not only in Populist circles. A small but enthusiastic audience had gathered to hear him speak.

Vorontsov spoke about the future of the peasant commune, taking a number of rather ponderous but good-natured side-swipes at his Marxist critics in the process. When he had finished, a number of young people raised objections but apparently to little effect. Volodya was standing at the back of the room by the door; he raised his hand to speak. Immediately he laid into Vorontsov's arguments, answering with more of the same, but also showering him with statistics and percentages. According to Viktor Chernov (future leader of the Socialist Revolutionary Party), Vorontsov at this point became heated, calling on the impertinent young man to produce written evidence in support of his arguments and drawing Volodya's attention to his own published works.

If his sister's account is to be believed, Volodya had not set out with the intention of hauling in such a big fish. As he was leaving the building, he asked a companion whom he had been arguing with. When told it was V.V., he 'became terribly angry': 'Why on earth didn't you say so earlier? If I'd known it was V.V. I would never have debated with him'.

A police spy was present at the meeting. A report dated 20 January 1894 stated: 'a certain Ulyanov (almost certainly the brother of the Ulyanov who was hanged) made a spirited attack against the writer V.V.'[32]

Volodya returned to Petersburg. On Shrove Tuesday he was invited to a pancake party at the home of an engineer called Klasson. One of the other guests takes up the story:

> There did not seem to be general agreement. Someone was saying – I think it was Shevalyin – that what was very important was to work in the Committee for Literacy. Vladimir Ilyich began laughing, and there was something dry and malicious in his laughter. I never heard him laugh that way again.
>
> 'Well,' he said, 'If anyone wants to save the fatherland in the Committee for Literacy, we won't stand in his way!'[33]

The name of the young woman who recalled this incident was Nadezhda (Nadya) Krupskaya. Life had been considerably less kind to her than it had been to Volodya. Nadya's father was an army officer who had taken part in the suppression of the Polish uprising in 1863, after which he had been appointed to a military governorship. Unlike most Russians, however, he was sympathetic to the Poles. His opposition to anti-semitism (Russian Poland had a large Jewish population), and to the government's policy of Russification, did not endear him to his superiors. Eventually, he was arrested on trumped-up charges. It took him ten years to clear his name, by which time he was a ruined man. Nadya, who was only 13 or 14 when her father died, had to help her mother look after the lodgers and also gave lessons to the neighbours' children to bring in extra income.

She was a year younger than Volodya. Pale in complexion with strong, regular features, she was not unprepossessing – though her lips protruded a little and her expression had a serious almost sullen quality. She and Volodya recognized in each other the same, passionate devotion to the revolutionary cause. Steeped, as they were, in the morality of *What Is To Be Done?*, this was enough to bind them together.

Nadya had been a Marxist for about two years though she quickly realized that she was far less well-informed than her new boy-friend. She did, however, have one advantage over Volodya: she knew real workers. For some time before the party at Klasson's house, Nadya had served as a volunteer at the Smolensk Sunday night-school for adults in the Nevsky factory district. She and a couple of Marxist colleagues used the school as a means of recruiting the brightest, most promising workers for the socialist cause. Once drawn into the orbit of the Social Democrats, they formed groups or 'circles' of about half a dozen people for purposes of instruction and discussion. The leaders came exclusively from the intelligentsia.

By the autumn of 1894 Volodya had his own workers' circle. They met on Sundays, usually in his room. If he did have to walk the 5 miles (8 km) to the Nevsky district, he would usually try to disguise himself, pulling his cap over his eyes and his collar about his ears. The sessions lasted from 10 a.m. to midday. The workers knew him by a pseudonym: to some he was 'Nikolai Petrovich'; to others, 'Fedor Petrovich'. Their affectionate name for him was *starik* (old man), for although he was still only 25, he looked much older. According to Krupskaya the sessions went something like this:

> Vladimir Ilyich read with the workers from Marx's *Capital* and explained it to them. The second half of the studies was devoted to the workers' questions about their work and labour conditions. He showed them how their life was linked up with the entire structure of society and told them in what manner the existing order could be transformed.[34]

One of the workers, Ivan Babushkin, recalled that he

> never consulted any notes and was continually pausing to provoke us to speak or start an argument and if we answered he would always make us justify our positions. We were always amazed by the learning of the lecturer. We used to say among ourselves that he had such big brains that they had pushed his hair out.[35]

Babushkin also remembers having to make detailed notes about working conditions at his factory for Volodya. He stuffed the bits of paper into his tool-box to avoid detection.

Of course, spreading socialist propaganda among the workers was strictly illegal and potentially dangerous. The security police were generally well-informed and could infiltrate almost any organization at will. Many revolutionaries were amazingly careless about covering their tracks. But not Volodya:

> Of all our group Vladimir Ilyich was the best equipped for conspiratorial work. He knew all the through courtyards and was a skilled hand at giving police spies the slip. He taught us how to write in books with invisible ink, or by the dot methods; how to mark secret signs, and gave us all manner of aliases.[36]

On one occasion he went with Nadya to Michael Silvin's home in the village of Tsarskoe Selo, outside Petersburg. Nadya took down the proceedings in cipher, filling half a notebook. When the couple returned home, however, Nadya was unable to decode the contents!

During the spring and summer of 1894 Volodya was working on a brochure with the title 'What Are "the Friends of the People"?'. Much of the tract was based on his Samara researches, but his analysis of capitalism and the political consequences for Russia (heavily influenced by Plekhanov) was becoming clearer and more incisive. This time Volodya had his sights trained on the great Populist mentor, N. K. Mikhailovsky. The work, in three parts, one of which has been lost, bears all the hallmarks of his later writings: forthright exposition, polemical tone, a text splashed with quotations from the works of his opponents (often surrounded by deprecatory exclamation marks) and studded with emphases to hammer home the line of argument.

Part one, completed in April, was first run off on a duplicator, then printed on an illegal press; parts two and three followed. About 200 copies were circulated in all.

Volodya thought his ideas merited a wider public than this and he sought the support of better-known Marxists whose views were regarded with slightly less hostility by the government and who had enough money and influence to get their work published legally. The doyen of this charmed circle was Petr Bernardovich Struve, a young man of German ancestry whose father was a senior government official. Struve, who described himself as 'an incorrigible litterateur and bookman' was converted to Marxism while studying at Petersburg University. He was much more the sophisticated man of the world than Volodya. After completing his education in Austria, he found a post as librarian with the Ministry of Finance. Struve contributed regularly to foreign as well as Russian journals and in 1894 he completed a book, *Critical Remarks*, which was published legally.

Struve shared Volodya's conviction that capitalism was ineradicably entrenched in Russia, but their views differed in several other respects. Struve placed more emphasis on the progressive face of capitalism than Volodya, who tended to stress its more destructive, exploitative features. Struve also allowed a greater role to the Russian bourgeoisie. He was an evolutionist. He believed that socialism might well triumph in Russia without recourse to violent revolution. His thinking in this respect was much influenced by developments in Germany where the Social Democratic Party (SPD), now legalized, had won 1.8 million votes in the elections of 1893 and captured 44 seats in the Reichstag. There seemed every chance that at some point in the future the SPD would come to power by parliamentary means. With the introduction of political freedoms, the same pattern might emerge in Russia.

While Volodya totally rejected the evolutionary scenario, he believed there was enough common ground (and potential advantage for himself and his associates) to establish ties with Struve. The two met at Lesnoe, outside Petersburg, at the end of 1894 and concluded a literary alliance. In April 1895 Struve and his close associate Alexander Potresov, with editorial assistance and contributions from Volodya, Radchenko and another member of his circle, V. V. Starkov, compiled a volume of essays for publication. The outcome, however, was disappointing. The censor was aroused by the tone and content of some of the essays which he denounced as 'pernicious' in intent. Save for about 100 copies, the entire print run of 2,000 was seized and burnt. This did not mark the end of the Ulyanov–Struve relationship. They met frequently during 1895–6 (though they were never entirely at ease in each other's company) and co-operated occasionally over the next few years.

Meanwhile, the Social-Democratic movement was by no means standing still. Small Marxist circles were forming in most of the major industrial centres and nowhere was the Social-Democratic ideology better received than among the impoverished Jewish artisans of western Russia, who were losing out in competition to the factory worker on the one hand and the peasant handicraftsman on the other. The Jews' social, cultural and political isolation left them no alternative but to band together; at the same time, many of them were coming to realize that their interests would best be served through co-operation with the broader socialist movement then emerging in other parts of the country.

Up until then, Jewish socialists had been content to propagandize workers in much the same way as Russian socialists elsewhere. In 1893, however, Arkadi Kremer produced a pamphlet 'On Agitation', which argued convincingly for a new tactic aimed at broadening socialism's base among workers by campaigning actively on bread-and-butter issues of pay, hours and conditions. Following the success of agitation in Vilno, a young associate of Kremer's, Iulii Martov (born Tsederbaum) visited Petersburg with the good news. In January 1895 Volodya and his worker-pupil Ivan Babushkin gave the tactic a trial run by composing an agitational leaflet addressed to workers at the Semyannikov (later Nevsky) shipbuilding plant. The following month agitation was discussed at a meeting attended by Social Democrats from Petersburg, Moscow, Kiev and Vilno. In the course of the same meeting, a decision was taken to establish closer links between Social-Democratic circles in Russia and Plekhanov's Emancipation of Labour Group in Geneva, in what was envisaged as a first step towards the creation of a Russian Marxist party. The two delegates elected to make the trip abroad were E. I. Sponti and V. I. Ulyanov.

Volodya was nearly unable to travel. In March he was struck down with pneumonia. His mother, fearful of losing yet another child, hurried to his side and nursed him to recovery. He used his convalescence as the pretext for requesting permission to go abroad. To his relief he was issued with the necessary travel documents and left Petersburg by train for Switzerland on 7 May.

This was his first taste of life overseas and he was determined to make the most of it. He was quickly disconcerted by the apparent gulf between his knowledge of written and spoken languages, especially German. During a short stay-over in Salzburg, he wrote to his mother:

> I understand the Germans with the greatest difficulty, or rather, I do not understand them at all. I do not understand even the simplest words – their pronunciation is unusual and they talk so fast. I ask the conductor a question – he answers; I do not understand. He repeats his answer louder. I still do not understand; he gets angry and goes away. In spite of such a disgraceful fiasco, I do not lose courage and fairly assiduously distort the German language.[37]

How many tourists have been through the same nightmare!

Eventually he managed to negotiate all the hazards and found himself in Geneva, where he was met by Alexander Potresov, a friend of Struve.

Potresov was entrusted with the task of conducting Volodya to Plekhanov's rural retreat at Les Ormonts.

One can easily imagine Volodya's feelings as he prepared to meet the 'Father of Russian Marxism'. He had a tendency to hero worship. Years before he had tried to start up a correspondence with Chernyshevsky, only to discover that his idol was already mortally ill. An ambition to meet Friederich Engels was about to be thwarted for the same reason (Engels died in August 1895). Marx had long preceded him to the grave. No one, however, would cheat Vladimir Ulyanov of his encounter with Plekhanov.

The founder of the Emancipation of Labour Group was a forbidding figure. Aged 39, he compensated for his short stature with a crisp, no-nonsense manner (he had been educated at military school) and a dapper appearance. His features increasingly came to resemble a stage Mephistopheles. Plekhanov's conversation was brilliant, urbane and sparking with sarcasm. If Volodya sometimes behaved like a headmaster, he had more than met his match in Plekhanov.

In the event, the meeting passed off quite well. Actually, Plekhanov was highly excited by the prospect of re-establishing links with the socialist movement on Russian soil, describing the visit of Volodya and Sponti as 'a tremendous event in the life of the Emancipation of Labour Group'. He praised his rather bashful visitor but at the same time gently admonished him for being too dismissive of the bourgeoisie in his assessment of revolutionary forces in Russia: 'We want to turn our faces to the liberals, while you turn your back'.[38]

From Geneva, Volodya moved on to Zurich, where he met another member of the Emancipation of Labour Group, Pavel Axelrod. A few years older than Plekhanov, Axelrod had lived abroad since 1874 and was something of an authority on the European socialist movement. He had recently been entertaining Sponti and noted that Volodya was 'also a young person, quite short, a rather colourless type'. Volodya introduced himself and made a presentation of the ill-fated Struve volume. Axelrod already knew about this project – he was originally to have been a contributor himself.

That evening, Axelrod leafed through the book he had been given and his attention rested on the contribution by 'K. Tulin'. This was actually Volodya's pseudonym but Axelrod did not know it at the time. Tulin's essay made 'the very best of impressions' even if the arguments were constructed in a 'somewhat discordant, ever careless way'. The author, it seemed to Axelrod, had 'the temperament of a fighting flame'; for him, Marxism was 'not an abstract doctrine but a weapon of revolutionary struggle'.[39]

When Axelrod found out that Tulin and Volodya were one and the same, he invited him to spend a few days in his alpine retreat near the village of Affoltern: 'It was May and the weather was fine. We walked for days at a time and together climbed the mountains around Zug'.

Both men got on splendidly. Axelrod noted approvingly that there was 'not the slightest trace of conceit or vanity' about Volodya. His companion was serious and attentive and soon conceded that he had been mistaken in his evaluation of the Russian liberals. As he confided to Axelrod: 'You know, Plekhanov made exactly the same remarks about my article'. The two went on to talk excitedly of the future of socialism in Russia and the splendid prospects for co-operation between the Emancipation of Labour Group and the Russian Marxists.

Volodya was in love with Switzerland. He had already written to his mother that 'The scenery here is splendid . . . it was impossible to tear oneself away from the carriage window'.[40]

Early in June, he travelled to Paris. Typically, he showed little interest in sightseeing, preferring to stroll through the suburbs observing the people – who behaved 'quite unrestrainedly' to someone grown accustomed to 'Petersburg respectability and severity'. He was also in the libraries again, this time doing some researches on the prototype for a workers' government, the Paris Commune. The highlight, however, was a meeting with Marx's son-in-law, Paul Lafargue. Lafargue made a good impression, but he was disappointingly sceptical when Volodya eagerly confided that Russian workers were already reading and understanding Marx.

At the beginning of July 1895, he returned to Switzerland, taking up residence at a health resort. He wrote to his mother: 'I have decided to take the opportunity of attending seriously to my tireless stomach trouble, especially as the specialist who runs this place had been strongly recommended to me as an expert'. Then came the bad news: 'Judging from all appearances, life here will be very expensive; the cure still more expensive, and I have already exceeded my budget and cannot hope to manage on my resources. If possible, send me another hundred rubles'.[41]

At the end of July, he made his way to Berlin where he studied for about six weeks at the Staatsbibliothek. 'I am quite happily settled here: the Tiergarten is only a few yards away (it is a beautiful park, the best and largest in Berlin), also the Spree, where I bathe every day'. But financial worries persisted. He wrote to his mother:

> Well, I shall live here for a while yet, but, to my great horror, I see I again have money difficulties; the temptation to buy books etc. is so great that my money goes the devil knows where. Again I have to turn to you for assistance: if you can, send me 50 to 100 rubles.[42]

Thanks to an introduction from Plekhanov, Volodya also met the leader of the German Social Democratic Party, Wilhelm Liebknecht. And he found time to attend a performance of Hauptmann's play *The Weavers*, not all of which he understood (he was still having trouble with German).

His first encounter with Western Europe was now drawing to a close. On 19 September 1895 he crossed the frontier into Russia, carrying with him a trunk with a double lining which was crammed with illegal literature. He escaped the notice of the border guards but his movements abroad had been closely observed. From now on he and his comrades would be under the closest surveillance.

He did not return directly to Petersburg. As he reported in a letter to Axelrod in Zurich, he stopped first in Vilno to discuss a projected workers' newspaper with local Social Democrats. Next he went to Moscow, where he failed to meet up with his contact, E. I. Sponti (known conspiratorially as the 'Master of Life'). Finally, he visited Orekhovo-Zuevo: 'one of those typical small mill towns with some tens of thousands of inhabitants where the life of the town depends on the factory'. Aware, perhaps, even at this stage (early November 1895) that the police were closing in, he was obsessed with conspiracy. He confided to Axelrod: 'I do not like the Zurich address. Can't you find another – not in Switzerland but in Germany? That would be safer'. Again, in the same letter: 'You must write in Indian ink. It would be better, if you were to add a small crystal of potassium bichromate ($K_2Cr_2O_7$); then it would not wash off. Use *thinner* paper'.

In another letter to Axelrod, written a week or two later, he said:

> It is essential [when hiding correspondence inside the binding of books] to use liquid paste: not more than a teaspoonful of starch to a glass of water (and moreover, potato flour, not the ordinary flour, which is too strong). The ordinary (good) paste is only necessary for the top sheet and for coloured paper, because the paper holds well together under a press, even with the thinnest of pastes.[43]

Back in Petersburg plans were afoot to unite the various Marxist circles around a campaign of agitation. A 'central circle' was formed which included Volodya, Martov, Krzhizhanovsky, Starkov and Vaneev. Volodya threw himself feverishly into the preparation of the agitational literature. His first effort, back in January, had been rather amateurish. Krupskaya recalled: 'The leaflet was copied out by hand in printed letters and distributed by Babushkin. Out of the four copies two were picked up by the watchmen, while two went round from hand to hand.'

The new batch of leaflets, 'To the Working Men and Women of the Thornton Factory', 'Explanation of the Law on Fines Imposed on Factory Workers' and 'The New Factory Law', was more informative and distributed more effectively by Nadya and two of her friends: Apollinaria Yakubova (on whom Volodya appears to have had a crush for a time) and Krzhizhanovsky's wife, Z .P. Nevzorova. Dressed as working women, they would roll up the leaflets in tubes hidden in their aprons and, when the factory hooter sounded, walk quickly among the emerging workers, pressing them into hands at random.

Speed was of the essence. The year 1895 marked the beginning of a strike movement which was to increase in scale and intensity over the next two years. Conveniently for Volodya's group, the unrest in Petersburg centred on the Thornton textile mill, just across the river from the Nevsky district. While the 'central circle' had no hand in directing the strike, nor any obvious influence in formulating the demands, it learned a lot about the mood of the workers, the nature of their grievances and their preferred methods of organization. This would be put to good use in the years to come. For the present, it was getting them into ever deeper waters. A police report noted:

> Members of the Petersburg social democratic circle took a direct part in the publication and distribution of appeals at the Thornton mill during the recent disturbances there. On the evening of 7 November of this year Ulyanov and Starkov went to see Nikita Merkulov, a worker at the Aleksandrovsky steel foundry, and handed over 40 rubles to assist the families of workers detained for disorders at the said factory. They instructed him to convince the workers to hold firm, not fearing for the future and promising to support them with financial help. On the following day the named agitators were constantly in the company of Merkulov and on 12 November supplied him with a large quantity of flysheets.[44]

Ulyanov and his friends were also busy preparing their own news-sheet, to be called *The Workers' Cause*. At the same time, they were collecting material for Plekhanov who hoped to bring out his own newspaper in Geneva. (They had already sent items on the Petersburg strikes via Axelrod.) Under the strain of this feverish activity, Volodya's nerves were becoming frayed. On 17 December he wrote to his mother:

> Life goes on as usual here. I am not very pleased with my room; first, because the landlady finds fault, and secondly, I have discovered there is the thinnest partition between my room and the one next door, so that everything is overheard and sometimes I am forced to escape from the balalaika with which my neighbour amuses himself immediately under my ear.[45]

On the evening of 8 December, the final revisions of the first number of *Workers' Cause* were completed at a meeting held in Krupskaya's house. One copy of the proofs was taken by Vaneev for a final check while Nadya took charge of the other. The next day she called at Vaneev's to pick up the corrected version. He was not at home. Becoming anxious, she hurried to the house of a colleague where Volodya was expected for his dinner. He did not arrive there either. She was sure he had been arrested, and she was not mistaken. During the night the police had swooped and seized more than 40 Social-Democrat activists, effectively cleaning up the Petersburg organization. Volodya was taken to the House of Preliminary Detention on Shpalernaya Street and confined in cell number 193. He would not be at liberty again for over four years.

3
Prison and exile

Accompanied by two, blue-uniformed policemen, Volodya was taken to prison in a police carriage, its windows curtained from public gaze. He was deposited in the grim, barrack-like remand centre and left to ponder his fate. A search of his apartment revealed several pieces of incriminating evidence: a duplicated leaflet addressed to spinning workers at the Kenig mill; a torn piece of paper containing the text of an appeal written by Zaporozhets to workers at a shoe factory; the text of an article by Volodya on the subject of a recent strike at Yaroslavl and a cutting from the *Moscow Gazette* on a strike by Jewish workers at a factory in Vilno. It hardly mattered; the police knew everything anyway.

On 21 December 1895 Volodya faced his first formal interrogation by Lieutenant-Colonel Klykov of the Special Branch in the presence of A. I. Kichin, Procurator of the Petersburg Chamber of Justice. In accordance with standard procedure in such cases, Volodya was not allowed legal representation. Then, and on each subsequent occasion, he denied all charges. This intransigence, plus the usual excesses of red tape, account for the 15 months he was to spend at the Shpalernaya Street gaol.

The family was informed of Volodya's arrest by Krupskaya, who travelled to Moscow to break the news in person. Anyuta arrived in Petersburg in January; his mother and Manyasha followed on later. (Anyuta had been ordered to leave Moscow in any case for the period of Nicholas II's coronation.)

Everyone did their best to help. Although her brother was no more than a nominal member of the legal community, Anyuta pressed his former employer, Volkenstein, to act. Eventually the president of the Petersburg bar association, V. O. Lyusnikh, wrote a letter to the police department requesting Volodya's release on bail, with Volkenstein offering to stand surety. The request was turned down.

The prison regulations allowed for twice-weekly visits from a month after arrest. Food parcels were accepted three times a week and his mother took advantage of this concession by preparing a special diet to ease Volodya's recurring stomach trouble. Books and other reading matter, including journals and magazines, could be deposited at the procurator's office on Wednesdays and Saturdays for inspection. As Nadya recalls:

> In those days prisoners under preliminary detention were allowed to have as many books sent them as they liked. These were subjected to a rather superficial examination, during which it was not possible to notice the minute dots placed inside various letters, or the hardly discernible change in the colour of the paper where inscriptions had been penned with milk.[46]

All this meant that Volodya could continue working much as before, though of course in less congenial surroundings. Like a hero out of Chernyshevsky, he brought his will-power and resourcefulness to bear on the situation. To combat the cold and damp of his cell, he devised a programme of exercises to keep him fit and to warm him up at night. (He was later in the habit of recommending this strategy to anyone who found themselves in the same predicament.) He invented a code which enabled him to play chess with the prisoner in the next cell and, assuming the role of senior captive officer in a POW camp, watched over the morale of his revolutionary comrades and was attentive to their needs. Contacts outside were commissioned to find 'girl-friends' for those without visitors, or to procure shoes or books. As his sister pointed out, this involved a great deal of time and effort on his part – and on that of his friends. Buoyant, but not superhuman, Volodya occasionally suffered from 'prison melancholy'. To stave this off, he once tried arranging a rather tortuous rendezvous with Krupskaya:

> When they were taken out for exercise, it was possible through one of the windows in the corridor to catch a momentary glimpse of a fragment of the Shpalernaya pavement. So he suggested that at a definite time I and Apollinaria Alexandrovna Yakubova should come and stand on this piece of pavement and then he would see us. Apollinaria was for some reason or other unable to go. I went several days and stood for a long while on that spot. Something went wrong with the plan, however, though I don't remember what.[47]

For Volodya, prison was above all a place for uninterrupted study. He was about to embark on one of his more important works, *The Development of Capitalism in Russia*, and some of the preliminary research was done at government expense. On his release, he complained to Nadya: 'It's a pity they let us out so soon . . . I would have liked to do a little more work on the book'.

This was not his only project while in detention. In July 1896 he completed the *Draft and Explanation of A Programme For the Social Democratic Party*, an expanded version of an earlier draft by Plekhanov.

Volodya focuses on the role of the working class in the coming revolution. He explains how capitalism has created a wage-dependent proletariat in Russia by tearing former peasants from their roots and concentrating them in large factories where their labour can most conveniently be exploited. He goes on to demonstrate how this concentration is also the source of the workers' strength, encouraging them to communicate, to analyse their experiences and to formulate grievances. And because the fluid, unstable nature of the labour market involves workers in constant movement from factory to factory in search of work, they come to appreciate that capitalist exploitation is not confined to one enterprise or industry, but is universal. This realization in turn promotes a wider, more effective, solidarity. Strikes become better organized and co-ordinated. The capitalists react by forming associations geared to protecting their own interests and to minimizing the impact of industrial action. The struggle has assumed a class dimension: the workers become 'class conscious'. But the contest remains an unequal one because the capitalist class has an ally in the government, which defends the employers' organizations while outlawing those of the workers. At this point the struggle takes on a political, revolutionary character: the workers come to realize that the only way

to put an end to the exploitation of labour by capital . . . is to abolish the private ownership of the instruments of labour, to hand over all the factories, mills, mines, and likewise all the large estates, etc. to society as a whole and introduce common socialist production that is directed by the workers themselves.[48]

However, as Plekhanov had described earlier, Russian workers faced an additional obstacle to those encountered by their comrades in Western Europe; namely, tsarist autocracy. Until this outmoded form of absolutism was swept away and the basic freedoms of speech, assembly and association introduced, the wider political struggle would be severely impeded. Fortunately, there were allies in the struggle to abolish autocracy: the bourgeoisie, which sought power for its own class interests, and the peasant masses, for whom the overthrow of tsarism effectively meant an end to exploitation by the landed nobility. But the proletariat alone must lead the struggle, under the guidance of the intelligentsia-led Social Democratic Party, whose role was to assist and enlighten the workers' movement: to advise on strategy and tactics, to educate and train leaders, to foster class consciousness among the rank and file and to lend material support. The party was in no way to substitute for the working class: 'The emancipation of the workers must be a matter for the workers themselves'.

This was the tenor of Volodya's thinking as he was condemned, along with most of his comrades, to three years' exile in eastern Siberia. He alone took advantage of the customary privilege of making the journey at his own expense and without a police escort. Ever adept at string-pulling, Mariya Ulyanov was working to have her son sent to a 'soft' location, arguing that his health was delicate (he had suffered previously from pneumonia). He was released from prison in mid-February 1897 and allowed a few days in Petersburg to put his affairs in order. Of course, he took full advantage of this heaven-sent opportunity to re-establish links with the revolutionary underground.

Much had happened in the 15 months since his incarceration. The recently unified party organization had survived, since Martov, Radchenko and a handful of others had evaded arrest. It was given a new name, the Union of Struggle for the Liberation of the Working Class. When Martov was arrested in January 1896, leadership passed to a former medical student, Fedor Dan, until he too was caught up in the police net. By now there were few of the original members left so, for the first time, workers were co-opted on to the Union's ruling body. While appreciating the intelligentsia's contribution to the movement, the workers were no longer prepared to play second fiddle. They had their own ideas of what the Union should be doing and began to assert themselves. They wanted to run their own newspaper and to direct their own strike fund. More important-ly, they were becoming resentful of attempts to superimpose political demands and slogans on to the strike movement. This new trend had the support of some intelligentsia newcomers to the movement – A. A. Yakubova and K. M. Takhtarev among them. They were known as the *molodye* (Youngsters); their opponents, led by Radchenko, as the *stariki* (Veterans). Volodya sided with his former colleague, Radchenko. He rejected the argument that the workers could grow 'spontaneously' to political consciousness through their own economic struggle without the help of the intelligentsia. On the other hand, he was by no means opposed to workers taking leading positions in the organization – providing, that is, they were up to the job intellectually as well as in other respects.

The Social Democrats had picked a bad moment to squabble among themselves. The strike movement, which had provoked the arrests of December 1895, broke out afresh in the following year. In May 1896 30,000 textile workers came out *en masse* in a dispute sparked off by a misunderstanding over paid leave on the occasion of Nicholas II's coro-nation. Unlike many previous strikes, however, discipline was maintained: there was no drunkeness, brawling or destruction of property. The workers held firm. Their principal demand was for a reduction in the working day from twelve or thirteen hours to ten and a half. When the government prevaricated, the textile workers threatened more strike action. Eventually, in June 1897, a new factory law reduced the length of the working day to eleven and a half hours.

While the Petersburg Marxists could not claim to have initiated or led the strike movement of 1896–7, they had helped to influence it. For some time, members of the Union of Struggle had been encouraging workers to discuss their grievances in the study circles. They now processed this information and presented it in leaflets which they printed themselves and distributed in the factories and mills. Members of the Union were also in contact with the strike committee and organized collections for its funds.

The trend was encouraging: the workers had shown themselves ready for struggle and, through a great show of solidarity, had won their first confrontation with the government. Everything, it seemed, was in line with Marxist predictions. The movement was becoming politicized.

So it was with mixed feelings that Volodya and his fellow-exiles said goodbye to their friends in February 1897. At that time Volodya was closest to Julius Martov, whose brother recalls their last days of freedom together:

> On the first day that [Volodya] came . . . he stayed overnight with us to talk his fill to Julius alone, for whom he showed great sympathy and respect. They did not even sleep but talked on into the morning. This night very probably marked the beginning of their close personal relationship while in exile, for until their arrest they had been acquainted only for a few months and had met mainly on an official footing.[49]

The leaders of the Union of Struggle had one final appointment – with Nadezhda Krupskaya, who photographed them for posterity, gathered around a table, gazing earnestly into the future. Her husband-to-be occupied the central position.

Russia had been exiling political prisoners since the sixteenth century. As the boundaries of the empire grew, so the places of exile became increasingly remote. The face of Siberia was scarred with hard-labour camps, factories, mines and prisons. The most notorious were Nerchinsk (where Chernyshevsky was incarcerated), Omsk (where Dostoevsky once served a term) and Sakhalin Island. Less serious offenders (like Volodya) were sentenced by Administrative Order – that is without trial – to spend a designated period in a specified location under surveillance. In their case, no compulsory labour was involved and there were few personal restrictions. By 1897 there were about 300,000 exiles scattered about the various provinces of Siberia, just over 5 per cent of the total population.

Volodya took about 11 weeks to reach his destination. After a short stop-over in Moscow, his mother and sisters travelled with him as far as Tula. Unlike exiles of an earlier generation, he was able to make use of the new Trans-Siberian railway which took him as far as Ob'. There he crossed the frozen river by horse-drawn sleigh before continuing by train to Krasnoyarsk. He stayed for nearly two months in the house of a radical sympathizer, Claudia Popova, waiting for the River Yenisei to become navigable. In Krasnoyarsk he had time to become acquainted with other 'politicals', as well as to visit the famous library of a local merchant called Yudin with its estimated 100,000 volumes. He was disappointed to find that it contained little in the way of economics and statistics.

In mid-April he was joined by Martov and other members of the Union of Struggle who had made the journey under police escort. Soon after-

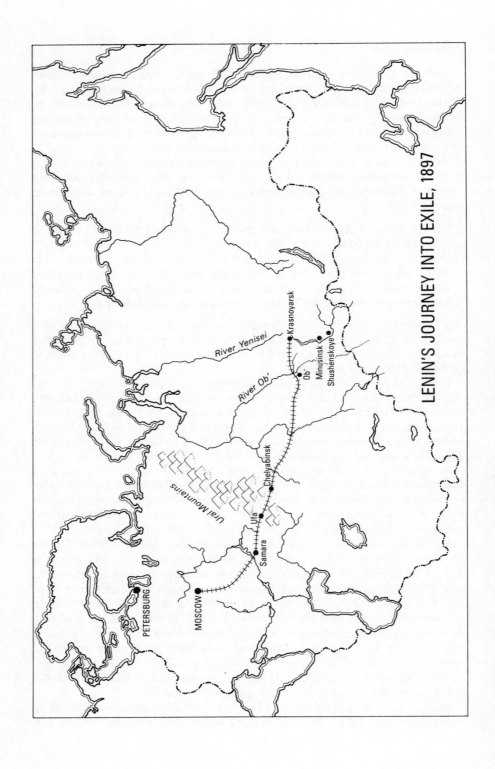

LENIN'S JOURNEY INTO EXILE, 1897

wards they were designated their various places of exile. The worst off was Martov, assigned to the bleak and remote settlement of Turukhansk, 700 miles (1,127 km) north of Yeniseisk and only just below the Arctic Circle. There he contracted tuberculosis, the disease which would ultimately kill him. The others were more fortunate. Volodya was to spend the next three years in the village of Shushenskoye in the district of Minusinsk, less than 300 miles (480 km) south of Krasnoyarsk. There the climate and surroundings were much more hospitable. Mariya Alexandrovna must have been relieved.

In the second week of May he set off by river steamer for Minusinsk, with Starkov and Krzhizhanovsky among his companions. This leg of the journey took seven days, so it was fortunate that he had plenty of reading matter with him. The wife of another exile, Lepeshinskaya, told her husband about this:

> Her bunk was near Vladimir Ilyich's. He had in his hands some kind of serious book (I think it was in a foreign language). Before half a minute had passed his fingers were already turning the page. She asked him, was he reading line by line or just skimming the pages with his eyes? Somewhat surprised by her question, he answered with a smile:
> 'Well, of course I'm reading . . . and very carefully, as this book is well worth –'
> 'But how are you able to read page after page so quickly?'
> Vladimir Ilyich replied that if he read at a slower rate, he wouldn't be able to get through everything he had to familiarise himself with.[50]

From Minusinsk it was only 30 miles (48 km) to Shushenskoye. Volodya was happy enough with his new surroundings when he finally arrived on 20 May. He wrote to Manyasha:

> You ask me to describe the village of Shu-shu-shu [his pet name for Shushenskoye]: Hm! Hm! It is a big village with several streets, rather muddy and dirty . . . It stands in the steppes – there are no orchards or greenery of any kind. The village is surrounded by dung, which the people here do not cart to the fields but dump outside, so that when you leave you always have to pass through a certain amount of dung. There is a stream called the Shush right beside the village; now it is very yellow. [A little distance away] the Shush joins the Yenisei which here breaks up into a large number of streams with islands between them, so that there is no way of reaching the mainstream on foot. On the other side . . . there is what the peasants quite seriously call 'the pine grove', really a very poor bit of woodland in which most of the trees have been felled so that there is no real shade (but lots of strawberries!) . . .
> Mountains . . . when I wrote about the mountains I was very inaccurate for they are *about 50 versts* (33 miles/53 km) from here so that you can only look at them when they are not hidden by clouds, in exactly the same way as you can see Mont Blanc from Geneva.[51]

He rented a room from a local peasant called Zyryanov. As Krupskaya tells us, all the cottages in the Minusinsk region were kept spotlessly clean. The walls were whitewashed and decorated with fir branches; brightly coloured mats were strewn on the floors. When Zyryanov saw the number of books Volodya had brought with him, he put up some shelves in his room.

Living in Shushenskoye was exceptionally cheap. Volodya received a State allowance of 8 roubles a week – quite sufficient to cover rent, food and laundry. The diet was rather monotonous but there were no shortages and he soon glowed with health.

Nor was there any lack of company. Apart from Zyryanov, who was something of a drinker, there were two worker-exiles: Prominsky, a Polish hatmaker who lived with his wife and six children, and a Finn called Oscar Enberg who had formerly been employed at the Putilov works in Petersburg – one of the largest factories in Europe. Prominsky had an impressive repertoire of Polish revolutionary songs which he liked to bawl at the top of his voice; he was also an enthusiastic hunter. Enberg had been exiled for taking part in a riot during a strike. His behaviour was unrestrained and unpredictable, but he could be a cheerful companion. Volodya was also friendly with a rough old peasant called Sosipatych who joined them on the regular hunting parties. No one else bothered him – the local school teacher spent most of his time playing cards with the priest and even the district policeman paid little attention to State criminal Ulyanov. Indeed, 'politicals' were generally treated with respect, even deference, by the host communities. Some policemen were quite happy to pay exiles to teach their children.

While he was adapting to his new circumstances, Volodya's friend Nadezhda Krupskaya had also been arrested, imprisoned and sentenced to three years' exile, but in her case to the much less remote town of Ufa in the Ural Mountains. In February 1898 Volodya petitioned the authorities to allow her to serve her exile in Shushenskoye instead. He describes her in the letter as his 'fiancée'. Permission was granted, with the proviso that they marry at the earliest opportunity. Nadya made the journey at her own expense and arrived, with her widowed mother Elizaveta Vasilyevna in tow, on 19 May. As Nadya recalled, Volodya was not at home:

At last Vladimir Ilyich returned from the hunt. He was surprised to see a light in his room. The master of the house told him that it was Oscar Alexandrovich [Enberg] . . . who had come home drunk and scattered all his books about. Vladimir Ilyich quickly bounded up the steps. At that moment I emerged from the *izba* [peasant cottage]. We talked for hours and hours that night. Ilyich looked much fitter and fairly vibrated with health.[52]

Inevitably, Nadya's arrival brought changes. She did not get on with the

Zyryanovs (too many drinking parties, for one thing) so the three of them moved into a house by themselves. To her delight there was a yard and kitchen garden where she managed to grow cucumbers, carrots, beetroots and pumpkins. She was not so successful in the kitchen: 'Two of us fought with the Russian stove. First I knocked over the soup and dumplings with the oven-hook, scattering them over the hearth. But afterwards I got used to it.'

They hired a 13-year-old girl, called Pasha, to help with the domestic chores. Nadya taught her to read and write. A kitten joined the household and there was a dog named Zhenka. Nadya's mother became particularly attached to a little boy from one of the neighbouring cottages who used to pay them impromptu visits.

Volodya married Nadya on 22 July 1898. The ceremony took place in church as Russian law demanded. This was obviously an embarrassment to the couple, though it would have pleased Elizaveta Vasilyevna, who was deeply religious.

Volodya was a devoted if undemonstrative husband and Nadya idolized him. Elizaveta Vasilyevna's feelings towards her son-in-law were mixed. She was willing to joke with him about his atheism but fundamentally of course she disapproved. To that extent, perhaps, she considered him a bad influence on her daughter. The same might be said about politics. Nadya's mother adapted to the world of social democracy readily enough, but she had no enthusiasm for Marxism. No doubt there were times when she wished her daughter had found a more conventional husband.

By far the most important product of Volodya's three years in exile was *The Development of Capitalism in Russia*. He had not written a work of this scale before and one senses in his correspondence an occasional feeling of impatience and frustration with the painstaking nature of the task. In July 1897, for example, he wrote home that work was 'progressing very, very slowly'. At the end of August he was 'distracted' from the main task by work on an article concerning handicraft industries. In April 1898 Volodya confessed to Mark Elizarov: 'My work [on the book] has come to a complete standstill'. However, the book was eventually finished on 11 February 1899 and sent on to Struve, who was liaising with the publishers in Petersburg. The book itself appeared in April, in a first edition of 1,200 copies. The text ran to 480 pages and cost 2 roubles 50 copecks.

The Development of Capitalism in Russia was the end-product of an interest which had begun six or seven years previously in Samara. Once again it was directed against the arguments of the Populists and, despite its unimpeachable academic content, its tone was polemical, as the title of the opening chapter, 'The Theoretical Mistakes of the Narodnik Economists', makes abundantly clear. Here, Volodya summarily dismisses his opponents' views as 'absolutely incorrect'; they 'fail absolutely to understand' the essence of the argument. Elsewhere he resorts to sarcasm: 'Mr. V. V. [Vorontsov] . . . cannot possibly be accused of "not understanding" theory; for it would be the height of injustice to suspect him of even the slightest acquaintance with it'. And this after he had agreed to follow the advice of his sister to tone down some of his remarks!

Thus *The Development of Capitalism* is, at one and the same time, a closely argued economic treatise and a political bludgeon. Actually, the book's title overstates the scope of the study, as Volodya himself was aware. The essence of the work is contained in the subheading: 'The Process of Formation of a Domestic Market for Large-Scale Industry'. Volodya wished to demonstrate that Russian agriculture, by creating a demand for large quantities of farming machinery and equipment, constituted an important market for capitalism. This assertion flatly contradicted the argument of Vorontsov and other Populists who maintained that by driving the peasants into further poverty through obliging them to pay for industrial development, capitalism was depriving itself of the very domestic markets it needed to survive. According to Volodya, commerce and capitalism were already active in the Russian countryside, challenging the traditional subsistence economy of the peasantry and promoting the process of differentiation into polarized classes.

The reception of *The Development of Capitalism* was initially disappointing. There was one hostile review by P. V. Skvortsov, a writer on the peasant commune, but the weightier pens of Struve, Plekhanov and Tugan-Baranovsky were not even put to paper. However, while the work has its shortcomings, it was a pioneering study of vital importance to Russian Marxism. And for many future revolutionaries graduating from school and university at the turn of the century, *The Development of Capitalism* was further proof of the irrefutability of Marx's economic analysis and of its relevance for the future of Russia.

Writing was a useful source of additional income for Volodya. Besides *The Development of Capitalism*, he was paid for a number of articles, half a dozen of which appeared in October 1898 under the title *Economic Studies and Essays*. Several other pieces came out separately in legal Marxist journals, largely thanks to Struve and his well-connected friends.

Translation work, though more tedious, was another way of earning money. Again with Struve's help, the Ulyanovs were commissioned to translate Beatrice and Sydney Webb's *History of Trade Unionism*. The two of them immersed themselves in grammars and dictionaries and, because their knowledge of English was not very good, they looked to the German edition for assistance. The worst part was writing out the 1,000 pages in fair copy by hand – there were few typewriters available in those days, fewer still in Siberia.

In order to be able to conduct this literary activity over such vast distances, Volodya needed to draw remorselessly on family and friends. Even before his arrival in Shushenskoye, he was writing to his mother: 'I am counting on exploiting [Manyasha] for letter-writing and even for literary work'. And in the same letter (dated 26 March 1897) there is a message for his other sister:

I am sending Anyuta a list of those books I should very much like to obtain and which, it seems, can be bought only in the Petersburg second-hand bookshops, so you will have to write to the 'director' [S. I. Radchenko] and ask him to do it or get somebody else to.

He also apologizes for sending her on a wild-goose chase after a work which he had detailed incorrectly. Still, now that he had corrected his mistake, 'Could not a search also be made in the Moscow libraries?'[53]

Even when the books had been found, there were the frustrations of the postal service to contend with – long delays, lost correspondence and confusion over addresses. Volodya was lucky: there were two posts a week in his district; Martov received letters only eight or nine times a year. Yet he could carp to his mother:

It's a pity that the books were sent so late (if they have been sent – you write that you will be sending them 'in a day or two'). I thought they were already on the way. Now I shall have to find out when they will arrive in Krasnoyarsk. Probably not before the end of summer![54]

Six months later it was the same story:

Up to now I have not received the L.G. [*Labour Gazette*] and *Bulletin*. I don't know the reason for the delay. If you happen to be near the shop in which you ordered them, look in and hurry them up.[55]

Manyasha's work was never done. In a letter to Mark Elizarov, Ulyanov writes:

I hope Manyasha will find time to undertake the proof-reading. In general, it is very important for the proofs to be read by one person from the beginning to end, otherwise there will be a muddle because of the signs the proof-readers use . . . Accurate printing and an elegant edition are very important.[56]

Nor was there any escape for her when she went abroad:

As for newspapers and books, please get hold of whatever you can. Send all sorts of catalogues from second-hand booksellers and bookshops in all languages.[57]

Obviously Volodya was keeping himself and everybody else busy. But he found plenty of time for relaxation and even his work routine could be flexible. As Nadya reported in a letter to Anyuta:

he asks me to wake him at 8 o'clock in the morning, or at half past seven, but my efforts are usually fruitless: He gives a couple of grunts, pulls the clothes over his head and goes to sleep again.[58]

He and Nadya spent as much time as possible out of doors. Skating and walking were the favoured pastimes during the long winter months:

Late in the autumn, when the snow had not yet begun to fall, but the rivers were already freezing, we went far up the streams. Every pebble, every little fish, was visible beneath the ice, just like some magic kingdom. And winter-time, when the mercury froze in the thermometers, when the rivers were frozen to the bottom, when the water, flowing over the ice, quickly froze into a thin upper ice-layer – one could skate two *versts* or so with the upper layer of ice crunching beneath one's feet. Vladimir Ilyich was tremendously fond of all this.[59]

In the summer, he liked nothing better than to go out hunting: from his earliest days in exile it was something of a craze. Even Nadya caught on: '. . . by the following spring I had also become capable of conversing about ducks – who had seen them, and where, and when.'[60]

The evenings were spent reading works of literature or philosophy. Volodya's favourite authors continued to be Pushkin, Lermontov, Nekrasov and Turgenev: the classics. Then there was an extensive correspondence to keep up, including chess games with Lepeshinsky and others. (Nadya sometimes heard him plan out moves in his sleep.) At one time he amused himself by carving a set of chessmen from bark.

Occasional opportunities to go visiting or to receive visitors also enlivened Volodya's exile. Permission was required for this, but it was usually forthcoming. His friend Gleb Krzhizhanovsky spent the New Year with them in 1898 and visited again the following November. In March 1899 the Ulyanovs entertained half a dozen of their exiled friends in Shushenskoye. Of course, the away-trips were more enjoyable. Volodya was in Tsesinskoye in August 1897 to attend the wedding of V. V. Starkov and visited fellow exiles there and in Minusinsk the following October. He made a couple of trips to Yermakovskoye where the Lepeshinskys, the Vaneevs, Silvin and one or two others were all serving out their sentences. And in September 1898 he travelled alone as far as Krasnoyarsk. Nadya wrote to Manyasha: 'Today I am going to write an enormously long letter; Volodya has gone off to Krasnoyarsk and the place seems empty without him; the "regime" has changed'. He took a shopping-list with him but had problems with some of the items:

I wanted to instruct him to buy material for a blouse for Prominsky's daughter but since Volodya went to mother to find out how many 'pounds' of cloth to buy for a blouse, he had to be relieved of that onerous duty.[61]

Perhaps the most enjoyable trip was to Minusinsk to celebrate the new year, 1899. In December Nadya had written excitedly to Volodya's mother:

We are now busy preparing for a trip to Minusinsk . . . Mother is not going with us – first she said 'no' because the road was bad; now she says it is too cold . . . I don't know whether Volodya told you that Kurnatovsky and the Lepeshinsky's are coming to Minusinsk for Christmas and that they intend to skate, play chess, sing, argue, etc. It looks as though we shall have a good time.

She was not disappointed as she again reported to Mariya Ulyanov:

> At Christmas almost the whole district was in town, so we saw the New Year in very pleasantly at a big party. When the company broke up everyone was saying 'A wonderful New Year's party!' The main thing was the splendid mood. We mulled some wine; when it was ready we put the hands of the clock at '12' and saw the old year out in proper style; everybody sang whatever they could and some fine toasts were pronounced – we drank 'To mothers', 'To All Our Friends' and so on and in the end danced to the guitar . . . Altogether it was a real holiday. Volodya battled on the chessboard from morning to night and won all the games of course; then we went skating.[62]

This atmosphere contrasted sharply with the larger exile colonies, where bickering and ill-founded suspicions preyed on nerves and often resulted in the kind of 'scandals' which Volodya detested. Martov, for example, suffered terribly from persecution at the hands of a Polish worker in Turukhansk, while accusations and innuendo led to the suicide of the precocious young Marxist, N. E. Fedoseev. 'May God save us from "exile colonies" and exile "dramas"!', Volodya lamented to his mother. However, the skirmishes in Siberia were a mere foretaste of the open warfare which was about to break out among Marxists elsewhere in Russia.

In March 1898 representatives of the Jewish Bund had met secretly in Minsk with Social Democrats from Petersburg, Kiev, Moscow and Ekaterinoslav to form the first united Russian Social Democratic Workers' Party. This considerable feat of organization was to count for nothing: within weeks, not only eight of the nine delegates but virtually every activist in Russia were behind bars (some 500 individuals in all).

Worse was to come. In 1899 a leading member of the German Social Democrats (SPD), Eduard Bernstein, challenged the foundations of Marxian orthodoxy in his book *Evolutionary Socialism*. Bernstein denied, among other things, that the capitalist economy was irremediably susceptible to crisis and anarchy, that workers would necessarily become poorer under capitalism and that socialism was attainable only through revolution. The situation in Germany lent weight to Bernstein's arguments. The economy was prospering and the prospects of the SPD eventually coming to power by legal means were good. Bernstein believed that the party could improve its electoral chances still further by attracting support from the bourgeoisie – but this was only possible if it jettisoned its revolutionary phraseology and adopted a reforming, gradualist strategy. Socialism would come about not because it was in any way 'inevitable' but because people wanted it.

Bernstein's frontal assault on Marx's theories (known as Revisionism) was immediately challenged not only by the leading theorist of the SPD, Karl Kautsky, but also by Georgi Plekhanov and other members of the Emancipation of Labour Group. But Bernstein had his Russian supporters. The coterie of Petersburg intellectuals around Peter Struve, for example, which included the economists Mikhail Tugan-Baranovsky and Sergei Bulgakov, was sympathetic to his views. So too was August Kok, an Estonian metalworker from the Caucasus who fell under the influence of Revisionist ideas while on a visit to Germany. When Kok returned to Russia, he began to edit a labour newspaper *Workers' Thought*. He was joined in this enterprise by K. M. Takhtarev and other Youngsters who had spoken out against the domination of the intelligentsia in the Union of Struggle just before Volodya had gone into exile. *Workers' Thought* was composed of material largely by and for the workers themselves, in line with Kok's view that the intelligentsia should be a mere handmaid of the proletariat. The paper was committed to furthering the workers' economic and professional demands but denied the need for an illegal revolutionary workers' party. In short, it represented the heretical deviation which Plekhanov and Volodya (together with their orthodox sympathizers) labelled 'Economism'.

Trouble was also brewing among the Russian Social Democrats abroad. In 1895 the younger generation of *émigrés* had formed the Union of Russian Social Democrats Abroad with the aim of assisting the Emancipation of Labour Group in its publishing activities. The Union's most prominent figures included the husband-and-wife team, Ekaterina Kuskova and Sergei Prokopovich, whose views became increasingly coloured by Economism and Revisionism. Naturally, this brought them into conflict with Plekhanov, whose autocratic manner had already made him unpopular with the Youngsters. Eventually the Emancipation of Labour Group and the Union parted company. In 1899 Kuskova and Prokopovich returned to Russia and caused another stir when the text of one of Kuskova's lectures was published (without her permission) in the newspaper *Workers' Cause*. It became known as her 'Credo'. Kuskova rejected such orthodox notions as the need for an independent working-class party and the inevitability of a revolutionary seizure of power as 'transplantations of alien aims and alien achievements to our soil'. In line with other Economists, she advocated that the intelligentsia should confine itself to backing the proletariat in industrial disputes. They should downplay socialist propaganda and support active co-operation with the liberals and other democratic elements.

Naturally, news of all these developments reached Siberia only fitfully and imperfectly. In April 1899 Volodya wrote with concern to Potresov: 'In general all this "new critical trend" in Marxism, espoused by Struve and Bulgakov . . . looks highly suspicious to me'. Later in the same letter he mentioned that he had ordered Bernstein's new book but was not hopeful of receiving a copy. A couple of weeks later he informed Anyuta that 'there is a very interesting discussion going on now in Germany over Bernstein's new book – and I have not seen that book or anything written about it (with the exception of some casual notes in the *Frankfurter Zeitung*). A great pity'.[63]

At the end of June, Potresov described the worrying impact Bernstein's ideas were having on social democrats in Petersburg. Volodya replied:

> Your information about the reaction against Marxism which has begun in St. Petersburg was news to me. I am puzzled. 'Reaction' – does that mean among the Marxists? And which ones? PB [Struve] again? . . . I fully agree that the 'critics' are only confusing our people . . . and that a serious fight with them (especially over Bernstein) will be necessary.[64]

Manyasha finally managed to get hold of a copy of Bernstein's book in August and her brother received it at the beginning of September. He wrote to his mother:

> Nadya and I started reading Bernstein's book immediately; we have read more than half and its contents astonish us more and more as we go on. It is unbelievably weak theoretically – mere repetition of someone else's ideas. There are phrases about criticism but no attempt at serious, independent criticism . . . Bernstein's statement that many Russians agree with him . . . made us very indignant.[65]

He was also seething about Kuskova's 'Credo', a copy of which he had received courtesy of Anyuta. Clearly it was time to act before the break-up of the entire movement became irreversible. He composed 'A Protest by Russian Social Democrats', aimed specifically at demolishing the arguments of the 'Credo'. In September 1899, 17 exiled Social Democrats gathered in Yermakovskoye to append their signatures to the protest. A copy was dispatched to Martov and the Turukhansk colony, who expressed solidarity with their Siberian comrades. Volodya then began writing a flurry of articles in the same vein and, in December, a new draft of a party programme based defiantly on the 1891 Erfurt programme of the German Social Democrats.

From his point of view, the issues were crystal clear, as was the necessary response. On the ideological front, orthodoxy must be reaffirmed without qualification: class struggle was synonymous with political struggle, the democratic revolution would be led, not by the liberals, but by the proletariat. New foundations for a Social Democratic Party must be laid immediately. The new organization must be disciplined, conspiratorial and unswervingly revolutionary; its duty was to lead the working class, not to be led by them.

Thus Volodya was imbued with a new sense of purpose as his long period of exile drew finally to a close. On 29 January 1900 he, Nadya and Ekaterina Vasilyevna left Shushenskoye for good.

4

Bolsheviks and Mensheviks

The long period of exile was at an end but Volodya was still not entirely free. He could expect to remain under police surveillance and was prohibited from residing in a string of 'sensitive' urban centres, including the two capitals. He eventually chose to settle in Pskov, a small town about 200 miles (322 km) south-west of Petersburg. This was a tolerably convenient location from which to resume revolutionary activity, only two hours' train journey from the capital. It proved impossible, however, for Nadya to join him. She had elected to serve the final year of her term in Ufa, in the Ural Mountains, and he was unable to persuade the authorities to allow her to transfer to Pskov. The alternative – that he petition to be allowed to live with his wife in Ufa – was not seriously considered: 'it did not even enter Vladimir Ilyich's head to remain in Ufa when there was a possibility of getting nearer to Petersburg', Nadya later wrote with warm approval. And so, after he had entrusted his wife and mother-in-law to the care of fellow-revolutionaries in Ufa, he moved on.

Volodya was bursting with energy and enthusiasm. His consuming idea was to launch a working-class newspaper which would simultaneously nail Economism, reassert Marxian orthodoxy and further the political struggle by exposing the tyrannic nature of the autocracy. Besides setting its readers straight on questions of theory and stimulating discussion about a future party programme, the new paper would, he hoped, contribute to reviving the party by giving isolated local groups a sense of belonging to a wider international labour movement.

He already had collaborators: Martov had endorsed the plan from his Turukhansk exile, as had Alexander Potresov, a committed if somewhat genteel Marxist, who had been among the founders of the Petersburg Union of Struggle back in 1895. Potresov too had recently been exiled to Vyatka in the Urals. He was, by arrangement, making for Pskov at the same time as Volodya. Potresov suggested a title for the paper – *Iskra* (*The Spark*), from an early revolutionary verse which contained the stirring line,

'Out of the spark will come a conflagration'. He also proposed launching a second, more abstract journal to be called *Zarya* (*The Dawn*). Volodya's confidence was proving infectious.

The two flouted the conditions of their release even before they reached Pskov. After spending a few days with his mother near Moscow, Volodya called on Social Democrats in Nizhni-Novgorod before making a lightning trip to Petersburg. Here he met up with Vera Zasulich who was also staying illegally in the capital. The backing of the Emancipation of Labour Group was a vital element in his strategy: to his delight, Zasulich assured him of the Group's support.

Support without money, however, was not enough. An initial investment of at least 30,000 roubles was needed to launch a paper like *Iskra*. Volodya began to cast about for likely backers. He himself had nothing to contribute – Nadya had fallen ill in Ufa and his first royalty payment from *The Development of Capitalism* went to pay her medical bills. Potresov donated 2,000 roubles and managed to get half that sum again from D. E. Zhukovsky, a wealthy landowner and childhood friend. Potresov also approached another acquaintance: Alexandra Kalmykova, the widow of a prominent judge and a former mistress of Peter Struve. Kalmykova was a leading figure in the Literacy Committee of the Free Economic Society – the same committee Krupskaya had heard her future husband disparage at their first meeting. Through Struve, Kalmykova had become sympathetic to the Social Democrats and her apartment on Petersburg's fashionable Liteiny Prospekt became something of a safe haven for them (Kalmykova's large and successful book business provided a useful front). Known as 'auntie' in these circles (she was more than 20 years older than Volodya and Struve), Kalmykova now promised 2,000 roubles to help launch *Iskra*. She may also have agreed to canvass support among her wide circle of influential friends. These would have included Struve himself and Mikhail Tugan-Baranovsky.

If Struve and his associates could be won over to the cause, they would prove extremely useful, but there was a problem. They were Revisionists and Volodya had only recently been berating them in print for their sins. How then could he court support from people whose views his journals were intended to attack?

He ruminated on this vexing question in Pskov. He was staying in a house on Archangel Street with his old Petersburg friends, the Radchenkos. Nadya's illness, gynaecological in nature, continued to trouble him. He was not in the best of health himself (he suffered persistently from catarrh). And he had not yet completed the index for the Webb translation he had been working on in Siberia. On the other hand, the news concerning *Iskra* was more encouraging. Feelers in Struve's direction had met a more promising response than might have been expected. Struve appeared willing to make a financial contribution providing he was allowed some space to put the Revisionist case. His apparent flexibility came as a pleasant surprise.

There was more good news to come. On one of his clandestine visits to Petersburg, Volodya met with emissaries from the Union of Russian Social Democrats Abroad who were hoping to take the initiative in arranging a second party congress in Smolensk. This news might have been calculated to raise his hackles. After all, the Union was the nursery of Economism, of those arch-heretics Kuskova and Prokopovich. Yet here again the sweet breeze of compromise was in the air. These Economists, at least, turned out to be less hostile to the political struggle than Volodya had expected; even better, they indicated that the Union might be willing to recognize *Iskra* as the literary organ of the newly reconstituted party. So it appeared that the forces of social democracy were not irreconcilable after all. Had Plekhanov and Axelrod been too intransigent in their dealings with these apparently quite reasonable people, Volodya began to wonder?

At the beginning of April, Volodya sat down to compose a 'Draft Declaration of the Editorial Board of *Iskra* and *Zarya*' intended to serve as a basis for negotiations with Struve. It was a muddled document, cobbled together with one overriding purpose in mind – to obtain funds. When Martov saw the statement he was appalled: he despised Struve and was opposed to any collaboration with him.

Nevertheless, negotiations went ahead. In April 1900 Struve and Tugan-Baranovsky met with Volodya and Potresov in the plain wooden house of the statistician Obolensky in Pskov. Martov attended as an observer. To Martov's considerable chagrin, an agreement was reached whereby the Revisionists would support *Iskra* and *Zarya* in return for discussion space in both newspapers. As a sign of his good faith, Struve pressed a 5 rouble coin into Volodya's palm as he left the meeting. Volodya later joked about this with his friends, telling them, 'I propose not to spend this gold half-imperial, but to put it in a little box and pray every day.'[66]

It was now time to consult with Plekhanov. Potresov left immediately for Europe on the understanding that Volodya would soon follow. On the eve of the latter's departure, however, disaster struck. On 20 May Volodya made one clandestine trip to Petersburg too many. The journey involved changing trains at the imperial residence of Tsarskoe Selo. All railway stations were dangerous places for revolutionaries but none more so than this one, which fairly bristled with policemen of all types. Volodya reached Petersburg safely but was arrested on the street the following day. Eventually he was allowed to travel, under police escort, to his mother's home near Moscow. The manner of his return was ignominious but he had been fortunate: the police had overlooked some incriminating evidence, probably on the instructions of the Okhrana (the security police) which was anxious that he should be allowed to proceed abroad.

For some time Volodya had been trying to get permission to see Nadya. Now at last his request was granted. He journeyed to Ufa in the company of his mother and elder sister. They took the steamer from Nizhni-Novgorod (where he brazenly contacted local Social Democrats) and travelled along the Volga, a magical trip which reminded them all of old times. After spending two weeks with his wife, Volodya returned to Moscow. Then, on 29 July 1900, he finally departed for Europe. It would be five years before he would set foot on Russian soil again.

He made for Zurich where he spent two days with Axelrod. Relations between them were as cordial as they had been on his first visit back in 1895. From Zurich he moved on to Geneva where the formal talks with the Emancipation of Labour Group were to take place. Here he met Potresov, who cautioned him to be wary of Plekhanov.

Plekhanov was indeed in a cantankerous mood. In the spring he had launched a fierce literary attack against the Economists only to see their supporters become the majority in the Union of Russian Social Democrats Abroad. Now he turned his attention to the Revisionists. Never had he been less in the mood to compromise with anyone, let alone renegades from orthodox Marxism.

Even at the preliminary meetings, Plekhanov ('a great man with an enormous number of petty traits' according to Martov's sister) was difficult to handle and sensitive to the most adroit attempts to divert him from the single-minded hatred he was nursing against his opponents. He raged against Struve and the 'Union Abroad people', resorting to the most extravagant hyperbole, even threatening to 'shoot them as traitors'. Yet he was evasive when Volodya invited him to write his criticisms into the text of the *Iskra* statement so that they could be discussed formally.

Things did not augur well for the conference which began at Corsier, near Geneva, on 24 August 1900. Present were Plekhanov, Axelrod, Zasulich, Volodya and Potresov (Martov was away in Russia). By this time Plekhanov's mood had become even darker. When *Iskra*'s relations with the Jewish socialist organization, the Bund, came up, he responded in the debased currency of anti-semitism. His embarrassed colleagues quickly moved on to other matters while Plekhanov folded his arms and feigned disinterest.

By the evening Volodya and Potresov realized that they were being presented with a scarcely veiled ultimatum: either Struve or Plekhanov. Axelrod and Zasulich sympathized with the younger men but their instinctive and long-standing loyalty to Plekhanov prevented them from saying so outright. Finding the situation impossible (as he was meant to), Volodya dropped his proposal to involve Struve.

More concessions were required, however. Up until now, Volodya and Potresov had assumed that they would head the *Iskra* editorial team (it was, after all, their project), but Plekhanov was not prepared to cede his customary pride of place without a struggle. Playing, as always, for the maximum dramatic effect, he suddenly announced his resignation as co-editor. The others were dismayed and pleaded with him to reconsider. Graciously he acquiesced, but at a price: two votes instead of one on the editorial board. Overnight the spell was broken. Volodya no longer saw

LENIN'S EUROPE

the great man in Plekhanov but the vain, mean-spirited one. The consequences for their relationship were dramatic:

> My 'infatuation' with Plekhanov disappeared as if by magic, and I felt
> offended and embittered to an unbelievable degree. Never, never in my
> life had I regarded any other man with such sincere respect and
> veneration, never had I stood before any man so 'humbly' and never
> before had I been so brutally 'kicked' . . . there could be no doubt that
> this man was bad, yes bad, inspired by petty motives of personal vanity
> and conceit – an insincere man.[67]

Rather than accept Plekhanov's humiliating conditions, Volodya and
Potresov decided to give the whole idea up and return to Russia. Axelrod
tried to dissuade them, so did Zasulich, who was said to be close to suicide.

In the end they did change their minds, but on their own terms. *Iskra*
would be produced in Munich, not in Geneva, making it difficult for
Plekhanov to interfere in everyday editorial decisions, even with his
second, casting vote. Effectively, the paper was controlled by the Youngsters – Volodya, Potresov and (from early 1901) Martov.

Plekhanov also backed down on the Struve issue, but here things did not
work out as Volodya had hoped. Struve turned out to be more interested in
forming a new liberal party than in serving the Social Democrats and there
could be no forgiveness for this treachery. Overnight, the man who had
done so much to help Volodya in his literary career became villified as 'Judas
Struve'. The two remained implacable enemies for the rest of their lives.

With the help of Potresov and a Polish socialist, Julian Marchlewski,
Volodya pressed on with the production arrangements for *Iskra* and *Zarya*.
After leaving Geneva in a highly nervous state, he travelled to Nuremberg
for a meeting with Adolf Braun, a German Social Democrat with considerable editorial experience. He also met Anyuta there. From Nuremberg
he continued to Munich, where he arrived on 7 September 1900.

Negotiating with the German socialists was far from easy, as he
complained in a letter to Axelrod: 'We [Ulyanov and Potresov] are both
quite well but very edgy: the main thing is the astonishing uncertainty;
these German rascals keep putting us off daily with "tomorrows". What I
could do to them!'[68]

In the end, perseverance was rewarded. The first issue of *Iskra* rolled off
the presses of the Leipzig printing works of Hermann Rauh on Christmas
Eve, 1900. *Zarya* was entrusted to the SPD's own publishing firm, J. H. W.
Dietz, and first appeared in March 1901. The launch of *Iskra*, in
particular, was a triumph for Volodya and he had reason to be pleased with
his brainchild. The first issue was legible, well-produced and informative.
Twenty-eight more followed over the next two years, making it the most
successful Russian underground publication since Herzen's *Bell* in the
1850s. Volodya (who began to use the pseudonym Lenin about this time)
went to great pains to attract contributors of stature, such as Karl Kautsky

and the Polish socialist Rosa Luxemburg. He also encouraged and brought on new Russian talent: Lev Bronstein (subsequently known as Trotsky) was a regular contributor from the autumn of 1902. *Iskra* also contained a regular column on the activities of local organizations in Russia, drawn from information supplied (erratically) by party members. The political message was trumpeted from the front page of the first issue in the article: 'Urgent Tasks of Our Movement', composed by Lenin himself. The aim of Russian Social Democrats, he proclaimed, was 'the overthrow of autocracy and the attainment of political freedom'.

The slogan was a timely one. A new tide of opposition to the tsarist regime was swelling up inside Russia, one which would gather in strength until it pounded with elemental force against the crumbling rock of absolutism. Student demonstrations at the turn of the century had provoked the government into introducing draconian legislation, which included drafting protesters into the army. Attempts to enforce the provision met with a storm of protest throughout the country, culminating in the assassination of the Minister of Education, N. P. Bogolepov, in 1901. No section of society remained unaffected. Doctors, teachers and agronomists working for the *zemstvos* came into conflict with the government over proposed restrictions on their powers; workers in towns as far apart as Petersburg, Kharkov and Tiflis clashed with troops and police as they took to the streets to proclaim their strike demands or to celebrate May Day; the spectre of peasant rebellion threatened to erupt in the Ukraine and there were nationalist stirrings in Poland and Finland. *Iskra* correspondents were not short of copy.

Each and every manifestation of discontent exhilarated the professional revolutionary in Lenin. But the physical and intellectual burdens imposed on him at this time were truly extraordinary. For the actual production of *Iskra* was only part of his responsibilities: he was also in charge of directing correspondence, of gathering and collating material sent from Russia and of maintaining the fragile distribution network which itself owed much to his formidable organizational skills.

Of course, he did not have to shoulder these burdens alone. Potresov and Zasulich also lived in Munich and helped with the paper's launch, though neither was a great organizer. In this respect, the situation greatly improved in the spring of 1901 when Martov finally arrived, accompanied by his sister, Lydia Osipovna. Despite being thoroughly undisciplined, Martov was a brilliant man, brimming over with energy and talent, while Lydia proved to be an invaluable editorial assistant. When Nadya arrived shortly afterwards, she became Lenin's secretary, replacing Inna ('Dimka') Smidovich.

His taste for routine soon imposed itself on his staff. Work began immediately after lunch, when someone would fetch the post. It was Lenin's prerogative, as editor-in-chief, to read through all correspondence first and he became irritated if Martov began reading over his shoulder or wandered off to the café with one of the Russian newspapers. Nadya's job was to iron the mail in search of secret messages written in milk or lemon juice. Then, either Lydia or Dimka would decode them. This was a hazardous operation, as Lenin 'absolutely couldn't tolerate a bad decoding'; nor, as Lydia recalled years afterwards, could he bear delays. He instructed his wife: 'Each letter should say in invisible ink, not in code, of course, "Please reply on day of receipt".'[69] Later in the afternoon, Lenin and Martov would discuss the correspondence and other administrative business.

Separate editorial meetings were convened to review material submitted for publication. Here, Lydia remembered, Lenin 'could be very severe and cruel in his opinions'. As editor-in-chief, he accorded himself the privilege of making marginal comments on manuscripts while the others had to make do with jotting down their observations on bits of paper. The articles were then sent off to Plekhanov and Axelrod. The latter, burdened with family and business cares and plagued by nervous illness, inevitably failed to meet deadlines. Plekhanov, on the other hand, supplied a multitude of corrections, many of them to the point. Generally speaking, however, he preferred the speculative world of *Zarya* to *Iskra*, with its obsessive regard for organizational questions.

Correspondence from Russia was directed to a variety of 'safe' addresses in Germany before being sent on to a single collecting point in Munich, ultimately to the home of Dr Lehmann on the Gabelsbergerstrasse (Lehmann was a German Social Democrat). Copies of *Iskra* were dispatched to a warehouse in Berlin. Packages were then handed over to professional smugglers who were entrusted with carrying them across the Russian border, together with other contraband goods (usually in double-bottomed suitcases). A Russian contact would pick up the material and deliver it to an *Iskra* agent – S. O. Tsederbaum in Vilno, for example (Tsederbaum was Martov's brother). The agent would await the arrival of a Social Democrat from some other Russian centre, say Moscow or Kazan, who would then take it away for local distribution. *Iskra* was always handed over in person, never through the post. Once in the hands of the local organizations, it was distributed by ordinary activists: pasted on walls, smuggled into factories, dumped in courtyards, even dropped from theatre galleries on to the unsuspecting public below.

However, not every delivery passed through the hands of professional smugglers. Sometimes ordinary travellers would agree to carry a small consignment. On one occasion a ship's cook took on a small load at Marseilles and travelled with it as far as the southern Russian port of Batum. There it was dumped into the sea in special water-proof packages, to be fished out by local Social Democrats and sent on to Baku. All kinds of routes were opened up in this way: packages arrived from places as far apart as Toulon, Alexandria, Tabriz and Lvov. Often the material was intercepted or lost; sometimes the carrier was a double agent or plain dishonest. One consignment was left unclaimed for years in a Stockholm warehouse. The *Iskra* team estimated that about 10 per cent of its deliveries eventually got through, enough to make the paper's production worthwhile.

The entire enterprise depended on the maintenance of secret, coded communication between Lenin in Munich and his agents inside Russia. There were nine of them by the end of 1901, but arrests ensured a rapid turnover in personnel. One-time agents included Elena Stasova in Petersburg, Lev Khinchuk and Nikolai Bauman in Moscow, the Krzhizhanovskys and Manyasha in Samara, the Lepeshinskys in Pskov and Lengnik in Poltava. In addition, there were a number of roving agents whose tasks included passing on vital information from abroad, issuing instructions to local groups and committees and restoring links with organizations cut off by arrests.

The traumatic negotiations with Plekhanov, the equally fraught business with Struve and the launching of *Iskra* all took place within a matter of months from the autumn of 1900 to the beginning of 1901. The biographer has to delve deep to uncover Lenin's personal life at this time (in the context the word 'private' hardly seems appropriate).

His first home in Munich adjoined a tavern on the Kaiserstrasse kept by a German Social Democrat, Georg Rittmeyer. The simple surroundings suited him, though presumably not the noise which carried across the yard into his room. He was served *mehlspeise* (a kind of pudding) and morning and evening tea in a tin mug which usually hung from a nail above the sink. He confessed to feeling lonely during these months, and longed for photographs of members of his family and for 'the real Russian winter, the sleigh rides and the clean frosty air'. He was contemptuous of those Germans who called ten degrees below zero a 'terrible frost'.

His health was not good: bouts of influenza laid him low; he was still troubled by catarrh and nervous exhaustion led to the insomnia that was to plague him, off and on, for the rest of his life.

Nevertheless, things began to improve after Christmas 1900. He was cheered by the Munich carnival ('People here do know how to make merry publicly in the streets') and he paid several visits to the threatre. He asked his mother about Chekhov's *Three Sisters*, of which he had just seen a review. In February 1901 he attended a performance of Halevy's opera *La Juive* (then highly popular) and recalled having heard it in Kazan when the tenor lead was taken by Zakrzhevsky ('Some of the tunes have remained in my memory').

What really raised his spirits, however, was the thought of Nadya's arrival. In March he had to travel to Vienna in order to have her passport witnessed by the Russian consul there. He loved the place: 'Vienna is a huge, lively and beautiful city', he wrote to his mother. 'There is something to look at here and it is worth while stopping off (should any of you be travelling this way). For this purpose I have sent Nadya a pocket *Fuhrer durch Wien*.[70]

But for Nadya the journey to Germany was a nightmare. She mistakenly thought her husband was living in Prague, using the name of Modraczek (actually the name of acquaintances), so she made her way there. The Modraczeks told her that Lenin was living in Munich under the name of Rittmeyer. She eventually found the tavern and asked the woman behind the bar for Rittmeyer. Rittmeyer was of course the landlord – Lenin actually called himself Meyer in Munich – but the mix-up was finally sorted out. Nadya found her husband in his room, chatting aimiably to Martov and Anyuta. Steaming in her winter furs (it was April), she was in no mood for sentimentality: 'Why the devil didn't you write and tell me where I could find you?'[71]

In May the Ulyanovs moved into a new flat, part of a modern housing development in Schwabing, then on the outskirts of Munich. In one of her chatty letters to Lenin's mother, Nadya enthused that Schwabing combined the advantages of town and countryside. Not only was there a tram route into the city but beyond them stretched a long, tree-lined road with fields and orchards on either side. They were able to go for the rambles and picnics they both enjoyed so much. The countryside had a beneficial effect on Lenin's health, Nadya reported to her mother-in-law in August 1901:

> Volodya is now working quite hard and I am glad for his sake; when he throws himself completely into some task he feels well and strong – that is one of his natural qualities; there does not seem to be a trace of the catarrh and no insomnia. Every day he takes a cold rub down and we bathe almost daily too.[72]

Mariya Ulyanov needed some cheering news. In February 1900, Manyasha and Mark Elizarov had been arrested with other Social Democrats in Moscow. The heart-rending cycle had begun again. Lenin had plenty of advice for his sister, based on his own prison experiences. The important thing was to establish a regime for oneself: 'On the physical side . . . do gymnastics every day and rub down with a wet towel'. For mental stimulation, he recommended 'translations, especially *both* ways – first do a written translation from the foreign language into Russian, then translate it back from Russian into the foreign language'. The evenings, he advised, were best spent reading fiction.[73]

Lenin's letters to his mother are full of concern and tenderness:

> I embrace you again and again, my dear, and wish you vigour and good health. You remember, when I was locked up, you imagined the case to be more serious than it was, and, of course, Manyasha's and Mark's case bears no comparison with mine! I kiss you again.[74]

He was in the middle of a small but highly significant treatise. It was completed at the end of 1901 and appeared in print several months later. The title, *What Is To Be Done?*, recalled Chernyshevsky's novel of the same name. Krupskaya has described Lenin's working method at this time:

> When he wrote anything he generally paced briskly from one corner of the room to the other and whispered what he was about to write. By that time I had already become used to his manner of working. When he was writing I never spoke to him about anything, nor asked him anything. Afterwards, when we went out for a walk, he told me what he was writing.[75]

What Is To Be Done? was conceived as a polemic against the Economists but it also contained Lenin's ideas on the role of the party as well as practical suggestions for building an effective revolutionary organization under autocratic conditions.

The Social Democrats, he asserted, must construct a party of revolution not reform and they must be ready to serve in the vanguard of the workers' movement, rather than follow along limply in its wake, like the Economists. The latter's obsession with strikes and bread-and-butter issues to the detriment of the political struggle would, Lenin warned, eventually place the working class under the tutelage of the bourgeoisie. This argument derived from his novel views concerning political consciousness. Marx had generally been understood to imply that workers would attain political consciousness through experiencing industrial conflict on the shop-floor. Lenin's interpretation was quite different. In *What Is To Be Done?* he states:

> The history of every country teaches us that by its own ability the working class can attain only a trade-union consciousness, that is to say, an appreciation of the need to fight the bosses, to wrest from the government this or that legislative enactment for the benefit of the workers.

Social-democratic theory, on the other hand, 'originated independently of the unconscious strivings of the labouring classes'. It was 'a natural and inevitable result of the development of the ideas of the revolutionary socialist intelligentsia'. In other words, only intellectuals were capable of leading the workers along the correct revolutionary road. So the Economists' conviction that workers would find their own route to socialism, through fighting for everyday improvements in the industrial environment, was hopelessly misguided and would have made the workers dupes of the bourgeoisie.

Lenin also invited controversy with his remarks about party organization. Under Russian conditions, he argued, it would be folly even to attempt to create a mass party like that of the German Social Democrats. Realism dictated that membership of the Russian organization must be confined to 'people who make revolutionary activity their profession'. This was not meant to imply, as some later alleged, that the party would be composed exclusively of intellectuals, although they, of course, had a head start. Lenin made it clear that 'our very first and most pressing duty is to help train working-class revolutionaries who will be on the same level regarding Party activity as the revolutionaries from among the intellectuals'. In other respects, he felt, special allowances might be made for candidates from the working class. But in practice, far fewer workers than intellectuals were in a position to make the kind of commitment he was demanding.

Lenin envisaged a centralized, closely knit and highly disciplined party organization, trained in the methods of conspiracy and able to operate effectively under autocratic conditions. Such an organization was capable of 'turning Russia upside-down'. Once autocracy had been swept aside and a constitutional regime installed in its place, then the party would be able to relax its controls and open its doors to a wider membership. Until that time, however, the conspiratorial imperative would severely restrict intra-party consultation and democracy. The directives of the *émigré* leadership, transmitted to activists in Russia by *Iskra* agents, were to be considered binding. Party posts might be filled by appointment or co-optation rather than open election.

What Is To Be Done? received a mixed reception. In writing the work, Lenin had the official approval of the *Iskra* board, though several of its members are known to have had reservations. Neither Axelrod nor Plekhanov actually specified their criticisms, but Potresov chided Lenin for his views on working-class consciousness. His political opponents were more forthright, pouring scorn on his vision of a centralized, conspiratorial party. Some argued that his views on organization were better suited to the People's Freedom party than to a social-democratic one; but there were more positive reactions, both inside and outside Russia. Perhaps the book's most enthusiastic adherents were the *Iskra* agents themselves, who admittedly had a vested interest in Lenin's organizational blueprint – people like S. I. Gusev, V. A. Noskov, P. A. Krasikov and M. N. Liadov. Generally, the younger people liked the book. The Kiev activist, Nikolai Valentinov (then 24) remembers the positive impact made by *What Is To Be Done?* on his circle, while Boris Nicolaevsky, a high-school convert to Marxism, later had this recollection of the book's reception in Samara: 'I saw how eagerly people read it and was told: "This is some book! Some book!"'[76] Evidently, Lenin had his finger on the pulse of the coming generation of Social Democrats.

He did not settle in Munich for long. The German printers were getting cold feet about producing material hostile to a foreign government on their presses, while the Russians themselves feared harrassment or even expulsion from Germany. A new location was sought. Predictably, Plekhanov and Axelrod argued for Geneva, but Lenin valued his hard-won independence too greatly to fall into line with his plan. London was chosen as an alternative.

Lenin and Krupskaya crossed over to England in mid-April 1901. They disembarked at Charing Cross Station and were promptly engulfed by fog. Lenin wrote to Axelrod: 'The first impression of London: hideous.' He had left a forwarding address with his sister: Mr Alexejeff, 14 Frederick Street, Gray's Inn Road. Alexejeff was Nikolai Alexeev, a former member of the Petersburg Union of Struggle who had escaped from Siberia in 1899. He did all he could to accommodate his bewildered and somewhat irascible guest. British socialists, too, were helpful. Harry Quelch, editor of the workers' newspaper, *Justice* , sectioned off a corner of his own printing works at 37a Clerkenwell Green for the *Iskra* staff, while the Secretary of the General Federation of Trade Unions, Isaac Mitchell, endorsed Lenin's application for a reader's ticket at the British Museum.

Martov and Zasulich were also in London, living just around the corner from Alexeev in a five-room apartment in Sidmouth Street. In October, 23-year-old Lev Trotsky moved in with them. He had recently escaped from Siberia and had come to London to report on the state of Social Democrat organizations in Russia. Trotsky was appalled by what he found in Sidmouth Street. Martov and Zasulich were notoriously untidy. Their living-room was permanently wreathed in smoke: Martov's pipe ash found its way into the sugar bowl, while Zasulich's (she chain-smoked roll-your-own cigarettes) settled evenly on window-sills, tables, tea-cups, herself and the person she was talking to. Her cooking methods too were unorthodox: 'I remember,' recalled Krupskaya, 'how she once cooked herself some meat on an oil stove, chipping off pieces to eat with a pair of scissors'. In the end, a visiting Russian worker tidied up for them, remarking laconically, 'The Russian intellectual is always dirty.'[77]

This could not be said of Lenin and his wife, who had no intention of sharing the communal life of Sidmouth Street. Instead, Alexeev found them an unfurnished, two-room apartment at 30 Holford Square, not far from King's Cross. Conditions were cramped, especially when Nadya's mother arrived, and water and coal had to be brought from downstairs. Lenin balked at the rent – 30 shillings a week, which was paid out of party funds.

The landlady, Mrs Yeo, could not quite make out her new tenants. Mr and Mrs Richter (as Lenin and his wife called themselves in London) seemed a quiet, respectable couple and kept reasonable hours, but they failed to put up the obligatory net curtains and – Mrs Yeo could not help noticing – Mrs Richter did not wear a wedding ring. It took the threat of a lawsuit to pacify her on the latter point.

Lenin did not warm to London but it did fascinate him. After all, it was the largest city in the world and the engine-room of the capitalist system. He and Krupskaya made their own private study of the city's working class. Their favourite observation post was the top deck of a bus, but they also frequented pubs, stopped off at market stalls and visited music-halls. Lenin was soon much more at home here than his other compatriots, even if he continued to find the language difficult and the inhabitants sometimes incomprehensible. On Sundays he took Nadya to join the crowd at Speakers' Corner in Hyde Park, or visited the socialist church in Seven Sisters where the Almighty was invoked in unusual terms: 'Lead us O Lord from the

Kingdom of Capitalism to the Kingdom of Socialism'. Then there was the countryside, in those days considerably more accessible than today. One of their favourite spots was Primrose Hill, from the summit of which Nadya could make out 'the vast, smoke-wreathed city receding into the distance'.

Her husband had other things on his mind. The previous year he had asked Plekhanov, as the party's most eminent theoretician, to compose a new draft programme (his own version was now considered to be out of date). Plekhanov had complied but neither Lenin nor Martov liked what they read. They had wanted something inspiriting, a vivid and forthright statement which could be read and discussed by workers as well as by intellectuals – an action programme. Perhaps this was a tall order; but Plekhanov's draft fell hopelessly wide of the mark. Its language was abstract and its tone remote. Lenin was no longer prepared to take account of Plekhanov's highly tuned sensitivities and he stated his objections bluntly. Plekhanov submitted a revised draft, but Lenin remained dissatisfied. Tension was mounting. The spark to the tinder-box was Plekhanov's reaction to an article Lenin had submitted for publication in *Zarya*, entitled 'The Agrarian Programme of Russian Social Democracy'. He covered it with more than 200 'corrections', provoking Lenin to fury:

> I have received the article with your remarks. You have a fine idea of tact with regard to your editorial colleagues. You do not hesitate to choose even the most contemptuous expressions, not to mention 'voting' on propositions which you do not take the trouble to formulate, and even 'voting' on style. I would like to know what you would say if I were to answer your article on the programme in the same way . . . As for personal, as distinct from business relations you have already completely ruined them, or more exactly: you have achieved their complete cessation.[78]

The quarrel was eventually patched up and a consensus reached on the party programme. But Lenin's nerves were, by his own admission, at 'breaking point'. He was in sore need of a holiday. Towards the end of June he left London to spend three weeks with his mother and Anyuta at Longuivy in Brittany. On returning to England, he wrote to his sister, thanking her for some photographs of Sasha she had sent him.

Work in London was becoming impossible – Zasulich was cheerfully ineffective; Potresov had fallen ill; Martov had wandered off to Paris. Lenin and Krupskaya were left to shoulder the burden alone. And the burden was daily becoming more onerous. It was not just a matter of preparing *Iskra* for publication and maintaining communications with Russia and the widely dispersed *émigré* community; there were also new and pressing organizational tasks, chief among them being the preparations for convening a second party congress, which everyone agreed was now urgent.

In the spring of 1903 the editorial board of *Iskra* overruled Lenin's objections and voted to transfer production of the paper from London to Geneva – back, that is, into the orbit of Axelrod and Plekhanov. There was nothing he could do but pack his bags. Immediately on arriving in Geneva, he developed shingles. The burning irritation was unintentionally aggravated by Nadya who, as a result of a mistaken diagnosis gleaned from a medical textbook, covered her husband's chest and back with iodine. He was in bed for two weeks before they could get around to looking for permanent accommodation.

Once he had recovered, thoughts of the congress occupied every second of his working day. Time was pressing because Marxism no longer held a monopoly over the opposition movement. In June 1902 Struve had launched his journal, *Liberation*, with the aim of attracting wider public support in favour of democratic change. A year later, inspired to no small degree by Struve's pen, liberal forces gathered to form the Union of Liberation: a broad alliance of professionals, forward-thinking members of the gentry and former subscribers to Revisionism.

The Social Democrats were also confronted by a rival on the left. Despite all prognostications of its demise, Populism had survived and re-entered the political arena, decked in a new set of clothes. Its supporters now called themselves Socialist Revolutionaries and a party of that name was formed at the end of 1901. Like the Social Democrats, the Socialist Revolutionaries were committed to overthrowing autocracy and laying the foundations for a new socialist order. But they had no special veneration for the proletariat. For the Socialist Revolutionaries, the term 'working class' incorporated peasants, artisans and socialist sympathizers among the intelligentsia as well as industrial workers – everyone, in fact, who worked by his or her own labour. They took particular exception to the Marxists' descriptions of the peasantry as backward and reactionary, believing, on the contrary, that the peasant masses had the potential to become a mighty arm of the revolutionary movement. The immediate political goal of both parties was a democratic republic, but at this point Social Democrats and Socialist Revolutionaries again parted company. While the former wished to promote capitalism in the countryside to accelerate class polarization, the latter wanted to undermine it. By 'socializing' the land (that is, transferring all landed property into 'the possession of all the people'), the Socialist Revolutionaries hoped to pull the rug from under capitalism. The land would be redistributed on an egalitarian basis, but private cultivation would continue until the peasants became convinced (by persuasion not compulsion) of the superiority of socialist co-operation.

The other major difference between the two parties was a tactical one. Like People's Freedom before them, the Socialist Revolutionaries advocated terror and their Fighting Organization carried out several assassinations of prominent government figures between 1902 and 1905. The Social Democrats rejected terror, not out of principle, but because they regarded it as superfluous. None the less, terror enjoyed considerable popularity among workers during this period and some Social Democrats, too, were sympathetic.

Lenin took the revival of Populism very seriously. Between June 1902 and March 1903 he campaigned against the Socialist Revolutionaries and their programme in a series of lectures delivered to *émigré* audiences in London, Paris, Geneva, Berne, Lausanne and Zurich. *Iskra* too published a flurry of articles against the new party.

If *Iskra* and its supporters were to triumph at the forthcoming congress, Lenin would have to keep a close eye on its rivals within the movement. The Economists had not been a real threat while their influence was confined to the Union of Russian Social Democrats Abroad, but in 1902 they began organizing in Russia itself, capturing the Kiev Committee from *Iskra* in December. This was tantamount to a declaration of war.

The Bund posed an indirect challenge to the *Iskra* line by demanding broad organizational autonomy for Jewish socialists within any reconstituted party. With a membership of thousands in the towns of western and southern Russia, it too was a force to be reckoned with.

And there was a third challenger to *Iskra*'s supremacy. In January 1900 Social Democrats in the southern Ukrainian town of Ekaterinoslav began publishing a journal called *Southern Worker*. It soon inspired an organization of considerable regional influence. *Southern Worker* could not be attacked on ideological or organizational grounds; it was orthodox, militant and uncorrupted by Economism, Revisionism or any other type of 'ism'.

To defeat these influences, Lenin and his editorial colleagues needed to control the organizational committee which was to oversee the selection of delegates to the congress. At one time this looked like a forlorn hope. In the spring of 1902 Social Democrats in Russia had stolen a march on *Iskra* by setting up a committee of their own. *Iskra* was represented (by Fedor Dan) but so too was the Bund, *Southern Worker* and the Union Abroad. Fate intervened, however, when everyone but the Bundist delegate, K. Portnoi, was arrested.

Lenin's response was swift. Operating through a trusted agent, F. V. Lengnik, he issued his instructions:

> And so your task is to turn *yourself* into a committee for preparing the congress, to accept the Bundist [Portnoi] into this committee (after assessing him *from every angle* – this N.B.,!) and to push your own [i.e. *Iskra*] people through into the largest number of committees possible, safeguarding yourself and your people more than the apple of your eye, until the congress.[79]

A second organizational committee was elected at a meeting at Pskov in November 1902: Portnoi was among those chosen, but the new committee was dominated by *Iskra* nominees.

The next stage was the election of delegates. Here too *Iskra* generally came out on top but only after considerable manoeuvring and not a little skulduggery. The battle raged most furiously in Petersburg where a group of Economists broke away from the *Iskra*-dominated committee at the beginning of 1903 to form a rival opposition. Lenin was furious, accusing the local *Iskra* agent, Elena Stasova, of being 'led by the nose'. Both he and Martov lashed the break-away group in print, but to no avail: the Petersburg organization split and was ultimately represented by rival delegates.

The congress was to take place in Brussels but many of the delegates called on Lenin in Geneva beforehand. He quizzed them in detail about their views, mentally dividing them into 'hard', 'soft' and 'wavering' supporters of the *Iskra* line. In the evenings the doubters were wooed tête-à-tête in the more relaxed atmosphere of the Café Landolt. Lenin was leaving nothing to chance.

In Brussels the delegates assembled at a hotel called the Coq d'Or where, cognac in hand, Gusev entertained them with his repertoire of operatic arias. Lenin applauded with the rest but privately he was racked by nerves. Unable to sleep, he lost his appetite – his Belgian landlady chided him for not eating his cheese and radishes at breakfast.

The second Congress of the Russian Social Democratic Labour Party opened on 30 July 1903 in a flour warehouse, the central window draped defiantly with red material. As Plekhanov gave the welcoming address, rats scurried about the delegates' feet. They were the first of many indignities. The police were soon on the delegates' trail, compelling them to move from one cheerless venue to another. After a few days, they were chased out of Belgium altogether.

The ragged caravan then made its way to London, meeting first at the English Club in Charlotte Street, then in a succession of premises made available by the trade unions. In England they were received with indifference rather than hostility, though some of them were pelted by street urchins on one occasion.

The mood of the congress darkened with the passage of time. The first cloud on the horizon was the Bund's refusal to back down on its demand for Jewish autonomy. The five-man delegation was already embittered by what it took to be *Iskra*'s low-key response to the recent bloody pogrom in the Ukrainian town of Kishinev. Now, to add salt to the wound, the principal speakers against the motion, Martov and Trotsky, were both Jews. They argued that, if acceded to, the Bund's demand would threaten the unity of the movement. The motion was heavily defeated.

The congress then moved on to debate the party programme. Two Economist delegates, Martynov and Akimov, attacked Lenin's view that, left to themselves, workers were capable of attaining only 'trade union' consciousness. Martynov read back at Lenin passages from *What Is To Be Done?* and countered with citations from Marx and Engels. Akimov took up the same theme, pointing out that in minimizing 'the active role of the proletariat' the *Iskra* draft was diverging fundamentally from the programmes of other European socialist parties. Lenin argued that his remarks had

1 Lenin's coffin
being carried to
the House of
Trade Unions by
(left to right)
Stalin, Kamenev,
Tomsky, an
unidentified man,
Molotov,
Zinoviev, (partly
hidden) Kalinin
and Bukharin.

2 Lenin's sisters,
Mariya
(Manyasha) on
the left and Anna
(Anyuta) on the
right, join the
guard of honour
during the lying in
state, January
1924.

3 The house in Moscow Street, Simbirsk, where Lenin spent much of his childhood. (*left*)

4 The ancient Russian city of Simbirsk on the banks of the Volga. (*below*)

5 Lenin, aged four, with his younger sister Olga (Olya). (*opposite*)

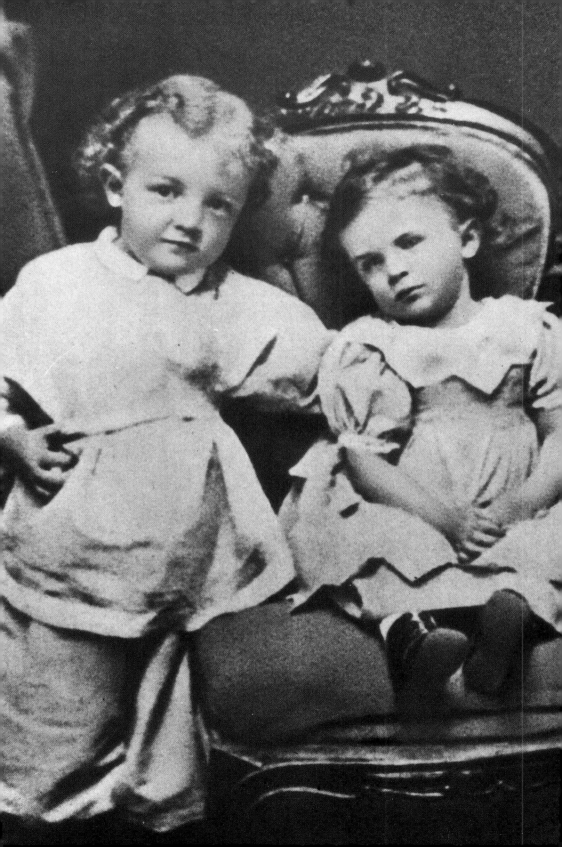

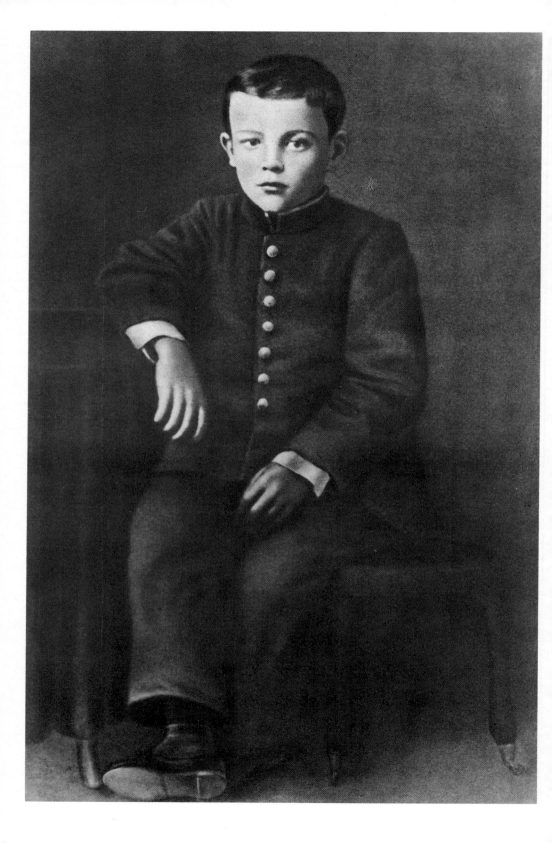

ПОХВАЛЬНЫЙ ЛИСТЪ

Педагогическій Совѣтъ Классической Гимназіи, уважая отличные успѣхи, прилежаніе и похвальное поведеніе воспитанника III ᵍᵒ класса *Ульянова Владиміра* наградилъ его симъ похвальнымъ листомъ. Симбирскъ, *Июня 10 дня 1882* года.

Директоръ Симбирской Гимназіи *Керенскій*

Инспекторъ *Христофоровъ*

Преподаватели:

6 Lenin was nine when he entered the first form at the Simbirsk Gymnasium, which he attended from 1879 to 1887. (*opposite*)

7 Certificate of Honour awarded to Lenin after completing his third year at Simbirsk Gymnasium, 1882. It refers to his 'outstanding success, constant effort and excellent conduct ...' (*above*)

8 Lenin's school-leaving medal.

9 Lenin aged 17, in 1887, the year he was sent into exile to Kokushkino.

10 The house in Kokushkino where Lenin lived until October 1888. He had been accepted into the Faculty of Law at Kazan University the previous year but was exiled that December for his part in organizing a student protest meeting.

11 Nadezhda Krupskaya (Nadya) in 1886, aged 17.

И. Шарыгинъ   САМАРА.

12 Lenin in Samara, 1891. (*opposite*)

13 Members of the Union of Struggle for the Liberation of the Working Class in Petersburg in 1897. Standing (left to right): A. L. Malchenko, P. L. Zaporozhets and A. A. Vaneev; seated: V. V. Starkov, G. N. Krzhizhanovsky, Lenin and I. O. Martov. (*above*)

14 Petersburg's Nevsky Prospekt in the 1890s. (*below*)

15 Zyryanov's house in the village of
Shushenskoye in Siberia, where Lenin was
exiled in 1897. Lenin lived here until the
arrival of Nadezhda Krupskaya in 1898.
(*above*)

16 Lenin in Moscow, 1900. (*right*)

17 The first issue of *Iskra*, published by Lenin
in Leipzig in December 1900. Between 1902
and 1903 *Iskra* was published from
Clerkenwell Green, London. (*opposite*)

РОССІЙСКАЯ СОЦІАЛЬ-ДЕМОКРАТИЧЕСКАЯ РАБОЧАЯ ПАРТІЯ

ИСКРА

„Изъ искры возгорится пламя!"...
Отвѣтъ декабристовъ Пушкину

№ 1. ДЕКАБРЬ 1900 ГОДА. № 1.

НАСУЩНЫЯ ЗАДАЧИ НАШЕГО ДВИЖЕНІЯ.

Русская соціалдемократія не разъ уже заявляла, что ближайшей политической задачей русской рабочей партіи должно быть ниспроверженіе самодержавія, завоеваніе политической свободы. Это заявляли больше 15 лѣтъ тому назадъ представители русской соціалдемократіи, члены группы „Освоб. Труда", это заявили два съ половиной года тому назадъ и представители русскихъ соціалдемократическихъ организацій, образовавшіе весной 1898 года Россійскую Соціалдемократическую Рабочую Партію. Но не смотря на эти неоднократныя заявленія, вопросъ о политическихъ задачахъ соціалдемократіи въ Россіи снова выступаетъ на очередь въ настоящее время. Многіе представители нашего движенія выражаютъ сомнѣніе въ правильности указаннаго рѣшенія вопроса. Говорятъ, что преобладающее значеніе имѣетъ экономическая борьба, отодвигаютъ на второй планъ политическія задачи пролетаріата, съуживаютъ и ограничиваютъ эти задачи, заявляютъ даже, что разговоры объ образованіи самостоятельной рабочей партіи въ Россіи просто повтореніе чужихъ словъ, что рабочимъ надо вести одну экономическую борьбу, предоставивъ политику интеллигентамъ въ союзѣ съ либералами. Это послѣднее заявленіе новаго символа вѣры (пресловутое credo) сводится уже прямо къ признанію русскаго пролетаріата несовершеннолѣтнимъ и къ полному отрицанію соціалдемократической программы. А „Рабочая Мысль" (особенно въ отдѣльномъ Приложеніи) высказалась въ сущности въ томъ же смыслѣ. Русская соціалдемократія переживаетъ періодъ колебаній, періодъ сомнѣній, доходящихъ до самоотрицанія. Съ одной стороны, рабочее движеніе отрывается отъ соціализма: рабочимъ помогаютъ вести экономическую борьбу, но имъ ничего не разъясняютъ при этомъ или недостаточно разъясняютъ соціалистическихъ цѣлей и политическихъ задачъ всего движенія въ цѣломъ. Съ другой стороны, соціализмъ отрывается отъ рабочаго движенія: русскіе соціалисты опять начинаютъ все больше и больше говорить о томъ, что борьбу съ правительствомъ должна вести одними своими силами интеллигенція, ибо рабочіе ограничиваются лишь экономической борьбой.

Трояко го рода обстоятельства подготовили, по нашему мнѣнію, почву для этихъ печальныхъ явленій. Во-первыхъ, въ началѣ своей дѣятельности русскіе соціалдемократы ограничивались одной кружковой пропагандистской работой. Перейдя къ агитаціи въ массахъ, мы не всегда могли удер[illegible]

Во-вторыхъ, въ началѣ своей дѣятельности намъ приходилось очень часто отстаивать свое право на существованіе въ борьбѣ съ народовольцами, которые понимали подъ „политикой" дѣятельность, оторванную отъ рабочаго движенія, которые съуживали политику до одной только заговорщицкой борьбы. Отвергая такую политику, соціалдемократы впадали въ крайность, отодвигая на второй планъ политику вообще. Въ-третьихъ, разрозненно дѣйствуя въ мѣстныхъ мелкихъ рабочихъ кружкахъ, соціалдемократы недостаточно обращали вниманія на необходимость организаціи революціонной партіи, объединяющей всю дѣятельность мѣстныхъ группъ и дающей возможность правильно поставить революціонную работу. А преобладаніе разрозненной работы естественно связано съ преобладаніемъ экономической борьбы.

Всѣ указанныя обстоятельства породили увлеченіе одной стороной движенія. „Экономическое" направленіе, (поскольку тутъ можно говорить о „направленіи") создало попытки возвести эту узость въ особую теорію, попытки воспользоваться для этой цѣли модной бернштейніадой, модной „критикой марксизма", проводящей старыя буржуазныя идеи подъ новымъ флагомъ. Лишь эти попытки породили опасность ослабленія связи между русскимъ рабочимъ движеніемъ и русской соціалдемократіей, какъ передовымъ борцомъ за политическую свободу. И самая насущная задача нашего движенія состоитъ въ укрѣпленіи этой связи.

Соціалдемократія есть соединеніе рабочаго движенія съ соціализмомъ, ея задача — не пассивное служеніе рабочему движенію на каждой его отдѣльной стадіи, а представительство интересовъ всего движенія въ цѣломъ, указаніе этому движенію его конечной цѣли, его политическихъ задачъ, охрана его политической и идейной самостоятельности. Оторванное отъ соціалдемократіи, рабочее движеніе мельчаетъ и необходимо впадаетъ въ буржуазность: ведя одну экономическую борьбу, рабочій классъ теряетъ свою политическую самостоятельность, становится хвостомъ другихъ партій, измѣняетъ великому завѣту: „освобожденіе рабочихъ должно быть дѣломъ самихъ рабочихъ". Во всѣхъ странахъ былъ такой періодъ, когда рабочее движеніе и соціализмъ существовали отдѣльно другъ отъ друга и шли особой дорогой, — и во всѣхъ странахъ такая оторванность приводила къ слабости соціализма и рабочаго движенія; во всѣхъ странахъ только соединеніе соціализма съ рабочимъ движеніемъ создавало прочную основу и для того и для другого. Но въ каждой странѣ это соединеніе соціализма съ рабочимъ движеніемъ вырабатывалось исторически, вырабатывалось особымъ путемъ, въ зависимости отъ условій мѣста и времени. Въ Россіи необходимость соединенія соціализма и рабочаго движенія теоретически провозглашена уже давно, — но практически это соединеніе вырабатывается лишь въ настоящее время. Процессъ этой выработки есть очень трудный процессъ, и нѣтъ ничего особенно удивительнаго въ томъ, что онъ сопровождается разными колебаніями и сомнѣніями.

Какой же урокъ вытекаетъ для насъ изъ прошлаго?

Исторія всего русскаго соціализма привела къ тому, что самой его насущной задачей оказалась борьба противъ самодержавнаго правительства, завоеваніе политической свободы; [illegible]

[illegible] ческой мысли отъ передовыхъ представителей трудящихся классовъ гораздо больше, чѣмъ въ другихъ странахъ, и что при такой оторванности русское революціонное движеніе осуждено на безсиліе. Отсюда сама собою вытекаетъ та задача, которую призвана осуществить русская соціалдемократія: внѣдрить соціалистическія идеи и политическое самосознаніе въ массу пролетаріата и организовать революціонную партію, неразрывно связанную съ стихійнымъ рабочимъ движеніемъ. Много уже сдѣлано въ этомъ отношеніи русской соціалдемократіей; но еще больше остается сдѣлать. Съ ростомъ движенія поприще дѣятельности для соціалдемократа становится все шире, работа все разностороннѣе, все большее число дѣятелей движенія сосредоточиваетъ свои силы на осуществленіи различныхъ частныхъ задачъ, которыя выдвигаются повседневными нуждами пропаганды и агитаціи. Это явленіе совершенно законное и неизбѣжное, но оно заставляетъ обращать особое вниманіе на то, чтобы частныя задачи дѣятельности и отдѣльные пріемы борьбы не становились чѣмъ-то самодовлѣющимъ, чтобы подготовительная работа не возводилась на степень главной и единственной работы.

Содѣйствовать политическому развитію и политической организаціи рабочаго класса — наша главная и основная задача. Всякій, кто отодвигаетъ эту задачу на второй планъ, кто не подчиняетъ ей всѣхъ частныхъ задачъ и отдѣльныхъ пріемовъ борьбы, тотъ становится на ложный путь и наноситъ серьезный вредъ движенію.

Отодвигаютъ эту задачу, во-первыхъ, тѣ, кто съуживаетъ содержаніе и размахъ политической пропаганды, агитаціи и организаціи, кто считаетъ возможнымъ и умѣстнымъ угощать рабочихъ „политикой" только въ исключительные моменты ихъ жизни, только въ торжественныхъ случаяхъ, кто слишкомъ заботливо размѣниваетъ политическую борьбу противъ самодержавія на требованіе отдѣльныхъ уступокъ отъ самодержавія и недостаточно заботится о томъ, чтобы эти требованія отдѣльныхъ уступокъ возвести въ систематическую и безповоротную борьбу революціонной рабочей партіи противъ самодержавія.

„Организуйтесь!", повторяетъ рабочимъ на разные лады газета „Рабочая Мысль", повторяютъ всѣ сторонники „экономическаго" направленія. И мы, конечно, всецѣло присоединяемся къ этому кличу, но мы непремѣнно добавимъ къ нему: организуйтесь не только въ общества взаимопомощи, стачечныя кассы и рабочіе кружки, организуйтесь также и въ политическую партію, организуйтесь для рѣшительной борьбы противъ самодержавнаго правительства и противъ всего капиталистическаго общества. Безъ такой организаціи пролетаріатъ не способенъ подняться до сознательной классовой борьбы, безъ такой организаціи рабочее движеніе осуждено на безсиліе, и одними только кассами, кружками и обществами взаимопомощи рабочему классу никогда не удастся исполнить лежащую на немъ великую историческую задачу: освободить себя и весь русскій народъ отъ его политическаго и экономическаго рабства. Ни одинъ классъ въ исторіи не достигалъ господства, если онъ не выдвигалъ своихъ политическихъ вождей, своихъ передовыхъ представителей, способныхъ организовать движеніе и руководить имъ. И русскій рабочій классъ показалъ уже, что онъ способенъ выдвигать такихъ людей: широко разлившаяся борьба русскихъ рабочихъ за 5-6 послѣднихъ лѣтъ показала, какая масса революціонныхъ силъ таится въ рабочемъ классѣ, какъ самыя отчаянныя правительственныя преслѣдованія не уменьшаютъ, а увеличиваютъ число рабочихъ, рвущихся къ соціализму, къ политическому сознанію и къ политической борьбѣ. Съѣздъ нашихъ товарищей въ 1898 г. вѣрно поставилъ задачу, а не повторилъ чужія слова, не выразилъ одно только увлеченіе „интеллигентовъ"... И мы должны рѣшительно взяться за выполненіе этихъ задачъ, поставивъ на очередь вопросъ о программѣ, организаціи и тактикѣ партіи. Какъ мы смотримъ на основныя положенія нашей программы, мы уже сказали, а подробно развивать эти положенія, здѣсь, конечно, не мѣсто. Вопросамъ организаціи мы намѣрены посвятить рядъ статей въ ближайшихъ номерахъ. Это одинъ изъ самыхъ больныхъ нашихъ вопросовъ. Мы сильно отстали въ этомъ отношеніи отъ старыхъ дѣятелей русскаго революціоннаго движенія: надо прямо признать этотъ недостатокъ и направить свои силы на выработку болѣе конспиративной постановки дѣла, на систематическую пропаганду правилъ веденія дѣла, пріемовъ надуванія жандармовъ и обхода сѣтей полиціи. Надо подготовлять людей, посвящающихъ революціи не одни только свободные вечера, а всю свою жизнь, надо подготовлять организацію, настолько крупную, чтобы въ ней можно было провести строгое раздѣленіе труда между различными видами нашей работы. Что касается, наконецъ, до вопросовъ тактики, то мы ограничимся здѣсь слѣдующимъ: соціалдемократія не связываетъ себѣ рукъ, не съуживаетъ своей дѣятельности однимъ какимъ-нибудь заранѣе придуманнымъ планомъ или пріемомъ политической борьбы, — она признаетъ всѣ средства борьбы, лишь бы они соотвѣтствовали наличнымъ силамъ партіи и давали возможность достигать наибольшихъ результатовъ, достижимыхъ при данныхъ условіяхъ. При крѣпкой организованной партіи отдѣльная стачка можетъ превратиться въ политическую демонстрацію, въ политическую побѣду надъ правительствомъ. При крѣпкой организованной партіи возстаніе въ отдѣльной мѣстности можетъ разростись въ побѣдоносную революцію. Мы должны помнить, что борьба съ правительствомъ за отдѣльныя требованія, отвоеваніе отдѣльныхъ уступокъ, это — только легкія стычки съ непріятелемъ, это — небольшія схватки на форпостахъ, а рѣшительная схватка еще впереди. Передъ нами стоитъ во всей своей силѣ непріятельская крѣпость, изъ которой осыпаютъ насъ тучи ядеръ и пуль, уносящія лучшихъ борцовъ. Мы должны взять эту крѣпость, и мы возьмемъ ее, если всѣ силы [illegible]

есть въ Россіи живого и честнаго. И только тогда исполнится великое пророчество русскаго рабочаго-революціонера Петра Алексѣева: „подымется мускулистая рука милліоновъ рабочаго люда, и ярмо деспотизма, огражденное солдатскими штыками, разлетится въ прахъ!"

ВИЛЬГЕЛЬМЪ ЛИБКНЕХТЪ

(родился 29-го марта 1826 г., умеръ 7-го августа 1900 г.)

Со смертью старѣйшаго вождя германской соціалдемократіи революціонный пролетаріатъ всего міра лишился одного изъ своихъ наиболѣе замѣчательныхъ и неутомимыхъ борцовъ и руководителей. Не даромъ вѣсть объ его внезапной кончинѣ, какъ громомъ поразила передовыхъ рабочихъ всѣхъ цивилизованныхъ странъ. Не только изъ всѣхъ концовъ Германіи, но и изъ другихъ странъ Европы, да и одной лишь Европы, а и Америки, Австраліи, и даже южной Африки, Японіи посланы были соболѣзновательные телеграммы, съ выраженіемъ глубокой скорби о незамѣнимой утратѣ, понесенной международной соціалдемократіей. Похороны Либкнехта приняли характеръ и размѣры величественной манифестаціи, въ которой приняли участіе сотни тысячъ, быть можетъ, около милліона нѣмецкихъ рабочихъ и представителей рабочихъ партій Англіи, Франціи, Австріи, Венгріи, Бельгіи, Даніи и разныхъ другихъ странъ. По единодушнымъ заявленіямъ всѣхъ добросовѣстныхъ газетныхъ корреспондентовъ, видѣвшихъ эту манифестацію, такихъ грандіозныхъ похоронъ не удостаивался еще ни одинъ король, ни одинъ императоръ.

Всеобщія глубокія симпатіи борющагося пролетаріата всего міра къ Либкнехту, съ такой силой и искренностью выразившіяся по случаю его кончины, пріобрѣтены были имъ многолѣтней службой дѣлу освобожденія рабочаго класса, неутомимыми усиліями его на пользу умственнаго и политическаго возвышенія эксплуатируемыхъ и угнетенныхъ рабочихъ массъ. Представить полную и разностороннюю оцѣнку его заслугъ передъ международнымъ пролетаріатомъ значитъ дать подробное описаніе его жизни и дѣятельности, по меньшей мѣрѣ, начиная съ шестидесятыхъ годовъ, т. е. приблизительно за сорокъ лѣтъ. Но начало его общественной дѣятельности относится къ революціи 1848 г., выработка его убѣжденій и идеаловъ, на служеніе которымъ онъ отдалъ свои способности, началась еще раньше, въ тѣ времена, когда въ Германіи, какъ теперь въ Россіи, не только рабочіе, но и буржуазные классы, въ особенности образованные ихъ слои, терпѣли отъ правительственнаго произвола и устарѣлыхъ государственныхъ и общественныхъ порядковъ. Исторія жизни и дѣятельности Либкнехта тѣснѣйшимъ образомъ связана, поэтому, съ исторіей Германіи и косвенно съ важнѣйшими моментами и событіями въ исторіи Европы, за періодъ болѣе продолжительный, чѣмъ полстолѣтіе. Для того, чтобы представить біографію Либкнехта въ такихъ широкихъ рамкахъ, надобно написать объемистую книгу. Здѣсь же мы ограничимся только сообщеніемъ нѣсколькихъ фактовъ изъ его, полной неутомимой дѣятельности и борьбы жизни, и, главнымъ образомъ, изъ того періода ея, въ теченіе котораго онъ воспитался и подготовился къ роли вождя германскихъ рабочихъ.

* * *

По своему рожденію и воспитанію, Либкнехтъ принадлежитъ къ буржуазіи и именно къ тѣмъ ея слоямъ, которые у насъ извѣстны подъ названіемъ „интеллигенція". Какъ я уже сказалъ, во времена его дѣтства и юности, въ Германіи господствовало монархическое и полицейское самовластіе, отъ котораго больше всего страдали, конечно, не [illegible] городскіе классы да деревенскія массы, находившіяся сверхъ того, подъ гнетомъ помѣщиковъ: но терпѣли также и буржуазные классы, — торговцы, фабриканты, а въ особенности образованные ихъ слои, врачи, адвокаты, учителя, профессора и учащіеся, по преимуществу, университетская молодежь. Вслѣдствіе этого, буржуазія вообще, а интеллигенція въ особенности, проникнута была духомъ недовольства и оппозиціи. Наиболѣе благородныя натуры и горячія головы изъ интеллигенціи проникнуты были сочувствіемъ къ народнымъ страданіямъ, мечтали о такихъ общественныхъ порядкахъ, при которыхъ не было бы мѣста неравенству и несправедливости и старались даже распространять революціонныя и соціалистическія идеи среди рабочихъ. Внутри самой Германіи пропаганда эта велась, конечно, тайно, подъ страхомъ строжайшихъ наказаній. Но нѣмецкіе рабочіе, главнымъ образомъ, молодые подмастерья, имѣли тогда обыкновеніе переселяться изъ одного города въ другой и даже изъ одной страны въ другую. Благодаря этому обстоятельству, нѣмецкихъ рабочихъ въ 30-хъ и 40-хъ годахъ можно было встрѣтить сотнями не только въ Швейцаріи, Франціи, Бельгіи, сосѣднихъ съ Германіей странахъ, но даже и въ Англіи. Во всѣхъ этихъ государствахъ, до революціи 1848 г. были конституціонные порядки, [illegible]

Что дѣлать?

Наболѣвшіе вопросы нашего движенія

Н. ЛЕНИНА.

... „Партійная борьба придаетъ партіи силу и жизненность, величайшимъ доказательствомъ слабости партіи является ея расплывчатость и притупленіе рѣзко обозначенныхъ границъ, партія укрѣпляется тѣмъ, что очищаетъ себя" ... (Изъ письма Лассаля къ Марксу отъ 24 іюня 1852 г).

Цѣна 1 руб.
Preis 2 Mark = 2.50 Francs.

STUTTGART
Verlag von J. H. W. Dietz Nachf. (G. m. b. H.)
1902

18 First edition of *What Is To Be Done?*, published in 1902. (*opposite*)

19 The Crown and Woolpack public house in Islington, a meeting place in London for Russian Social Democrats in 1905. (*above*)

20 A press photograph of Matyushenko and fellow mutineers from the *Potemkin*, the *Graphic*, 22 July 1905. (*above*)

21 Bloody Sunday, 22 January 1905, from the *Graphic*. British press reports referred to the 'murderous onslaught'. (*opposite above*)

22 Students outside Petersburg University welcome the announcement of the Imperial Manifesto, October 1905. (*opposite below*)

23 Members of the Soviet of Workers' Deputies about to be sent into exile, December 1905. Trotsky is marked with a cross.

been taken out of context but he conceded (grudgingly) that he had been guilty of exaggeration.

A speech of Plekhanov's aroused greater controversy. The delegates were debating a reference in the programme to 'the dictatorship of the proletariat' (the stage in revolutionary strategy which was to follow the party's conquest of power from the bourgeoisie). Plekhanov spelled out the implications of this dictatorship for traditional notions of democracy. Every democratic principle, he argued, had to be judged in the light of a higher law: the good of the revolution. If this could be guaranteed only by depriving the upper classes of their political rights, then so be it. The same was true for parliaments and assemblies:

> If, in an outburst of revolutionary enthusiasm, the people should elect a very good parliament . . . it would suit us to try and make that a Long Parliament; but if the elections turned out badly for us, we should have to try to disperse the resulting parliament not after two years but, if possible, after two weeks.[80]

Lenin applauded enthusiastically but there was hissing from those delegates who envisaged a constitutional transfer of power.

One of the more remarkable aspects of the congress was the closeness of these two obdurate individuals. Not only did Plekhanov and Lenin support one another's speeches – this was hardly surprising as Plekhanov had once calculated that they were in agreement on '75 per cent' of the issues – but their personal relations appeared to have improved. At one point in the proceedings, when Plekhanov joked that none of his opponents would succeed in 'divorcing' him from his colleague, Lenin had laughed good-naturedly and shaken his head. The full implications of their *rapprochement* were about to become apparent. Lenin had decided on a proposal to reduce the number of *Iskra*'s editors from six to three. He justified the removal of Axelrod, Potresov and Zasulich by totting up their contributions to the paper – just 18 articles between them. By contrast, Plekhanov had written 24, Lenin 32 and Martov 39. Martov knew of the plan and had tacitly assented; Plekhanov was handed the details while the congress was in session and had slipped the piece of paper into his pocket without comment.

However, when Lenin raised the matter at the congress, he found himself wrong-footed by Martov's unexpected opposition. For some time now Martov had been uneasy about certain aspects of Lenin's behaviour: his increasing remoteness from his editorial colleagues; his refusal to countenance any proposal aimed at limiting the powers of *Iskra* agents over local committees; and his apparent indifference to personal ethics (Lenin had refused to censure a party member, Nikolai Bauman, for allegedly provoking a former mistress to suicide). Now, somewhat belatedly and to little avail, Martov sprung to the defence of the aggrieved veterans, Axelrod and Zasulich, as Plekhanov looked on in silence.

The *Iskra* majority was threatened by a second issue. Martov and Lenin each submitted their own definitions of party membership for the consideration of the delegates. For Martov, a member was someone 'who recognises the Party programme and supports it by material means and *by regular personal assistance* under the direction of one of the Party's organisations'. Lenin defined a member as someone 'who recognises the Party programme and supports it by material means and *by personal participation* in one of the Party's organisations'.

It is doubtful, to say the least, whether anyone trying to gain entry to the party would have been accepted on the basis of the one definition and rejected by the other. However, both speakers were clear about what was implied. Martov wished to open the doors of the party a little wider than his colleague. As he put it:

> The more widespread the title of Party member the better. We could only rejoice if every striker, every demonstrator, answering for his actions, could proclaim himself a Party member. For me a conspiratorial organisation only has meaning when it is enveloped by a broad Social Democratic working-class party.[81]

Lenin suffered a defeat. Martov's version was preferred by 28 votes to 23; the *Iskra* majority had split.

The atmosphere was becoming more acrimonious by the day. One young delegate, A. V. Shotman, planned to beat up another who had changed sides, and had to be restrained by Lenin himself. Axelrod brought the bumptious Nikolai Bauman to the verge of tears by alluding venemously to his dead mistress. And Krupskaya recalled an altercation between the veteran Lev Deutsch and the young Leninist, V. A. Noskov, which ended with the latter retorting: 'You just keep your mouth shut, you old dodderer!'

Lenin's strategy appeared to be in ruins; he was saved by a tactical manoeuvre of the Bund. On 18 August the five Jewish delegates and two of the Economists staged a walk-out. At one stroke the opposition was deprived of its majority. A series of votes now went Lenin's way. The congress approved his plan for an *Iskra* board consisting of himself, Martov and Plekhanov. Indignant, Martov refused to serve and his supporters, faced with certain defeat, abstained from electing the Central Committee, a new body charged with overseeing day-to-day affairs within Russia. Consequently, the committee was packed with Lenin's nominees. Finally, Plekhanov was elected to preside over the Party Council which was to liaise between *Iskra* and the Central Committee and to arbitrate on disputes arising between them. Lenin's supporters came to be known as *bolsheviki* (members of the majority) and Martov's as *mensheviki* (members of the minority).

After 37 exhausting sessions, spread over three weeks and two cities, the second Congress of the Russian Social Democratic Labour Party broke up in bitterness and rancour; rather than cementing the various factions into one party, it had sown the seeds of two. The question then on everyone's mind was – who was to blame?

On returning to Geneva, the rival camps dug themselves in and began hurling abuse. Martov's supporters were disparaged as 'disorganisers', 'opportunists', 'Girondists' and 'reformists' while the Martovites accused Lenin of being a 'Robespierre', a 'Jacobin', a 'terrorist', a 'despot', an 'autocrat', a 'bureaucrat', a 'formalist', a 'centrist' and more. Both sides indulged in satire and lampoon. The Mensheviks drew up a mock 'Short Constitution of the All-Russian Social Democratic Workers' Party', point one of which read: 'The Party is divided into those who sit and those who are sat upon'. Lenin replied by calling on the talents of the amateur cartoonist, P. N. Lepeshinsky, who produced the tale 'How the mice buried the tom-cat' in which Lenin is portrayed as the cat, Plekhanov (who had since joined the Mensheviks) as the 'all-wise rat' and Martov, Axelrod and Trotsky as the mice. It was not long before the mud-slinging assumed more vicious forms. The Mensheviks castigated Lenin for cavorting with the likes of the 'forger', S. I. Gusev (he had circulated a bogus list purporting to be Martov's nominees to the Central Committee), N. E. Bauman, of 'cruelty to mistresses' fame and M. N. Liadov, who was known to have squandered party funds in a brothel. For his part, Lenin attempted to win Dan over to his cause by promising to show him a 'secret dossier' said to contain salacious details on the private lives of prominent Mensheviks.

Of course, there were attempts at a more serious analysis of the dispute, though even these were sullied with invective. The Martovites re-examined the pages of *What Is To Be Done?* to discover that Lenin's vision of the party was full of sinister implications for the working class, promising, not a dictatorship of the proletariat, but a dictatorship over the proletariat by an intelligentsia élite whose leaders (Lenin first and foremost) were already corrupted by a dangerous moral relativism. In an extravagant pamphlet entitled *Our Political Tasks*, Trostsky spoke in prophetic terms, describing a situation in which 'The organisation of the Party takes the place of the Party itself; the Central Committee takes the place of the Party organisation; and finally "the dictator" takes the place of the Central Committee'.[82] Rosa Luxemburg agreed with him.

Lenin dismissed all this as a smoke-screen to hide the blatant fact that the Martovites were refusing to obey decisions, arrived at democratically, simply in order to get their own way. He denounced them as anarchists, incapable of understanding the need for party discipline. Lenin gave his own account of the second congress in *One Step Forward, Two Steps Back*, an almost unreadable work, written in a state bordering on rage, in which he itemized every jot and tittle of the proceedings to prove himself right and his opponents wrong. He ridiculed 'their tendency to proceed [building the party] from the bottom upwards, which would allow every professor, every high-school student and "every striker" to declare himself a member of the Party'.

In calmer moments, Lenin was at least prepared to admit that he had 'often behaved and acted in a state of frightful irritation, frenziedly' and he denied imputing Martov's 'integrity and sincerity'. But the stakes were high – nothing short of control of the party – and Lenin was not prepared to concede ground so patiently and painfully acquired. 'War has been declared', he wrote on 5 October 1903.

The first battle was fought at a meeting of the Foreign League (the party's official *émigré* association) towards the end of October. Fearing that the Martovites would hold the whip hand, Lenin first tried to prevent the assembly from taking place, then attempted to engineer a majority in his favour. Both strategies failed. To add to his problems, he had recently cycled into the back of a tram and arrived at the meeting looking slightly ridiculous with his head swathed in bandages. Martov, not always an effective speaker (he tended to stutter), used this platform well, repenting of the trust he had misplaced in Lenin and criticizing Plekhanov's congress speech on proletarian dictatorship. Martov had something much more damaging up his sleeve, however. He revealed the argument Lenin had used to persuade him to take up his seat on the new *Iskra* board: 'Don't you see that if we stick together, we shall keep Plekhanov always in a minority and he will not be able to do anything about it?' At this point, Lenin stormed out to a barrage of catcalls and abuse.

It was indeed a damaging revelation and it gave Plekhanov the excuse he was looking for to distance himself from his one-time ally. He began to preach reconciliation. Lenin resigned from *Iskra* in protest. It was a tactical error: shortly afterwards, Plekhanov co-opted Axelrod, Potresov, Zasulich and Martov on to the board. Thanks to some adroit manoeuvring, Lenin managed to get himself a place on the Central Committee, but he was an isolated figure by the end of the year. Even former close colleagues, like Krzhizhanovsky, Noskov and L. B. Krasin, now urged him to trim his demands for the sake of the party. He denounced them as 'conciliators' and demanded the convening of a third congress. The majority of the Central Committee would have none of this. Early in 1904 they wrote begging him to 'give up his quarrel and start work'. Their appeal fell on deaf ears and in May they took more drastic action, sending Noskov to Geneva with an instruction forbidding Lenin to continue campaigning for a new congress.

While the leaders abroad presided over the disintegration of the party, activists in Russia looked on in bemused horror. There was total confusion about the origins of the dispute and about which side to take. Lydia Dan heard about the split in remote Siberia and could not believe what had happened. She joined the Mensheviks mainly out of loyalty to her brother. Boris Nicolaevsky, living in Ufa, decided that, as the 'minority' had refused to submit, it was they who had broken discipline and were therefore in the wrong. Generally speaking, people joined whichever group was in the ascendancy in their home town.

At the end of 1903 Nikolai Valentinov was sent to Geneva by the Kiev Committee to find out what was going on. He remained there for some time and came to know Lenin well. Valentinov encountered 'a short, well-built man with a bald head, a sparse, dark-red beard, and a moustache'. Lenin's eyes, though small and unattractive, 'shone with intellect'. His face was mobile and expressive; when he was angry it became taut and his cheeks flushed. Lenin denounced his opponents in a voice that was hoarse and high-pitched; a speech impediment forced him to gutturalize his 'r's. When he spoke, he rocked on his heels, thrusting his thumbs into his waistcoat and extending his fingers like fans.

Valentinov used to join Lenin for his daily walk. They left at precisely 3.55 in the afternoon and took the same route, along the Quai du Mont Blanc as far as the bridge, then back along the Route de Lausanne. They talked about the Mensheviks. On one occasion they nearly ran into Vera Zasulich, approaching from the other direction. Anticipating the danger, Lenin pulled his friend into a neighbouring doorway.[83]

Krupskaya was worried about her husband's health. He had become thin, his skin was sallow, his eyes bloodshot and ringed with blue. She persuaded him to take a holiday. They left for the mountains at the end of June 1904, travelling by steamer as far as Montreux. The trip was idyllic and restored both their spirits. They walked, swam and, perhaps most importantly, slept ten hours a day. Lausanne, Chinon and Lucerne were all on the itinerary. Nadya recalled that they took dictionaries and other books in their rucksacks but never opened them. There was a rule about talking politics: it was absolutely forbidden.

The rule lapsed in August when Lenin sojourned on Lac de Bre with a new recruit, the writer and philosopher A. A. Bogdanov. Lenin longed to continue the war against the Mensheviks but, on the face of it, the prospects looked bleak. The conciliators had taken advantage of arrests and resignations to strengthen their position on the Central Committee. In their 'July Declaration' Noskov and his supporters demanded a *rapprochement* between Bolsheviks and Mensheviks and peace in the party. Lenin responded by calling a meeting of 22 Bolshevik 'hards', including M. S. Olminsky, A. V. Lunacharsky, Bogdanov and R. S. Zemlyachka. They issued a protest demanding the convocation of a third party congress. During the autumn, Lenin's allies rallied the local committees inside Russia and formed a 'Bureau of Committees of the Majority'. Noskov's Central Committee was left high and dry, unable to command sufficient grass-roots support. Lenin now intended to start publishing a rival newspaper to the Menshevik-controlled *Iskra*. Bogdanov was charged with rustling up the money and the first issue of *Vpered* (*Forward*) appeared early in January 1905. The first revolutionary upheaval in Russia was only days away.

5
Dress rehearsal

Geneva, 23 January 1905: on their way to the library, Lenin and Krupskaya catch sight of Anatoly Lunacharsky and his wife, Anna Alexandrovna, hurrying towards them. Anna appears out of her mind, laughing and shrieking hysterically and waving her muff at her astonished friends. It turns out that the Lunacharskys have seen the newspapers: they say that revolution has broken out in Russia!

Unable to disentangle Anna's maddeningly garbled version, Lenin takes her arm and the four of them make for Lepeshinsky's Russian café on the rue de Carouge, the centre of Bolshevik life in Geneva. Inside, they are unable to hear themselves speak. Friends and acquaintances are shouting at them, their faces distorted with excitement. A crumpled newspaper is shoved under Lenin's nose and fingers point to a single, densely printed column, announcing that Russian soldiers have fired on unarmed demonstrators in Petersburg.

The day will go down in history as 'Bloody Sunday'.

On the morning of Sunday 22 January 1905, hundreds of workers, accompanied by their wives and children, had gathered at branches of the Assembly of Russian Factory and Mill Workers in the industrial suburbs of the capital and begun making their way towards Palace Square. The crowd was calm and restrained but the atmosphere in the city was tense. The authorities had forbidden the march and troops blocked major thoroughfares, bridgeheads, public buildings and the approaches to the square itself. The protesters, hastily furnished with icons and crosses in an effort to reassure the soldiers of their peaceful intentions, continued to press forward. A bugler sounded a warning, but to no effect. On the command of their officers, the troops fired repeatedly into the oncoming marchers – at the Narva Gate, at Troitskaya Square behind the Peter–Paul Fortress and in the vicinity of Palace Square itself. This was only the beginning. Skirmishes continued throughout the day, bringing the total number of fatalities to 1,000. During the evening the situation deteriorated further as break-away elements from within the crowd, blind with fury, rampaged through the streets, smashing lamps and windows and attacking isolated military units. The officers were dragged aside and beaten to within an inch of their lives.

The Assembly of Russian Factory and Mill Workers of the City of St Petersburg was the fruit of an experiment launched in 1900 by the head of the Moscow Okhrana, S. V. Zubatov, to create 'official' trade unions under the discreet supervision of the police. Members were encouraged in monarchist and patriotic sentiments and were absolutely forbidden to engage in politics. In return, they received assistance in negotiating improvements in their pay and conditions. Initially successful, the contradictions inherent in this highly idiosyncratic strategy were dramatically revealed in the summer of 1903 when a police-sponsored union haplessly found itself at the forefront of a general strike in Odessa. Zubatov was dismissed as a result but the experiment survived in Petersburg where the Assembly of Russian Factory and Mill Workers received official approval early in 1904. By the end of the year it had grown to 8,000 members, dwarfing Bolshevik and Menshevik organizations in the city.

The leader of the Assembly was an orthodox priest, Father Georgi Gapon. A charismatic figure in his mid-thirties with a haunting face and dark, flowing beard, Gapon's authority stemmed from his considerable oratorical gifts, peasant-like simplicity and genuine love of the poor. He was also ambitious, wayward and dangerously confused in his plans for the Assembly.

At the beginning of January 1905, four members of Gapon's organization were dismissed from the vast Putilov engineering works on the outskirts of the city. Their claim to have been victimized by a heavy-handed foreman provoked a strike which, in a matter of days, brought industrial production in Petersburg to a standstill.

Gapon and his advisers decided on a peaceful march to the Winter Palace, where they intended to present a petition to the Tsar in person (in fact, Nicholas II was in Tsarskoe Selo). While some of the demands were bold ones – the introduction of the eight-hour day, freedom to strike and to form unions, the transfer of land to the peasants and popular representation in government – they were couched in humble, even reverential language: 'We, workers of St Petersburg, have come to Thee, Sovereign, to seek justice and protection; we are destitute, oppressed, overburdened with heavy toil, cursed at, not treated as human beings, but as slaves . . .'[84]

It was a critical moment for the Tsar and his government. In October 1904 a 'Conference of Oppositional and Revolutionary Organisations of the Russian Empire' had gathered in Paris to plan a united strategy. Representatives of the Union of Liberation, the Socialist Revolutionary Party and various nationalist organizations called for the abolition of

autocracy, the introduction of universal suffrage, the election of a parliamentary assembly and national self-determination. Following the
French example of 1848, a campaign of banquets was initiated in Russia by
the Union and its *zemstvo* partners, ostensibly to commemorate the legal
reforms of 1864, really to discuss the need for constitutional change. There
was little the government could to. The gaols were already full.

The final humiliation occurred over foreign policy. Russia had blustered
into a colonial war with an adversary it had mistakenly assessed as a
push-over. From the time of the Boxer Rising, Japan had watched with
alarm as its gargantuan neighbour occupied Manchuria and disputed the
Korean frontier. On 8 February 1904, Japanese naval forces launched a
pre-emptive strike on Russia's Far Eastern fleet at Port Arthur on the
Liaotung Peninsula. This was what the Russian war party (including the
Tsar himself) had been waiting for. They would teach the 'yellow monkeys'
a lesson and drown internal discontent in a wave of patriotic fervour. It was
not to be. Russian land forces were defeated at the Yalu River at the
beginning of May and the navy received a drubbing off Vladivostok in
August. Back home, rumours of corruption in high places, gross military
incompetence, even treason, abounded. Dissatisfaction was rife as news
arrived, in the early days of 1905, that the besieged garrison at Port Arthur
had surrendered.

The events of Bloody Sunday acted as catalyst to the ripening crisis.
Sympathy strikes and demonstrations broke out in Petersburg, Moscow
and a number of smaller provincial centres, but these were dwarfed by the
reactions at the empire's periphery, where nationalist strivings added to
the explosive mix. Troops opened fire on demonstrators in Riga; street
fighting accompanied strikes in Warsaw and Lodz; Finland was seething
with incipient rebellion. At the other end of the country, Tiflis was rocked
by a general strike and racial tension was mounting in the oil city of Baku.
Agrarian disturbances erupted in Georgia and in some areas law and order
relied on the authority of village elders. Everywhere, communications
were paralysed by a week-long railway strike which eventually led to the
introduction of martial law. By the end of February, Russia had still not
returned to normal. Strikes continued to erupt, protest meetings and
demonstrations were daily occurrences. There was a spate of assassinations, the most prominent victim being the Tsar's uncle, the Governor of
Moscow, Grand Duke Sergei Nikolaevich. Most ominously of all for the
regime, peasants in the Russian heartland began raiding landowners' estates.

There was no doubt in Lenin's mind that these momentous events did
indeed presage the longed-for revolution:

The uprising has begun. Force against Force. Street fighting is raging,
barricades are being thrown up, rifles are crackling, guns are booming.
Rivers of blood are flowing, the civil war for freedom is blazing up.
Moscow and the South, the Caucasus and Poland are ready to join the

proletariat of St Petersburg. The slogan of the workers has become: Death or Freedom![85]

The art of insurrection preoccupied him. He scanned the works of Marx and Engels for guidance. He re-read the history of the Paris Commune. His articles and correspondence were peppered with references to barricade fighting, stone throwing, shooting, attacks on police stations and raids on armouries.

Lenin's admiration for the Russian proletariat knew no bounds, but it was disturbing to learn that the 'Party of the working class' had played little part in the January events. On the contrary, there were many instances of workers scorning the 'politicals', even ejecting them from meetings. It was no accident that in the march which led to the tragedy of Bloody Sunday, the Social Democrat contingent was assigned the rear of the procession – so much for the vanguard party!

Lenin now set about remedying the situation. He bullied, scolded and insulted his lieutenants into action. 'Rakhmetov' (Bogdanov) was berated for sending only two bulletins in 30 days, whereas Gusev had managed six in ten. The Bolshevik committees were accused of 'Oblomovism' (a reference to a character in a Goncharov novel synonymous with sloth and procrastination). Lenin begged his activists to work harder, to broaden the ranks of the organization (expressly the Bolshevik one) with all possible speed:

> This is a time of war. The youth – the students and still more so the young workers – will decide the issue of the whole struggle. Get rid of all the old habits of immobility, of respect for rank and so on. Form *hundreds* of circles of vperedists from among the youth and encourage them to work at full pelt. Enlarge the committee *threefold* by accepting young people onto it. Set up half a dozen or a dozen sub-committees. 'Co-opt' each and every honest and energetic person.[86]

The urgency betrayed a fear of losing ground to the Mensheviks. Both factions, of course, had been equally exhilarated by the prospect of revolution and one might have expected them to sink their differences. They did manage a joint appearance, at an *émigré* meeting at the Cirque Ranci, Geneva, in January 1905. The two sides foreswore polemics but, despite the joyousness of the occasion, the co-editor of *Iskra*, Fedor Dan, managed to upset the Bolsheviks in the hall. Taking their cue from Lenin, they reacted in time-honoured fashion by staging a walk-out.

The prospects for resolving the split looked bleaker than ever, notwithstanding the earnest desire of many Bolsheviks and Mensheviks inside Russia to come to an agreement and resume common work. The fractiousness which continued to pervade the personal relations of the *émigré* leaders concealed real differences of approach and emphasis in the realm of revolutionary strategy. Lenin continued to oppose any overtures in the direction of the liberals, set greater store by illegal underground activity than his rivals and believed that the party should give more concern to the practicalities of organizing the anticipated insurrection. These differences inevitably spilled over into other areas, complicating intra-party relations still further. Only a congress, in Lenin's opinion, had the authority to pronounce on these and other issues. In the meantime, the split must not only be tolerated but actively encouraged in order to ensure Bolshevik ideological purity.

Lenin's obsession with the congress (even insurrection seemed to take second place at times) irritated even close colleagues like Gusev and Zemlyachka. And they were disturbed by the lengths to which he was prepared to go in order to get his own way. In his fiercest moments, he talked of ignoring *Iskra*, the Party Council and the Central Committee altogether and calling a congress unilaterally on the authority of the Bolshevik Bureau. Zemlyachka and Bogdanov would not hear of such a provocative step and insisted that the Central Committee in Russia (which included three Mensheviks) be consulted first. Lenin fumed, but he was forced to assent.

When the Central Committee finally did meet to discuss the proposal, all but two of its members were arrested. However, the survivors agreed to co-operate with the Bureau in organizing the congress and preparations went ahead.

Lenin's theoretical appraisal of the recent events in Russia, *Two Tactics of Social Democracy in the Democratic Revolution*, was published in pamphlet form in August 1905. Up until now the Russian Social Democrats had constructed their revolutionary strategy on the basis of various Marxian blueprints whose main reference points had been the great social upheavals of the late eighteenth and nineteenth centuries: the French Revolution, the revolutions of 1848 and the Paris Commune of 1871. Now history was unveiling, fragment by fragment, a fresh canvas of startling originality: every Social Democrat thinker, Lenin included, was compelled to respond.

In *Two Tactics*, Lenin excluded the bourgeoisie from the revolutionary camp entirely. While most Social Democrats viewed this class with suspicion and a certain condescension, few regarded them with as jaundiced an eye as Lenin. He predicted that the liberals would betray the revolutionary cause by settling for a constitutional monarchy rather than a republic and sought a new ally for the proletariat in carrying out the bourgeois–democratic revolution. Influenced by the revival of rural unrest which peaked in the early summer of 1905, he reassessed the peasantry as a potentially revolutionary force. Now, he envisaged a scenario in which autocracy was swept from power by the proletariat and peasantry acting in concert. Introducing a 'revolutionary–democratic dictatorship', the allies would then drive through the necessary programme of economic and political reforms, dealing mercilessly with whatever opposition they encountered. Only when the situation had stabilized would a constituent assembly be elected and democracy restored. This 'provisional government' must not attempt to introduce socialism – such a step would be fatally premature.

Lenin's strategy, though bold, was not the most radical on offer in the summer of 1905. Trotsky's concept of 'permanent revolution' did away altogether with the distinction between democratic and socialist revolutions. He argued that socialist measures could indeed be introduced at an earlier stage, though only if the revolution in Russia were accompanied by similar developments abroad.

Lenin now proposed revising the agrarian section of the party programme to take account of this major change of emphasis. The 1903 Programme had promised relatively little to the peasants: the abolition of redemption payments, an end to compulsory membership of the rural communes and the restoration of the 'cut-offs', small parcels of land which the peasants had formerly cultivated but had lost to the gentry in the course of emancipation. Now, Lenin advocated the nationalization of all agricultural land and its redistribution among the peasantry by elected village committees.

The third Congress of the Russian Social Democratic Labour Party finally met in London in April 1905. It could not claim to be representative of the party as a whole; neither, strictly speaking, was it constitutional. Only 21 out of 33 committees sent delegates and many of these arrived with highly dubious mandates. The Party Council (nominally the supreme body) refused to legitimize the congress. The Menshevik leadership, needless to say, boycotted the proceedings and the handful of Russian-based Menshevik delegates who did turn up soon made off for Geneva where a rival gathering had been organized with comic haste. Lenin was unperturbed. He conceded that the congress was technically illegal but insisted that it had the support of most local committees and that the urgency of the moment made further delay impermissible.

The congress sessions were held in the back rooms of various pubs and dining-rooms in the vicinity of King's Cross. Lenin and Krupskaya rented rooms nearby, at 16 Percy Circus, but most of their colleagues were housed in Whitechapel, where there was a large Russian community. On Sundays they rested and Lenin, an old London hand, acted as tour guide. Karl Marx's grave at Highgate was *de rigueur* of course, but they also found time to visit the Natural History Museum and the zoo.

From Lenin's point of view, the congress could hardly have turned out better. There was no Plekhanov, no Martov, no Dan, no Trotsky: everyone present had solid Bolshevik credentials and this gratifying news helped to put him in a much more relaxed frame of mind than in 1903. But, as the proceedings revealed, he was far from being surrounded by yes-men. The delegates, who included Lev Kamenev, Alexei Rykov and Maxim Litvinov, all future leading figures in the Soviet Government, turned out to have minds of their own. Many of them, like Krasin, disparaged the *émigré* leaders (which included Lenin, of course). Some, like the Caucasian, Tskhakaya, held rigidly to the line of *What Is To Be Done?* and opposed Lenin's demand that more workers be elected on to committees. Most were unwilling to go as far as Lenin in advocating the expulsion of the Mensheviks from the party. Not everyone was happy with his revised view of the peasantry. Nevertheless, the atmosphere was good-natured and Lenin was reasonably content with the outcome. The delegates threw out Martov's contentious rule on party membership and agreed to the abolition of the Party Council. They approved the substance of Lenin's revolutionary strategy and agreed that the peasantry should be supported in seizing the gentry estates. On the practical front, *Vpered* (shortly to reappear as *Proletari* [*The Proletarian*]) was adopted as the official party organ in place of *Iskra* and an all-Bolshevik Central Committee, consisting of Lenin, Krasin, Bogdanov, Rykov and D. S. Postolovsky, was elected.

On the way home, Lenin's group, consisting of Krupskaya, Zemlyachka and Tskhakaya stopped over in Paris, where they visited the Eiffel Tower, the Louvre and the Wall of the Communards at the cemetery of Père Lachaise. They were briefly detained at Boulogne by customs officials searching for contraband tobacco. However, on an assurance from Lenin that he and his friends were not on business, they were released without an inspection of their suitcases which happened to contain the minutes of the third congress.

Back in Geneva, the offices of the new party newspaper, *Proletari*, became Lenin's centre of operations from which he monitored events in Russia closely. He received regular information from a host of correspondents and contributors and was occasionally briefed in person by activists in the field. He kept an up-to-the minute file of Press cuttings from foreign newspapers, including *The Times*, the *Frankfurter Zeitung*, *Le Matin* and the *Journal de Geneve*. And he still found time to pen dozens of articles and scores of letters, to edit the contributions of others, to advise, to negotiate and to lecture. In terms of sheer intellectual energy, Lenin had few equals.

The news from Russia made compelling reading for any revolutionary. The forces of opposition were gaining in strength and self-confidence; they were also becoming better organized. In May, nearly a dozen professional associations joined with railwaymen, *zemstvo* activists and organizations fighting for Jewish and female emancipation to form a single Union of Unions. A Peasant Union was founded in the same month and its first congress in July was attended by more than 100 delegates from 22 provinces. Simultaneously, factory workers were electing committees to present their demands: the first 'soviet' (association of factory committees) was established in May in the textile town of Ivanovo-Voznesensk.

Meanwhile, the war with Japan was going from bad to worse. In February, Russian land forces had suffered nearly 120,000 casualties at the Battle of Mukden. Three months later the Japanese Navy routed Admiral

Rozhdestvensky's Baltic fleet in the Straits of Tsushima. This was the knock-out blow. Shortly afterwards, Lenin read reports in the *Frankfurter Zeitung* of impending peace negotiations.

It was Gusev who informed him of the *Potemkin* mutiny. The newest battleship in the Black Sea fleet had put into Odessa, where there was already a turbulent general strike in progress. The infection quickly spread to the Sevastopol naval base and for several days in June it seemed possible, even likely, that the incipient rebellion might develop into an armed uprising. Anticipating just such an eventuality, Lenin dispatched his agent, M. I. Vasil'ev-Yuzhin, to the scene with instructions to board the *Potemkin*, spread the mutiny to other vessels in the fleet, arm the workers, co-ordinate the efforts of local Bolsheviks and fan the flames of peasant unrest. In the event, Yuzhin's blushes were spared – by the time he reached Odessa, the *Potemkin* was already bound for Romania where it subsequently lowered the red flag. The general strike disintegrated about the same time and the opportunity had been lost.

Three months later, a peace treaty was signed with Japan. This left half a million reservists in the Far East impatiently awaiting demobilization. Bad treatment and appalling conditions of service increased their volatility. Mutinies and riots broke out in Vladivostok, Harbin, Chita and other points along the Trans-Siberian railway and the disaffection soon spread to garrisons closer to home.

The Tsar's advisers worked feverishly to shore up the crumbling imperial edifice. In March the newly appointed Interior Minister, A. G. Bulygin, had announced that elected representatives would be consulted in the formulation of new laws, though this promise, vague as it was, seemed inconsistent with a simultaneous appeal to rally to the existing order. Even so it was six months before Bulygin fleshed out his constitutional proposals. These envisaged a Duma (Parliament) with consultative rights only, elected indirectly and on a restricted franchise weighted heavily in favour of the more conservative sections of society. The reforms were dismissed out of hand by revolutionaries and reactionaries alike. Only the moderates were divided, some advocating a boycott, others arguing that the Duma could be used as a platform to push the boundaries of freedom further.

Once again, events overtook the politicians. A strike by Moscow printers in September provoked sympathy action from their colleagues in Petersburg. Railwaymen in Moscow struck shortly afterwards and it was not long before the entire network was brought to a standstill. Telegraph and telephone services were badly disrupted as the strike movement spread beyond the two capitals, paralysing a succession of towns and cities across the length and breadth of the country.

Russia was plunged into chaos. University campuses were converted from academic institutions into centres for organizing anti-government resistance. Dissatisfaction with the 'Bulygin Duma' led to calls for a legislative assembly and full civil rights. The streets of the major cities filled with crowds carrying red flags and banners. By late October the government was faced with an empire-wide general strike. Shops, schools, hospitals, factories, law courts and local-government offices closed down. Newspapers ceased to appear. Armed workers acted as vigilantes in place of the police, who were increasingly incapable of maintaining order. In Petersburg, workers formed an elected council, the Soviet of Workers' Deputies, to co-ordinate industrial action in the capital; colleagues in other towns and cities were quick to follow suit. Meanwhile, the rash of mutinies continued unabated, peasant unrest flared up in the south and the peripheral regions descended into anarchy. The empire was coming apart at the seams.

Bewildered, Nicholas II turned for advice to the architect of the peace treaty with Japan, Count Sergei Witte. The former Minister of Finance offered the Tsar a choice: either reform or a military dictatorship. Nicholas toyed with the latter solution but his preferred candidate for the role of dictator, the Grand Duke Nikolai Nikolaevich, threatend to shoot himself rather than plunge the country into a blood-bath. On 30 October 1905 a manifesto, issued in the Tsar's name, promised Russian citizens freedom of speech, assembly and organization and accorded the forthcoming Duma legislative powers. The abolition of preliminary Press censorship and a partial amnesty for political prisoners followed later. Russians were to look back with nostalgia on the ensuing weeks as the 'days of freedom'.

News of the manifesto reached Lenin late in the evening of 30 October. At the time he was busy drafting the leader for the latest issue of *Proletari*. Clearly, this piece was now out of date and had to be discarded. He hastily apprised himself of the new situation by culling material from the foreign Press; more detailed communications from Russia followed. Among them was a telegram informing him of the death of his most experienced agent, N. E. Bauman, in Moscow. (Bauman was killed in a street skirmish immediately after being released from prison). Shortly afterwards, he learned of the wounding of another Bolshevik, N. I. Podvoisky, during a demonstration in Yaroslavl. Evidently things were hotting up.

In view of the more relaxed political climate, Lenin decided to risk returning to Russia. Krupskaya helped him sort through his papers. They were then placed in sealed envelopes and packed into a trunk ready for storage. Highly complicated arrangements were made for him to travel via Stockholm, where he was to wait for his contact. He waited . . . and waited. Two weeks later(!) the man showed up with the necessary false passport. When he eventually reached the Finnish capital, he was taken to the apartment of a teacher at the university, Gunnar Kastren, for meetings with prominent Social Democrats. From there he boarded the train bound for Petersburg's Finland Station.

Lenin moved in with P. P. Rumyantsev, an old acquaintance of Krupskaya's, on Rozhdestvensky Street. Before attending his first meeting of the Petersburg Committee, he visited the graves of the victims of Bloody

Sunday at the Preobrazhensky Cemetery. He was invited to join the editorial board of *Novaya Zhizn* (*New Life*), a legal daily newspaper published by M. F. Andreyeva, the wife of the radical writer, Maxim Gorky. The contributors included prominent Bolsheviks like Bogdanov, Rumyantsev, Lunacharsky (summoned by Lenin from Florence) and Kamenev, but also well-known writers and poets, including N. M. Minsky (editor-in-chief) and Leonid Andreev. Lenin was at the newspaper offices on the Nevsky Prospekt almost every day.

Life was developing with bewildering speed and it took some time for the returning revolutionaries to acclimatize and take stock of events. Lenin's priority (as always) was the development of the party. His first contribution to *Novaya Zhizn*, in fact, was entitled 'The Reorganisation of the Party'. It was an impassioned appeal to broaden the party's ranks: Lenin wanted to see a new influx of worker-recruits 'in two or three weeks'. It was time to leave the 'suffocation' of the underground and exploit the new freedoms to the full. Other innovations were advocated: the injection of more democracy into party affairs and the setting up of new types of organization. Even reconciliation with the Mensheviks was in the air once more. But there was a note of caution. The party must ensure that every new member was a genuine Social Democrat, subscribing whole-heartedly to party (Bolshevik?) policies. And, while supporting participation in semi-legal organizations, like trade unions and soviets, Lenin was careful to avoid calling for the wholesale abandonment of conspiracy. After all, as Trotsky pointed out, the political situation remained highly ambiguous: troops still patrolled the streets, armed gangs attacked demonstrators with impunity, newspaper editors were harrassed and the promises of constitutional reform were as yet no more than that – promises.

The most important mass organization in Petersburg at this time was the Soviet of Workers' Deputies. In the course of the general strike, the Soviet's authority had increased to a remarkable degree. Its 562 members, representing more than 150 of the city's most important factories, negotiated almost as a matter of course with employers, the city council, postal and railway officials, even the police. The Soviet even had its own militia which stood guard outside meetings and helped maintain public order. When Lenin returned to Petersburg, he was somewhat dismayed to find that many Bolsheviks were indifferent, even hostile, to the Soviet, partly because Menshevik agitators had played a major role in setting it up, partly because the Executive refused to subordinate itself to any one political party. Latterly, some local activists had tried to infiltrate the organization but with a view to turning it into a Bolshevik adjunct (in practice, a hopeless aim). Lenin called for a more flexible approach. He was impressed by the Soviet's power and its apparently radical aims. In his most sanguine moments, he even referred to it as an 'organ of revolutionary power', a provisional revolutionary government in embryo.

However, his attitude cooled considerably over time. He attended few sessions of the Executive (to which party representatives were invited as advisers or guests) and spoke only once at a full session, on 26 November. There were several reasons for his growing disillusionment. It rankled that the Soviet's origins and character owed more to the Mensheviks than to any other party, and that its leading orator was none other than Lev Trotsky, an outspoken opponent from 1903 days. The Soviet also seemed prone to tactical errors. Its attempts to impose the eight-hour day by unilateral action, for example, only served to unify employers, who replied with lock-outs and wage-cuts until the movement fizzled out. A similar fate befell the general strike called to oppose the introduction of martial law in Poland and the bloody suppression of a mutiny at the Kronstadt naval base. These defeats devalued the Soviet in Lenin's eyes, reducing it to the status of a 'talking shop'. There was little chance now of transforming it into an organ of insurrection.

In truth, the Bolsheviks were ill-prepared to launch an armed uprising in the winter of 1905. L. B. Krasin's 'combat group', set up by Lenin to oversee military operations in the wake of the London congress, had been able to amass only small quantities of weapons of dubious quality. There was no overall military strategy and operational planning at local level was purely fanciful. Worker militias had been formed in a considerable number of factories and plants by the end of the summer, but their training was rudimentary and sporadic. Some practical experience was gained during the October days when the detachments took to the streets to patrol political meetings and to defend revolutionary speakers from right-wing opponents, but this was hardly adequate preparation for a force contemplating insurrection. Certainly, Lenin was unimpressed. He wrote to the Petersburg combat organization in October: 'It horrifies me – I give you my word – it horrifies me to find that there has been talk about bombs for over six months yet not one has been made . . .'[87]

His correspondence is replete with 'practical' suggestions: start fires with rags soaked in kerosene; blow up a police station; carry out a bank raid to obtain funds; amass every kind of weapon immediately at any cost: rifles, revolvers, knives, knuckledusters, sticks – and shovels to build barricades!

On returning to Petersburg in November, he threw himself into insurrectionary preparations, attending meetings of the Bolshevik combat organization at the Wittmeyer secondary school for girls on Angliisky Prospekt, even visiting the polytechnic to inspect a secret workshop for manufacturing bombs. His clarion calls from the pages of *Novaya Zhizn* were couched in language so brazen that Minsky was threatened with prosecution. Lenin himself was placed under increasingly close police surveillance. Consequently, he never spent long at the same address and often lived under an assumed name. He and Krupskaya rarely shared the same accommodation and met only occasionally at their favourite restaurant, the Vienna on Gogol Street.

Meanwhile, the political situation was becoming more tense. On 8

December, the Chairman of the Soviet, G. S. Khrustalev-Nosar, was arrested. The following day, Trotsky arrogantly announced that the Soviet 'was continuing its preparations for armed insurrection'. On 15 December the entire radical Press called on the population to refuse to pay taxes and to withdraw savings' deposits in an effort to bring down the Witte administration. The Interior Minister, P. N. Durnovo, decided to take the bull by the horns. Troops were ordered to surround the Soviet and arrest the delegates. On the same day, the police raided the *Novaya Zhizn* offices and closed down the newspaper. Once again, Lenin was forced to move house.

To Witte's immeasurable relief, the workers of Petersburg were too strike-weary and demoralized to respond effectively to Durnovo's bold but provocative action. It was a very different story in Moscow, where a mutiny by local troops had convinced Bolsheviks and Mensheviks alike that the moment for insurrection had finally arrived. The Socialist Revolutionaries also agreed to collaborate. Hastily drawn-up plans were approved by party organizations and by the Moscow Soviet. The insurgents disposed of about 1,000 militiamen in all. When the Moscow Soviet announced a general strike in response to the arrest of the Petersburg deputies, the Governor-General, Admiral F. V. Dubasov, declared a state of emergency. Makeshift barricades now appeared and militiamen harrassed the troops with sniper fire and well-laid ambushes. For a few days the rebels appeared to have the upper hand and the sympathy of the city's workers.

On 23 December Lenin attended a joint meeting of the Bolshevik Central Committee and the combat organization, held in Krasin's apartment on the Fontanka Embankment in Petersburg. Support for the Moscow comrades was naturally top of the agenda – there was talk of blowing up the railway line linking the two cities in order to delay the arrival of troop reinforcements. But by then the issue was already decided. The leaders of the insurrection, including the Bolsheviks, Vasil'ev-Yuzhin and Liadov, had no plans to capture the key strategic points in the city and squandered their momentary advantage. The Semenovsky Regiment, under the resolute command of Colonel Min, now arrived to bolster the garrison forces. In the face of overwhelming odds, the rebels decided they had no alternative but to abort the uprising and disperse. The militiamen of the fiercely militant Presnya district, which included the huge Prokhorov textile mill, held out for a day or two more. They were bombarded into submission by concentrated artillery fire. About 700 civilians died in the abortive uprising – but only ten soldiers.

Similar insurgencies (but on a smaller scale) took place in a number of cities including Nizhni-Novgorod, Saratov, Rostov and Ekaterinoslav. All were put down with varying degrees of brutality.

The issue of the Moscow uprising was still undetermined when Lenin and Krupskaya left Petersburg for the Finnish town of Tampere (Tammerfors) to attend a Bolshevik conference. Among those present was the 26-year-old son of an impoverished Georgian cobbler, Iosif Vissarionovich Djugashvili, better known to his comrades as Koba and later, to the world, as Stalin. Anticipating his first encounter with the Bolshevik leader, the unpreprossessing but self-assured delegate from Tiflis (now Tbilisi) imagined meeting 'a great man, great physically as well as politically', the 'mountain eagle of our Party'; instead, Lenin turned out to be 'a most ordinary man, below average height, in no way, literally in no way distinguishable from ordinary mortals'. A second source of disappointment was Lenin's unpretentiousness. Stalin had arrived expecting a carefully measured theatrical entrance from the Bolshevik leader; instead, he found him already ensconced in a corner, chatting casually to some unknowns.[88]

Most of the delegates at Tampere were too excited by the situation at home to pay much attention to Lenin's mannerisms. Thoroughly convinced that revolution was just around the corner, they kept their hand in by retiring to the woods for shooting practice in between sessions.

High on the agenda was the business of reuniting the party. Reconciliation between Bolsheviks and Mensheviks in Russia, forged in the heat of battle, had shaken the leadership into the realization that the hoary disputes of the second congress were nothing but an impediment to the progress of the revolution. Many local organizations had already merged without consulting their *émigré* bosses and even the Bolshevik Central Committee, elected at the London congress, was now in sympathy with the conciliatory mood. Lenin was least of all susceptible to the heady atmosphere but, conscious that he was swimming against the tide, set himself the more modest aim of ensuring that his faction predominated in any newly constructed party organization. At Tampere it was decided to convene yet another congress (this time attended by Bolsheviks and Mensheviks together) in order to complete reunification. The Mensheviks concurred with these arrangements.

The Duma was the other major item of discussion. Despite some reservations on Lenin's part, the assembly voted to reject out of hand the recently published electoral law and to boycott the new parliament, which they dismissed as a sham.

The euphoria of Tampere was short-lived. Having successfully rid itself of the soviets, routed the Moscow insurrectionaries and split the democratic opposition with the October Manifesto, the government felt its confidence restored. The twilight world of semi-constitutionalism now gave way to naked repression. In towns and cities across the country revolutionary organizations were systematically destroyed, their members arrested and imprisoned, their printing presses silenced.

The authorities acted with much greater brutality in the countryside. Punitive expeditions were dispatched to the Baltic provinces, the Caucasus and along the Trans-Siberian railway. They were given *carte blanche* to terrorize with every means available to them and they used their powers assiduously. Villages were burnt to the ground, hostages taken, mass beatings and floggings administered, rapes and other acts of brutality committed wholesale. Suspected activists were rounded up and either taken to prison or publicly executed without trial. The actions of the generals who led the expeditions – Rennenkampf, Bezobrazov, Orlov, Meller-Zakomelsky and Alikhanov – received the unconditional approval of their political masters: Durnovo, Witte and the Tsar himself.

On returning to Petersburg, Lenin was forced to go into hiding. He took refuge in nearby Finland, commuting across the frontier whenever necessary. His name appeared on a police wanted-list, circulated among secret agents scouring the countryside for 'politicals' who had gone to ground in this traditional safe haven. In Petersburg, after a short, clandestine visit to Moscow, he noticed that his apartment was being watched. He left immediately for another, changing cabs three times to avoid detection – Lenin was a practised conspirator! All the while, he was up to his ears in party work: coming to terms with the lessons of the Moscow uprising, explaining his stance on the Duma to local activists and preparing draft resolutions for the approaching congress.

The fourth (unity) Congress of the Russian Social Democratic Labour Party met in Stockholm from 23 April to 8 May 1906. Lenin was already resigned to the fact that the Mensheviks would arrive with a majority: 62 votes against the Bolsheviks' 46 as it turned out; but he could derive comfort from the knowledge that party membership had increased from 12,000 in 1905 to 100,000 on the eve of the congress. He was elected to the Presidium, together with Plekhanov, who had not returned to Russia during the revolution, and Fedor Dan. Two of Lenin's other former opponents, Martov and Trotsky, were in police custody and could not attend. The atmosphere at the congress was businesslike rather than cordial: there was no sentimentality, no emotional reunions and the factional divide was still very much alive in the minds of the delegates.

The agrarian question topped the agenda. The winter of 1905 had seen a new wave of peasant unrest sweep the Russian countryside: strikes, grain seizures, timber theft and rent boycotts plagued the gentry estates. Manor houses and outbuildings were set alight. In some places, peasants helped themselves to land, anticipating a general repartition. Renewed disturbances on an even larger scale were expected in the spring.

Lenin's confidence in the revolutionary instincts of the peasantry appeared to be fully justified. But when he put forward his project for land nationalization, it encountered stiff opposition. Plekhanov was the most effective critic among his traditional opponents. He held to the orthodox belief that a future revolution would place the bourgeoisie in power, not the proletariat and peasantry in alliance. But he found other grounds for doubting the soundness of Lenin's strategy. What would happen, he enquired of the Bolshevik leader, if a counter-revolution were to restore the monarchy to power after the land had been nationalized? Surely, nationalization would then deliver the land into the hands of a hostile State, thus increasing its power. This would be a particularly dangerous development in Russia, Plekhanov argued, because historically the Russian State shared a kinship with oriental despotism: serfdom itself was rooted in State ownership of the land. Plekhanov went on to accuse Lenin of wishing to dispense with the bourgeois phase of the revolution altogether in favour of a direct route march to socialism. Such a move, he believed, would be criminally premature in a country as backward as Russia.

Lenin defended himself vigorously against these charges. He denied any intention of jettisoning the bourgeois revolution, insisting, on the contrary, that nationalization would greatly facilitate the development of a modern, capitalist agricultural system. And there was an additional advantage, in Lenin's view: by promoting market forces, nationalization would simultaneously accelerate social differentiation in the countryside, thus helping to bring class war to a head.

The agrarian debate seemed sterile and unreal to rank-and-file Bolsheviks like S. A. Suvorov and Stalin. They were convinced that the peasants would reject nationalization out of hand, from a belief that the land belonged to them, not to the State. It would be better, therefore, if the bulk of the land was handed over directly to peasant committees who would distribute it without any outside interference.

The balance of forces at the congress ensured that no Bolshevik proposal would obtain a majority. In the event, it was the Menshevik project of P. P. Maslov which was approved. Maslov argued that the land should be transferred into the hands of elected local-government authorities for redistribution (municipalization).

While the congress was still in session, the elections to the Duma were taking place in Russia. The Bolsheviks carried out their decision to boycott them, but the Mensheviks, who had initially left it to local organizations to make up their own minds, now belatedly came down in favour of participation, believing that this was the best way of increasing the political experience of workers while at the same time convincing them of the Duma's inadequacy.

The elections were contested by a number of newly formed parties and organizations, ranging from the Union of the Russian People on the right to the Menshevik Social Democrats on the Left. The more progressive liberals coalesced into the Constitutional Democratic (Kadet) Party, while moderate conservatives were represented by the Union of 17 October.

To the dismay of the government, the Kadets emerged as the single largest party with over one-third of the seats. Although the peasantry was also well represented (in line with official hopes), about 100 of their deputies formed a coalition of *Trudoviki* (Labourites) committed to land socialization. With the Duma cast in such an oppositionist mould (many of the delegates representing national minorities were also hostile to the government), head-on confrontation seemed almost inevitable.

The opening ceremony took place in the presence of the Tsar and Tsarina on 10 May 1906. The setting was the opulent splendour of the St George's Hall of the Winter Palace. Nicholas's address from the throne offered nothing of substance. The opposition replied by reiterating their demands for an end to all forms of martial law and emergency rule, for direct elections on the basis of universal male suffrage and for the strict observance of civil liberties. The new prime minister, I. L. Goremykin, dismissed the Kadet-inspired programme in a speech delivered in a provocative monotone. When behind-the-scenes negotiations failed to break the deadlock, the Tsar ordered the dissolution of the Duma on 21 July: it had been in session for just 70 days.

The Kadet deputies withdrew to a wood outside the Finnish town of Vyborg (about 80 miles [130 km] from Petersburg), where they called on the Russian people to refuse to pay taxes or to furnish conscripts until the Duma was reconvened.

The response of the Social Democrats was less circumspect. Lenin was holidaying in the Petersburg resort of Sablino when he learned of the Duma's dissolution. Hastening back to the capital, he rejected the Mensheviks' call for a general strike in favour of agitation for an armed uprising. He made frantic attempts to obtain from his Bolshevik colleagues details concerning the numbers and state of preparedness of the party's fighting units, the extent and effectiveness of their propaganda work among the armed forces and the mood of the railwaymen. Lenin failed, however, to make contact with Bolshevik activists in the naval bases of Kronstadt and Sveaborg when mutinies broke out there several days later. He and Krupskaya were compelled to wait anxiously for news in the home of their friends the Menzhinskys. When the news did arrive, it was bad. Not only had the rebellion been crushed, but the Bolshevik's military organization in Petersburg had been broken up and its members (including Menzhinsky) arrested.

The government resumed the offensive once more. Goremykin was replaced as prime minister by a relatively young but vigorous and self-confident administrator, P. A. Stolypin. A tried and trusted hardliner, Stolypin had impressed the Tsar with the way he had dealt with civil disturbances as Governor of Saratov in 1905. Shortly after his new appointment, Socialist Revolutionary terrorists blew up his house near Petersburg, injuring two of his children. If Stolypin was looking for an excuse to impose a clamp-down, then the perpetrators of the Aptekarsky Island attack had served him well. In August 1906, the government introduced a network of field courts martial and armed them with draconian powers. Suspect political offenders were picked up off the street and immediately tried in secret by an anonymous military tribunal. All cases were dealt with in the space of 48 hours and death sentences carried out before the following day – without recourse to appeal. By April 1907 the tally of executions had reached 1,144. In retaliation, the revolutionaries (Socialist Revolutionaries and anarchists for the most part) stepped up their own terror campaign, killing or injuring several thousand paid informers, police officers, military personnel and administrators of varying degrees of importance and seniority during the same period.

Stolypin's strategy was not all mailed fist, however. In November 1906 he introduced a programme of agrarian reforms designed to give the regime a new stability and vitality. Stolypin envisaged making land available to the peasants. This land would be drawn from the imperial domains, not the estates of the gentry, which were to remain intact. He also wanted to make it possible for peasants to leave the commune, an institution he regarded as a burden on the rural economy, and establish their own consolidated farmholdings outside. In the long term, Stolypin hoped to revitalize Russian agriculture and, in the process, create a class of prosperous, independent farmers with a stake in maintaining the existing social order.

While Stolypin was prepared to govern by emergency decree if necessary, he preferred to rule by consent. He intended to court moderate opinion by offering a broader framework of reforming measures to a new Duma, scheduled to convene in March 1907. Stolypin also promised to uphold civil liberties and the rule of law.

The Social Democrats discussed their attitude to the second Duma at Tampere in November 1906. Lenin now declared himself unreservedly in favour of participation, a position supported by the Mensheviks. He was unable, however, to win over his more militant colleagues, Krasin and Bogdanov. Lenin's change of heart did not mean that he had lost faith in insurrection, as his writings in the wake of the Kronstadt and Sveaborg mutinies make clear. Support for the Duma – 'not a parliament [but] a police headquarters' – was never intended as more than a tactical device, a means of ridding the working class of 'constitutional illusions'. Meanwhile, Lenin argued, the party should be working towards more effective agitation among the troops, better channels of communication, new tactics of guerrilla warfare to offset the technological superiority of enemy forces and the acquisition of new weapons, like the hand-grenade, used recently to great effect in the Japanese war. 'Insurrection is an art', Lenin reminded his comrades-in-arms.[89]

The second Duma opened on 5 March 1907. The electorate had returned an assembly even more hostile to the government than the first, despite a considerable amount of harrassment of left-wing candidates. Besides 65 Social Democrats (18 of whom were Bolsheviks) there were 37 Socialist Revolutionaries and 98 Trudoviki. The parties of the right were also well represented, with more than 50 seats. These gains at the extremes of the political spectrum were made at the expense of the Kadets, whose representation was halved. The debates in the chamber quickly descended into a slanging match, making fruitful legislative work impossible. Once Stolypin turned down a Kadet demand to dispense with the field courts martial and other extraordinary measures, it became clear that the prime minister's programme would fall largely on deaf ears.

This was exactly the kind of Duma Lenin had been hoping for: the revolutionaries had their soap-box, while the government was being pushed ever further back into reaction, making a mockery of their supposedly reformist leanings. Another confrontation was in the offing.

Lenin was living with G. D. Leitezen and his family at Vaza, their rambling country house near Kuokkala Station in Finland. Vaza had previously belonged to the Socialist Revolutionaries, who had set up a bomb factory there. Krasin and Bogdanov shared the house and a steady stream of Bolshevik activists commuted from Petersburg, so many in fact that Nadya left the door unbolted and refreshments and bedding in the dining-room for unexpected guests who had arrived by the night train. Lenin occupied a room at the side of the house and turned it into a makeshift office. From here he reeled off his newspaper articles, advised, instructed and drafted speeches for the Bolshevik Duma deputies and attended party meetings.

Preparations were under way for a fifth party congress. The Mensheviks were lukewarm, to say the least, about holding yet another congress so soon after the last one. Lenin, on the other hand, was as anxious as ever to air controversy, expose flaws in the tactical positions of his opponents and (most importantly) improve Bolshevik representation in party organizations.

Arranging the congress presented formidable obstacles, finding a venue not least among them. The original intention had been to meet in Copenhagen, but permission was refused. Lenin then sent a telegram to the Norwegian labour leader, Oskar Nissen, asking him to sound out foreign-ministry officials there. Again his request was turned down. Sweden was also ruled out. In desperation, Lenin turned to London (not one of the Russians' favourite cities) and received a positive response. He arrived there in the company of Maxim Gorky and was most solicitous about the writer's health, drawing his attention to the damp sheets in his Russell Square hotel. He confided to Gorky: 'I believe you're fond of a scrap? There's going to be a fine old scuffle here'.[90]

The congress took place in the Brotherhood Church in Southgate Road, bordering the grimy, working-class neighbourhoods of Hoxton and Islington. The church belonged to a socialist clergyman, the Reverend F. R. Swann. Unlike previous gatherings, the London congress attracted considerable coverage in the English Press. The *Morning Post* reported the arrival of the Russians and printed a paragraph supplied by Lenin. Reporters and photographers jostled for position outside the entrance in an effort to capture the names and faces of the Tsar's most desperate enemies.

The Brotherhood Church was filled to capacity: there were well over 300 delegates, representing not only Russian social democracy but its Latvian, Lithuanian and Polish counterparts. Jewish members of the Bund and

Armenian socialists were also present. Among the old hands were Dan and
Martov, Axelrod and Plekhanov, Trotsky, Bogdanov and Stalin. Gorky
noted how Plekhanov, dressed 'in a frock coat, closely buttoned up like a
Protestant pastor', delivered the opening address 'like a preacher confident
that his ideas are incontrovertible, every word and every pause of great
value'. Gorky also had his eye on Lenin:

> At one time he hunched himself up as though he were cold, then he
> sprawled as if he felt hot. He poked his fingers in his armholes, rubbed
> his chin, shook his head and whispered something to M. P. Tomsky.
> When Plekhanov declared that there were no 'revisionists' in the Party,
> Lenin bent down, the bald spot on his head grew red, and his shoulders
> shook with silent laughter.[91]

The debates were verbose; the atmosphere cantankerous. On the Menshevik side there was now a consensus that the revolution, for the time being
at least, was over. Insurrection should be removed from the agenda along
with its trappings: conspiracies, troop agitation, arms' seizures, fighting
detachments and all kinds of 'adventurism'. Instead, attempts should
be made to co-operate with more progressive elements among the
bourgeoisie, to work actively in the Duma, the trade unions and other
non-party organizations. Despite the inhospitable terrain, the Mensheviks
persisted in their vision of a socialist party in the Western-European
mould. To Lenin, of course, such conciliatory views were anathema: 'the
purest revisionism'.

The outcome of the debates usually depended on the non-Russian
delegations, which gave Lenin and his supporters the edge. The Mensheviks were defeated on the question of co-operating with the bourgeoisie
and on Axelrod's proposal for a workers' congress in the tradition of the
soviets. The resolution on the Duma was also framed to the Bolsheviks'
liking. But they failed to deflect discussion on what was, for them, the most
embarrassing issue of all – expropriations.

Expropriations (politically motivated armed robberies) had already been
condemned by the Stockholm congress in 1906 but the Bolsheviks found
the practice too lucrative to give up easily, especially in view of the party's
increasingly shaky financial position. There was an additional advantage,
in Lenin's view: expropriations provided his armed detachments with
valuable experience in the art of guerrilla warfare. Bolshevik bands vied
with anarchists and Socialist Revolutionaries to carry out the most daring
raids on banks, post offices, military-pay convoys, mail trains, even ships.
Favourite centres of operations were the Urals (where hunting rifles were
in plentiful supply and the hilly, densely wooded terrain provided ideal
cover) and the Caucasus. In June 1907, a team led by S. A. Ter-Petrosyan
(known as Kamo) netted over 300,000 roubles in a raid carried out at the
State bank in Tiflis. But the serial numbers were known to the police and
when the *émigrés* tried to change them abroad, there were arrests. Kamo

visited Lenin at Kuokkala just a few months before the Tiflis robbery. A big-hearted bear of a man, thoroughly devoted to the cause, he was a particular favourite of Krupskaya's mother, who used to help him strap on his revolvers!

Lenin's underhandedness was fully exposed at the London congress. His opponents castigated him for ignoring the Stockholm resolution of 1906, for bringing the party into disrepute and for diverting it from more important tasks. A fresh resolution, roundly condemning expropriations, was passed by a large majority; Lenin contented himself with abstaining.

In line with tradition, the congress ran out of time long before it had run out of steam. It was also out of funds. Lenin was forced to go cap in hand in search of more money, with Gorky and Plekhanov providing moral support. The situation was urgent: many of the delegates, especially the workers among them, lacked the finances to return home. Lenin's first port of call was the painter, Felix Moschelles, but he refused to help. Eventually, an American soap manufacturer, named Joseph Fels, was persuaded to contribute £1,700. The debt was repaid with interest, but only after repeated threats and demands, and not until after the Revolution, by which time Fels himself had died.

The delegates hurried through the remainder of the agenda. Five Bolsheviks and four Mensheviks were elected to the new Central Committee, but this was not sufficient to give Lenin an overall majority: the balance of power rested with the Latvian, Polish and Jewish representatives who occupied the remaining six seats. Thus, the situation remained one of stalemate.

Lenin returned to Russia during the second week in June. On the 16th the second Duma was abruptly dissolved. Stolypin's decision, though hardly unexpected, was, strictly speaking, unconstitutional and is therefore usually described as a *coup d'état*. He claimed to have uncovered a conspiracy by the Social Democrats to murder the Tsar and foment rebellion among the armed forces, and demanded the lifting of their parliamentary immunity. Late on the night of 15 June Lenin discussed the situation with the Bolshevik deputies at Kuokkala and advised them to agitate among the factory workers of the capital. The session finished at 3 a.m. Hours later, Stolypin acted.

The revolution was finally over. Stolypin gave notice of his intention to summon a third Duma but, in the same breath, he issued a new electoral law which effectively gave the most wealthy one per cent of the population control over almost 70 per cent of the seats. Needless to say, the results this time fully accorded with the government's wishes: 154 Octobrists and 97 conservatives were returned, as opposed to 19 Social Democrats and 54 Kadets. The third Duma convened on 1 November 1907 and it was destined to serve out its full five-year term.

Lenin had taken a much-needed holiday after his return from Europe. He spent it in the peace and quiet of Styrs Udde, in Finland, with its pine forests, sea and 'magnificent weather'. Krupskaya wrote to Manyasha: 'We are bathing in the sea, cycling . . . Volodya plays chess, fetches water, at one time we had a craze for the English game of "Donkey" '.[92]

In August, Lenin travelled to Stuttgart to attend the congress of the Socialist International. As a member of the commission charged with preparing the resolution on militarism and international conflicts, he worked closely with Rosa Luxemburg, another sometime visitor to the Vaza country house. Their resolution committed the international socialist movement and the workers of all countries to do everything in their power to prevent a European war; should war nevertheless break out, their duty would be to hasten its end and, in the process, actively promote the transition from a capitalist to a socialist order.

Returning to Russia, Lenin re-immersed himself in party work. He was elected editor-in-chief of the newspaper *Sotsial Demokrat* (*Social Democrat*) and was preparing an edition of his selected works, to be called *12 Years*. But his days in Russia were numbered. The Paris branch of the Okhrana, the Finnish police and the authorities in Petersburg were all keeping close tabs on him. Throughout the country, revolutionaries were being arrested in droves: it would only be a matter of time before Stolypin's agents caught up with Lenin himself. Lenin was ordered by the party to go to ground. Early in December, he moved from Kuokkala to a hideaway at Oglbu, close to the Finnish capital of Helsingfors. Several days later, he took the train to Abo, with the intention of boarding the steamer bound for Sweden. To avoid detection, he even walked the last part of the journey on foot. But the port was already being watched. Relying on Finnish Social Democrats for help, Lenin took a zigzag course across the islands at the base of the Gulf of Bothnia. He travelled only at night: now on foot, now on horseback, now by sleigh. Eventually, he arrived within sight of Nagu, the steamer's next port of call, but he had to wait several days for the intervening waters to freeze over. Two local fishermen agreed to guide him over the ice-floes. In mid-journey, disaster struck as the ice began to give way beneath his feet. The thought occurred to him: 'What a silly way to die!' Precisely at that moment (seemingly his last), Lenin spotted a raft of ice nudging towards him and managed to scramble aboard it. His obsessive concern with physical fitness had served him well in his hour of need. Breathless, his heart pounding, he finally made it to Nagu. On 25 December 1907 he left for Stockholm, where Nadya joined him nine days later. They had had their first taste of revolution.

6
Return to the wilderness

The postcards for sale on the promenade offered unrivalled views of the 'latest avalanche sensation' but Geneva itself was damp and grey. A bitter wind whipped up from the lake, stinging the faces of the two fugitive revolutionaries as they struggled with their cases towards their new lodgings. Lenin turned to his wife and muttered, 'I feel as if I'd come here to be buried'.[93]

His natural resilience resurfaced in the end but never was it challenged as severely as during those first years of reimposed exile. The Ulyanovs were cold and lonely in their single-room apartment. They spent their evenings wandering aimlessly through the streets, sometimes stopping off at the theatre or calling in at a cinema. They rarely stayed until the end.

Once again, Lenin took refuge in routine. He buried his disappointments under a mountain of work and soon felt better for it. His first concern was to get *Proletari* back on the rails. Bogdanov and I. F. Dubrovinsky agreed to join him as editors. His sister Manyasha offered to supply him with newsworthy materials from home. Lunacharsky and Gorky were persuaded to contribute occasional articles. The logistics of smuggling the paper into Russia via Italy and Austria were discussed. By March, Lenin was back in business.

The news from Russia could hardly have been more discouraging. Hundreds of activists had already been executed, exiled or sentenced to long terms of imprisonment. Anxious to avoid a similar fate, the rank and file now deserted the party in droves, reducing membership by 95 per cent between 1907 and 1910. Spies and *agents provocateur* were everywhere: in the Duma, attending congresses abroad, serving on committees, on trade-union boards, on the staffs of newspapers and in party schools. No one knew whom to trust.

On top of this, the *émigré* leaders found it impossible to agree on tactics. Convinced that insurrection was, for the time being, unrealistic, Lenin, nevertheless, continued to insist on the preservation of the party underground. He advocated a mix of conspiratorial work of the *What Is To Be Done?* variety with agitational activity in the Duma and in the newly emerging, quasi-legal labour organizations, such as trade unions, co-operative societies and workers' education clubs. For once, the Martovites, now based in Paris, were in broad agreement with Lenin, but he was vigorously opposed by dissenters in both the Bolshevik and Menshevik camps. On the extreme right of the party, a group, disparaged by Lenin as 'Liquidators', demanded jettisoning the underground entirely, on the grounds that it had become little more than a spy-infested shambles. Diametrically opposed to this group was a new alignment of left-wing Bolsheviks who dismissed the legal organizations in much the same terms.

Controversy, never far from Lenin's side, broke out immediately on his return to Switzerland. Bolshevik comrades in Stockholm, Munich, Paris and Geneva were suddenly arrested as part of an international police operation while they were attempting to off-load some of the marked notes from the Tiflis bank robbery the previous summer. Simultaneously, Kamo was picked up in Berlin with a suitcase crammed with explosives. Menshevik fury knew no bounds. For Lenin there was no defence: in persisting with expropriations, the Bolsheviks had defied the resolutions of not one but two party congresses and Social Democracy had, as the Mensheviks warned, been brought into disrepute. Martov demanded an immediate break with the Bolsheviks and, for good measure, Lenin's personal expulsion from the party. He was overruled by those, like Dan, who wanted unity preserved at any price. In the end, Lenin got away with a severe reprimand. For the Mensheviks, it was an opportunity missed.

Somewhat chastened, Lenin now decided to abandon expropriations, but he did so in the teeth of fierce opposition from Bogdanov. This was by no means the first policy disagreement between the Bolshevik leader and his chief lieutenant. In 1905 they had differed on the soviets and on trade-union policy; two years later it was participation in the Duma which would divide them. On the latter occasion, Lenin had been successful in overcoming Bogdanov's demands for an electoral boycott, but the issue remained a controversial one. During 1908 a number of Bolshevik leftists began demanding the recall of the Social Democrat deputies on the grounds that they had failed to adhere to Central Committee policy. By the summer the 'Recallists' had taken control of the Petersburg party committee and were even stronger in Moscow. Bogdanov now adopted a more conciliatory approach: the deputies should be issued with an 'ultimatum' – either follow the line of the Central Committee, or face recall. He was supported by G. A. Alexinsky, V. L. Shantser (one of the leaders of the Moscow rebellion) and L. B. Krasin, the Bolsheviks' explosives expert who combined his party activities with a professional career as an engineer (he was currently engaged in laying the cable network for the electrification of Petersburg). Together, they became known as 'Ultimatists'.

Concentrating his fire on Bogdanov, Lenin chose for his ground a field of debate which at first sight appears singularly inapposite – philosophy.

A highly cultivated man of diverse intellectual interests, Bogdanov was a doctor by profession, a calling he never wholly abandoned (he was to die carrying out an experiment on himself while serving as director of a Soviet medical institute). At the time Lenin first encountered him, Bogdanov had already written a highly original handbook on economics (which Lenin approved of) and a treatise on philosophy (which he did not). When the two became political allies, in 1904, they agreed to put their philosophical differences to one side, but they were not forgotten. Now, in 1908, Lenin dragged the issue out into the open.

Bogdanov was one of a number of Russian intellectuals to become interested in providing Marxism with a more secure metaphysical base. He was greatly influenced by two prominent exponents of 'empiriocriticism', the Austrian, Ernst Mach and the German, Richard Avenarius. Bogdanov called his own adaptation of their teachings 'empiriomonism' and completed a three-volume work with that title in 1906. Equally displeasing to Lenin was a collection of *Essays on the Philosophy of Marxism* which appeared early in 1908 and included contributions by Bogdanov and Lunacharsky. Lenin wrote:

> Every article made me furiously indignant. No, no, this is not Marxism! Our empiriocritics, empiriomonists and empiriosymbolists are floundering in a bog . . . To be sure, we ordinary Marxists are not well up in philosophy, but why insult us by serving this stuff up to us as the philosophy of Marxism![94]

Empiriomonism was an attempt to overcome the shortcomings of materialism and scientific determinism at the heart of Marxist philosophy by grafting on the insights of the empiriocritics. It was unsatisfactory to Lenin, not only because it presumed to correct Marx and Engels but because it represented a dangerous digression along the path of 'subjectivism' and 'voluntarism'. Lunacharsky was adjudged to have sinned even more grievously. His philosophy, described somewhat crudely as 'god-building', was an attempt to furnish Marxism with a system of moral values independent of the material world. Lunacharsky envisaged a humanist religion with the search for the perfectability of mankind as its central goal. As far as Lenin was concerned, any attempt to rehabilitate religion, in whatever shape or form, was bound to obfuscate rather than enlighten. Religion, he believed, had been correctly presented by Marx as one of the great bastions of reaction, an obstacle impeding the development of socialist consciousness. Unadorned atheism was a *sine qua non* of orthodoxy.

The development of Lenin's battle with the wayward philosophers can be traced through his correspondence with Gorky, another sympathizer with the new trends. In a letter of March 1908, he complained to the writer: 'I am neglecting the newspaper [*Proletari*] because of my hard bout of

philosophy. One day I read one of the empiriocritics and swear like a
fish-wife, the next I read another and swear still worse.'[95] The following
month, he accepted a long-standing invitation to visit Gorky on the idyllic
island of Capri, though the trip was undertaken 'on condition' that
questions of religion and philosophy were excluded from the conversation.
Some hope, given that Gorky's other guests included Bogdanov,
Lunacharsky and another empiriocritic, V. A. Bazarov! Lenin set the tone
immediately on disembarking at the Marina Grande. He announced to
Gorky: 'I know Alexei Maximych that you are always hoping that it will be
possible to reconcile me with the Machists but I warned you of the futility
of it in my letter. So don't make any attempts.'[96] The visit did have its
lighter moments: chess tournaments on the terrace of Gorky's splendid
villa and excursions to Naples, Pompeii and Mount Vesuvius. Lenin even
tried his hand at fishing and his infectious laughter made him a favourite
with the locals. However, behind the scenes the atmosphere was as acrid
and threatening as the crater of the great volcano itself.

On returning to Paris, Lenin entered into battle. The enemy was
softened up with a sustained barrage of abuse in *Proletari* as Bogdanov was
elbowed from the editorial team. Lenin made no apology for his intransigence: 'Our supporters should not be afraid of an internal ideological
struggle, once it is necessary. They will be all the stronger for it. It is our
duty to bring our disagreement out into the open.'[97]

Personal relations with Bogdanov were broken off in February 1909.
By now, Recallism and Ultimatism had lost much of their appeal inside
Russia, but Lenin did not let up. He was equally assiduous with his
philosophy. Though no expert on the subject, as he readily admitted, he
had begun a detailed study of empiriocriticism the previous year. In May
1908 he made a brief visit to London to further his researches in the British
Museum. His rooms, in Tavistock Place, were only a stone's throw from
the house in Sidmouth Street which Martov, Trotsky and Zasulich had
occupied six years earlier. Did he succumb, just a little, to nostalgia as he
re-explored the dingy, ill-lit streets off the Gray's Inn Road? One would
like to think so.

The fruit of his London labours, *Materialism and Empiriocriticism*,
appeared a year later, in May 1909. More a statement of faith than a
serious epistemological discourse, the tone of the original manuscript can
best be gauged by the reaction of Lenin's sister, Anyuta, who undertook to
arrange its publication. In a letter written in November 1908 she advised:

> a lot of the abuse must be taken out or toned down. Heavens above,
> Volodek, there is an enormous amount of it, comparable to the 'Victory
> of the Kadets'. Especially for a study of philosophy it is stuffed full . . .
> *il ne faut pas outrer* [one must not exaggerate].[98]

Accounts with Bogdanov were finally settled at a meeting of the Bolshevik
'Centre' in Paris in June 1909. Recallism and Ultimatism were condemned

along with 'god-building' and other 'deviations from revolutionary Marxism'. Bogdanov's newly founded party school on Capri was placed out of bounds and he himself adjudged to have broken with Bolshevism. However, the outcome of the meeting, which dragged on for a week, was not all to Lenin's liking. The Russian contingent criticized his divisive methods and behind-the-scenes manoeuvring and objected to his blatant manipulation of party funds. They let him know that the workers found his paper (*Proletari*) unreadable and almost succeeded in having it closed down. Worse was to come. Two of Lenin's closest associates, Alexei Rykov and Lev Kamenev, began enthusing about Trotsky's recently launched, non-factional newspaper, *Pravda* (*Truth*) and suggested joining forces. Lenin balked at this suggestion, dismissing Trotsky as a 'poseur', but, once again, was overruled. The Russians also insisted on, and won, the right to take their own decisions without referring to the *émigré* leaders. Lenin could hardly have missed the hint that the foreign contingent had lost touch with domestic realities.

By now he was no longer living in Geneva. In the autumn of 1908 a party acquaintance, Dr Zhitomirsky, had advised a move to Paris on the grounds that police surveillance would be rendered more difficult in a large city; rather a strange argument, given that Paris was the overseas headquarters of the Russian security police. In time, all would be revealed: Zhitomirsky was himself one of the Okhrana's most highly valued agents!

After spending several days in a hotel on the Boulevard Saint-Marcel, Lenin and his family (Manyasha, Nadya and Elizaveta Vasilyevna) rented a large, attractive apartment on the rue Beaunier, close to the Parc Montsouris on the southern fringes of the city. Nadya was particularly struck by the mirrors over the fireplaces. However, this accommodation proved inconvenient and expensive, and in June 1909 they moved to a smaller flat on the second floor of an apartment block at 4 rue Marie-Rose.

Lenin came to loathe Paris. The city's more obvious charms had never held much appeal for him. The boulevards fairly reeked of bourgeois profligacy and pleasure-seeking ostentation, the heady product of the planned *embourgeoisement*, begun under Napoleon III, which had removed the working class to more appropriate quarters. It was to these remote, unglamorous suburbs that Lenin was drawn on his long evening walks. Paris was least congenial as a working environment. The Bibliothèque Nationale lacked both the intimacy of the Geneva libraries and the unobtrusive efficiency of the British Museum. It was far removed from his apartment; the staff were unhelpful and the cataloguing system incomprehensible. Even the opening hours changed according to the seasons of the year. When his bicycle was stolen from under the nose of a concierge who had promised to look after it while he was studying, he came close to despair. Life was no less fretful at home. The cafés along the Avenue d'Orleans were the favoured haunt of more than one band of noisy Russian *émigrés* and on one notorious occasion a fist-fight broke out between

Bogdanovists and Leninists which ended only when the terrified proprietor extinguished the lights. Lenin's health took a turn for the worse, and no wonder. His headaches and insomnia returned, he became tongue-tied and developed tremors. He was in urgent need of a rest.

A new friend had moved in next door. At 35, she was several years younger than Lenin, who, despite his well-turned-out appearance and fashionable moustache (he had shaved off his beard) was beginning to show signs of ageing. Bright and vivacious with long, chestnut-coloured hair and large, almond-shaped eyes, Inessa Armand was at the same time serious-minded, hard-working and thoroughly devoted to the causes she espoused. A Parisian by birth, she was brought up on the estate of a Moscow textile magnate, Evgeny Armand, by a maiden aunt who served as governess to his children. Inessa was educated with them, growing up to become an accomplished pianist as well as a gifted linguist. At the age of 19, she married Armand's second son, Alexander, who appears to have tolerated, if not encouraged, her growing involvement with philanthropic causes. An instinctive feminist, Inessa worked first with destitute women, becoming president of the Moscow Society for Improving the Lot of Women in 1900. Like Lenin, she owed her conversion to socialism to Chernyshevsky's *What Is To Be Done?*. She joined the party in 1903 and, after her third arrest in 1907, was exiled but escaped and fled abroad. By this time, Inessa had left her first husband, by whom she had five children, and had begun living with his younger bother, Vladimir. He died of tuberculosis in 1909. After studying in Brussels for a year, Inessa settled in Paris, where she became an active member of the Bolshevik *émigré* community.

Both Lenin and Nadya were extremely fond of her, especially valuing her sense of fun in what were, after all, trying times. But Lenin also appreciated her intellectual abilities (particularly her linguistic skills) and her capacity for unstinting work.

In August 1909 the Ulyanovs fled Paris for the peace and quiet of Bombon, a village deep in the surrounding countryside. They were joined by Manyasha, who was recovering from acute appendicitis. Their landlady, Madame Lecreux, assigned them a cottage of their own and detailed a servant to bring them coffee every morning. The Clamart Forest was only a cycle-ride away and there was a seventeenth-century château close to the village where, in 1918, Foch would be presented with his marshal's baton.

While Lenin was vacationing in Bombon, plans were already underfoot to call a joint conference of underground and trade-union activists in Russia as a first step to restoring party unity. These moves, initiated by rank-and-file workers alienated by the pathological disputatiousness of the *émigré* leaders, were supported by a group of Bolshevik 'Conciliators', including Rykov (who was eventually to succeed Lenin as Soviet prime minister), V. P. Nogin, A. I. Lyubimov and I. P. Goldenberg-Meshkovsky. Stalin was also sympathetic to this point of view, having privately dismissed Lenin's feud with Bogdanov as a 'storm in a teacup'.

Towards the end of 1909 the Conciliators won over Trotsky, Martov and Lenin's hitherto staunch allies, the Poles, to the idea of a meeting of all Social Democratic factions, to be held abroad. Extremely disapproving, Lenin gave his consent with the utmost reluctance.

Shortly before the conference took place, Lenin was involved in a collision with a car while cycling home from an air display at Juvissy-sur-Orge, an aerodrome about 12 miles (19 km) from Paris. He escaped serious injury but was, not unreasonably, indignant with the driver, who turned out to be a viscount ('the devil take him!'). Vladimir Ulyanov, experienced lawyer of the Samara circuit, was not one to let such an opportunity pass. Armed with the driver's number and the testimony of several onlookers, he took his case to court – and won. Bourgeois justice had its uses!

The Central Committee finally convened in Paris on 15 January 1910. Lenin remembered the following three weeks as 'torture'. Across the table sat his rogues' gallery incarnate: Martov, Bogdanov, Trotsky. The atmosphere was tense and ill-tempered and while nominal unity was achieved, it was delivered with a bad grace. Agreement was reached to disband all factional organizations and newspapers. Bolsheviks and Mensheviks were to be equally represented on the various party bodies, the balance of power being held by the non-Russians: Poles, Lithuanians, Latvians and the Jewish members of the Bund. The Liquidators and Recallists were censured but, to Lenin's chagrin, not expelled. There was to be a full party conference of all factions and associations within six months. While Lenin was adjusting to these new realities, the Mensheviks were preparing an unpleasant surprise. G. V. Chicherin had brought along a dossier itemizing Bolshevik involvement in expropriations and substantiating allegations that they had dishonestly misappropriated party funds. Lenin was compelled to hear out Chicherin's rendition of the tale of the Shmidt inheritance: how, in 1907, the owner of a Moscow furniture factory, Nikolai Shmidt, had left the party 280,000 roubles in his will and how two Bolsheviks, one of them a candidate member of the Central Committee, had cynically courted Shmidt's two sisters, the executrices of the will, in order to get their hands on the money. Since that time, Chicherin went on, the Mensheviks had been unable to persuade Lenin to share the bequest with them. Now the Central Committee intervened: the Bolshevik leader was persuaded to hand over the fund to a trust composed of three German Social Democrats, Karl Kautsky, Clara Zetkin and Franz Mehring. The delegates stopped short of summoning Lenin before a party court, where he might well have faced expulsion. Here at least, the spirit of compromise worked in his favour.

Lenin was never one to take defeat lying down. His formula for reversing the situation (the possibility of accepting it was not entertained) can be expressed succinctly: do not whine; work to frustrate the implementation of ill-advised decisions; exploit the divisions among one's opponents; engineer a majority at the next conference. As always Lenin acted on the conviction that he, better than anyone, knew what was best for the party. Absolute self-assuredness was his trade mark. As Lydia Dan recalled:

> Lenin knew, he was convinced, that he knew the truth and that this gave him the right not only to win you over but to make you act as he wished, not because he was doing it for himself but because he knew what was needed. Lenin had this ability to win over and command.[99]

All in all, the year 1910 was kind to Lenin. In June, he put the worst excesses of the previous French winter behind him (torrential rain had produced flooding in Paris) and holidayed for two weeks at Gorky's villa on Capri. The balmy steamer crossing from Marseilles to Naples was slightly marred by the knowledge that the writer's other guests again included Bogdanov and Lunacharsky. But, as his eyes feasted on the shimmering summit of Monte Solaro, towering above the jagged limestone cliffs clothed in their luxuriant maritime pine, Lenin's anxiety melted away.

Capri was followed by a vacation on the Bay of Biscay. Lenin chose the charming fishing village of Pornic, south of St Nazaire, where he was joined by Krupskaya and her mother. The three of them stayed in the house of the local coastguard. For four weeks Lenin did nothing but cycle, swim and go for walks. In the evenings he was regaled by the coastguard's wife, who fed him with freshly dressed crab and anti-clerical gossip. Lenin was much amused.

His next trip combined business with pleasure. After depositing his relatives in Paris, he embarked immediately for Copenhagen, venue of the eighth International Socialist Congress. This was a welcome opportunity to meet socialists from other countries in congenial surroundings. Over the next few days Lenin (who represented his party on the International Bureau) had meetings with the Belgian, Camille Huysmans, the Frenchman, Jules Guesde, the Poles, Marchlewski and Luxemburg, the German, Karl Kautsky and the Finn, Sirola. Relations with his own contingent were more strained. Trotsky had written some uncomplimentary remarks about him in the German socialist Press. Harsh words were now exchanged as Plekhanov, who detested Trotsky, lined up with Lenin against Lunacharsky and David Ryazanov. Eventually, the slanging-match petered out, amidst mutual recriminations. No wonder the international socialist community despaired of its Russian colleagues!

On 11 September Lenin left Copenhagen for Stockholm. Two days later he was reunited with his mother. Mariya Ulyanov was now a frail but bright-eyed old lady of 75. She had not seen her son for many years but he had never been far from her thoughts. Now he had an opportunity to justify her faith in him, if only in a small way. On 24 September he gave a lecture on the recent congress to an audience of about 60 people. His mother and Manyasha were among them. It was the first time his mother had heard him speak in public:

> She listened quite attentively . . . and apparently became very excited. He spoke so well, 'so impressively and skilfully', she then said to me, 'but why does he exert himself so much, why does he speak so loudly, that is so harmful. He is not looking after himself![100]

By now the party's leading protagonists had their daggers drawn again. Bogdanov had gone off to launch his own party school; the Liquidators were making their own organizational arrangements in Petersburg; Martov and Dan had broken with Lenin over an editorial for the party newspaper called – a supreme irony this – 'Towards Unity'; Trotsky was mistrusted by everybody and most of the Conciliators were too preoccupied with dodging arrest to pick up the pieces.

Lenin was now determined to go his own way and set about securing his long-term objective: the convening of a party conference with an in-built Bolshevik majority. The route he took was a devious one involving manoeuvres of dizzying complexity. With all his organizational experience, he realized that the best way to ensure the exclusion or under-representation of his factional opponents at the conference was to wrest control of the Central Committee, the body responsible for convening it. He was prepared, if need be, to drive a coach and horses through the party's constitution in the process.

In June 1911 a 'central committee' of Lenin's own choosing met at 110 Avenue d'Orleans, in Paris. Only eight of the forty-five members of the elected Committee were present; of these, two walked out when they realized what was afoot and a third, the Latvian representative, M. V. Ozolin, refused to vote. That left five: Lenin, Zinoviev, the Conciliator Rykov (who thought he was doing the party a service by hurrying the conference along) and two Poles – Leo Jogiches, ally, friend and sometime lover of Rosa Luxemburg, and Felix Dzerzhinsky, future head of the Soviet secret police. Even this quintet failed to play in tune, but they did agree to set up the necessary commissions to arrange the conference.

Meanwhile, Lenin had set up his own party school. In May 1911, 18 worker-students arrived in the village of Longjumeau, 11 miles (18 km) south of Paris and not far from the present Orly airport. Krupskaya remembered it as 'a straggling French village stretching along the highroad on which cartloads of farm produce rumbled all night carrying food to fill "the belly of Paris" '. Classes were held in an abandoned workshop and a communal canteen was set up nearby. The students and several of their teachers rented rooms in the village, Lenin and Krupskaya staying with a local tanner.

The students came from Petersburg, Moscow, Kiev, Baku, Ekaterinoslav and Ivanovo. Most were in their early to mid-twenties. All had been screened in Russia, at Lenin's behest, to ensure their political reliability.

Even so, one Conciliator, one Bogdanovite and one *provocateur* showed up. The star pupil was a 25-year-old Georgian, 'Sergo' Ordzhonikidze, a long-standing friend of Stalin's and later his Commissar for Heavy Industry. Sergo would subsequently perform many services for Lenin.

The syllabus at Longjumeau was a daunting one for workers without much formal education. Lenin himself lectured on political economy, the agrarian question and the theory and practice of socialism (45 lectures in all), but there were also classes on the history of the party, the history of the Western labour movement, law, finance and journalism. The other mainstays of the school were Lenin's closest supporters at the time, Zinoviev, Kamenev and Armand, who also contributed to the financing. Krupskaya commuted between Longjumeau and Paris, where she continued to look after the party's day-to-day business.

Despite the seriousness of the study programme, the atmosphere was relaxed. It was a refreshingly healthy environment for the students, many of whom had weak constitutions resulting from the deprivations of factory and prison life. The summer of 1911 was a hot one, so everyone wandered around with bare feet, while the Zinovievs' 3-year-old son romped among the outhouses. In the evenings, as the students stretched out on the grass and swapped stories or sang, Lenin engaged his most trusted colleagues in sensitive political discussions.

Lenin returned to Paris during the second half of September. He had already dispatched three Longjumeau students, including Ordzhonikidze, to Russia with the delicate mission of ensuring that enough of the delegates attending the forthcoming conference were dependable Leninists. All that remained was to fix a time and a place. At the beginning of November, he wrote to the Czech representative on the International Socialist Bureau, Anton Nemecs, with a request to provide facilities in Prague. Lenin stressed the need for absolute secrecy. Nemecs acquiesced.

The conference began on 18 January 1912. It was held in the club premises of the Czech Social Democratic Party at 7 Hybernska Street. The building, a former palace, was an imposing one. The delegates met in a room on the third floor, under the watchful eye of Karl Marx whose bust perched on a bookcase in the corner. Those who found their attention wandering could enjoy the view over the roof-tops of the Bohemian capital. Of the eighteen representatives present, eight had attended Longjumeau and very few had been elected in any meaningful sense of the term. Two were *provocateurs*. The only non-Bolsheviks present were two party Mensheviks representing Kiev and Ekaterinoslav (Plekhanov, the leader of their group, declined his invitation). The absence of all other factions worried a number of the delegates, who had expected a more representative show. On their own initiative, they now sent off ten new invitations post haste. Lenin was far from amused by this prank and threatened to walk out if any unwelcome guests turned up. In the event, the invitations either arrived too late or were ignored.

Awarding itself the status of party congress, the Prague gathering drew up a new set of regulations requiring all Social Democrats to subordinate themselves to a newly elected Central Committee. As the elections could hardly fail to produce an all-Bolshevik committee, the implications for the Mensheviks and other factions were obvious: tow the line or form a separate party.

The debates reveal a testiness and independence of spirit perhaps surprising in such an overwhelmingly hand-picked body. The most touchy issue turned out to be the behaviour of the Russians living abroad. Here, no one was more forthright than the 'loyal' Leninist, Ordzhonikidze, who pronounced the contribution of the *émigrés* to be 'zero'. The energetic but impetuous Georgian complained that there would be much more co-operation between Bolsheviks and Mensheviks were it not for the 'damned abroad' with their leaders 'who sit in Paris, San Remo and elsewhere and, understanding nothing, issue directives and create splits'. Lenin began to chuckle when Ordzhonikidze's Armenian colleague, Spandaryan, made a similar complaint. Irritated by this unseemly intervention, Spandaryan rebuked Lenin: 'This [quarrelling abroad] is terrible, comrades, and no laughing matter.' In his defence, Lenin pointed out that issues of substance lay behind the *émigré* squabbles and that, for as long as there were two distinct parties in Russia (Liquidators and others), it was his duty to struggle for the victory of his own side. His critics held their ground, convinced now that he was hopelessly out of touch with the realities of the situation inside Russia.[101]

At the end of the conference, new elections were held for the Central Committee: Lenin, Zinoviev and Ordzhonikidze were among the successful candidates. The name of J. V. Stalin, then in gaol, was added to the names on the Committee's Russian bureau – seven of the eighteen delegates at Prague were to die during the height of Stalin's purges.

The sense of urgency which drove Lenin on was only partly motivated by a desire to steal a march on his opponents. He was also anxious to exploit the first stirrings of discontent in Russia since the imposition of the Stolypin regime in 1907. His timing could not have been better. In April 1912 troops opened fire on striking miners in the Lena gold-fields of Siberia, killing 200 and wounding perhaps twice that number. The ghost of 1905 was reawakened. Protest strikes involving half a million men occurred in April alone, twice as many as during the previous four years combined. The May Day proclamation of the Bolshevik Central Committee thundered: 'The sea of proletarian anger is rising in high waves and striking ever more menacingly at the toppling rocks of capitalism'. Lenin urged the workers on: 'Without a victorious revolution there will be no freedom in Russia. Without the overthrow of the Tsarist monarchy by a proletarian and peasant uprising there will be no victorious revolution in Russia'.[102]

The striking workers of Petersburg were kept informed by a new

Bolshevik newspaper. *Pravda* made its first appearance on 5 May 1912. It was the only labour daily then being produced in Russia. Lenin stole the title (and much of the format) from Trotsky, who waxed indignant at this shameless 'usurpation'. But when he issued a formal complaint, Lenin advised the editors to respond with the following curt statement: 'To Trotsky in Vienna: We shall leave your quibbling and pettifogging letters without reply'. *Pravda* was no more popular with the Association of Petersburg Factory Owners. However, when they protested to the Interior Minister, A. A. Makarov, he could only apologize that such a subversive venture should be allowed to appear legally, admitting ruefully that 'it is no longer as in the past, when the Ministry had almost unlimited power in relation to the daily press'. Even so, *Pravda* was not given an easy ride by the authorities. Closed temporarily in 1913, it reappeared in a succession of barely modified guises (*Workers' Truth, Northern Truth, Proletarian Truth, The Way of Truth* – eight titles in all) before being finally suppressed on the outbreak of the First World War. The editorial staff included Kamenev, V. M. Molotov (cousin of the composer Scriabin and later Stalin's foreign minister), the overall director of the legal Bolshevik Press, V. D. Bonch-Bruevich and M. S. Olminsky, a statistician with the Petersburg city council. As Lenin was not on the spot, it fell to Stalin, only recently returned from exile, to pen the first editorial. He took a more conciliatory tone than Lenin would have liked: 'Just as we ought to be irreconcilable *vis-à-vis* our enemies [advised Stalin] so we must make concessions towards one another. War to the enemies of the workers' movement, peace and friendly collaboration inside the movement.'[103]

In his overseeing of *Pravda*, Lenin was at his most exacting. 'We were extremely sorry to see two blunders in Sunday's *Pravda*,' he wrote in November 1912. A month later he lamented to G. L. Shklovsky: 'We've not had a single letter from the spot while the liquidators had several in *The Ray*. Isn't it shameful? Of course, so long as we sleep and the liquidators work, they will make more headway.' Lenin was quick to react when the editors declined to publish his own pieces without informing him: 'Having just come home after a journey "on business",' he wrote in February 1914, 'I looked through all the published issues and have *failed to find* two articles which I sent (about a month ago!) . . .' His complaints were not confined to the editorial staff. The mailing department was in hot water when Lenin's own copies of *Pravda* were delayed: 'Clearly the mailing department is working carelessly. I earnestly request you to see that they display greater care with the daily post.'[104]

In June 1912 he moved from Paris to the Polish city of Cracow, then in Austria-Hungary. He gave his reasons in a letter to Gorky: the Russian frontier was nearby, communications with Petersburg were easier and the quiet provincialism of the ancient cathedral town made a welcome change after the clamour of Paris.

The practical arrangements were made by a Polish socialist, S. J.

Bagocki. He later recalled waiting for the Ulyanovs to arrive opposite the long, red-brick façade of the university building:

> Half an hour had passed since the agreed time. The benches around me were filling up. On one nearby sat a middle-aged couple – the man in a bowler hat with a small beard, and a modestly dressed woman. But I did not pay much attention to them.[105]

The couple, it turned out, were indeed Lenin and his wife. Bagocki first settled them on the Ulica Zwierzyniecka. While the location was a pleasant one, close to the River Vistula and not far from the enchanting Volsky Woods, it was very muddy and, more importantly, far from the station and the post office. In September, therefore, they moved into an imposing new apartment block at the other side of town, 17 Ulica Lubomirskiego. Lenin found Cracow's proximity to Russia a great tonic. He wrote to his mother: 'This summer we have moved a long way from Paris – to Cracow. Almost in Russia! Even the Jews are like Russians and the frontier is eight *versts* away.'[106] For Nadya, whose earliest years had been spent in Poland, their stay acquired a nostalgic quality. Her knowledge of the language (though only a smattering) came in useful. The Ulyanovs found the relative simplicity of Polish life refreshing after Paris, though they were dismayed by the anti-semitism and the all-prevailing influence of the Roman Catholic Church.

Lenin established a similar routine to the *Iskra* days. At his desk until noon, he would collect the post and discuss the news with colleagues. (Zinoviev had moved with him to Cracow and Kamenev joined them in 1913.) At 5 in the afternoon he broke for a walk (or went skating in winter), then relaxed for a while, chatting with friends or playing chess. He was fond of Zinoviev's little son, Stepa, and would play ball with him or carry him on his shoulders until the moment came for the child to hurry off to bed. 'What a pity we haven't a boy like Stepa,' he once remarked to Nadya. Returning to his desk in the evening, he would read over the articles intended for Petersburg and at 9 p.m. take them down to the post office for dispatch.

'Organization and again organization' was Lenin's watchword. If the party hoped to exploit the rising tide of social and industrial unrest it would have to rebuild and extend its contacts among the masses. The task was a mammoth one. Undaunted, he set to work.

His first priority was to get Bolsheviks elected to the fourth Duma, which was to convene in January 1913. Stalin, who had just escaped from Siberia, played an important role in the campaign. To assist him, Lenin sent Armand and G. V. Safarov (both soon arrested) with specific instructions to see that the Prague resolutions were implemented in full. On their arrival, however, they discovered that, while the labour leaders were eager to campaign on behalf of the Social Democrats, they were far less enthusiastic about fighting the Mensheviks. As one activist put it to

Safarov: 'We believe in [Prague] as Protestants do; we are quite prepared to pray on Sundays, but every other day of the week we have to sin.' Evidently, the editors of *Pravda* felt the same way. To Lenin's fury they began excising all references in his articles to the Liquidators, as well as making conciliatory noises in the direction of Plekhanov. Later, he condemned *Pravda*'s attitude as being that of an 'old maid'. Fortunately there were more heartening developments. Unrest was reported among the sailors of the Baltic fleet and Lenin found it necessary to counsel against a premature armed uprising. The elections too, went according to plan. Six Bolsheviks and seven Mensheviks were elected, a considerable achievement given the heavily skewed franchise and the campaign of harrassment which accompanied it. Furthermore, the six Bolsheviks had all been elected by workers, whereas the Mensheviks had garnered much of their support from middle-class voters. The distinction did not escape Lenin's notice.

The elections had taken place in November 1912. The following January he summoned 'his' deputies to attend a conference of the Central Committee in Cracow. Among them was a new favourite, Roman Malinovsky. Malinovsky's attractions were lost on many of Lenin's colleagues. Of a decidedly unprepossessing appearance, with coarse red hair, a face scarred by smallpox and narrow, scowling eyes, Malinovsky spoke Russian with a marked Polish accent. Very little was known of his background. In fact he was a former guardsman who had enlisted following a number of convictions for petty crime. His career as a labour leader began after 1905, when he had been employed as a lathe-operator in a Petersburg metalworking factory. Appointed secretary of the Metalworkers' Union, he quickly gained a reputation as an energetic and gifted activist. Arrests in 1909 and 1910 changed the course of his life. He was blackmailed by the police into becoming an *agent provocateur* with a regular monthly salary of 100 roubles, plus expenses. Malinovsky was as assiduous in his police work as he had been as a trade-union leader. After helping to destroy the party organization in Moscow, he was instructed to announce his 'conversion' from Menshevism to Bolshevism. Lenin, who always had a weakness for 'genuine' proletarians, welcomed him enthusiastically and managed to conjure up a mandate for him to attend the Prague conference. To the amazement of the other delegates, Lenin pushed Malinovsky's candidacy to to the Central Committee and he was duly elected (some said the ballot was rigged). By the end of the year he was not only a member of the Duma, but the leader of the Bolshevik faction.

Lenin was well-nigh infatuated with his new discovery. In October 1912 he enthused to Shklovsky: 'For the *first* time we have an *outstanding leader* from among the workers representing us in the Duma'.[107] And undeniably, Malinovsky stood out at the January conference as a labour leader of great potential. Articulate, quick on his feet and brimming over with confidence, he was streets ahead of honest plodders like Badaev, Petrovsky and the other members of the Bolshevik Duma faction. Lenin quickly conferred on him the most responsible tasks, even that of investigating police penetration among the Bolshevik ranks! His first contribution in this direction was to secure the arrest of Stalin a month or so later at a fund-raising matinée in Petersburg. Lenin wrote to Kamenev in March 1913: 'Koba [Stalin] has been arrested. We have discussed with Malinovsky what measures to take'.[108]

Lenin impressed on his Bolsheviks in Cracow the need to distance themselves from the Menshevik deputies in the Duma and to continue the fight against those denying the need for an illegal, conspiratorial party apparatus. Though this clearly factional line was unpopular in Russia, Lenin persisted with it until, in November 1913, the Bolshevik deputies declared themselves to be the exclusive representatives of the Social Democratic Party in the chamber. He was also bent on securing a less independent-minded editorial team for *Pravda*. After the Cracow meeting, Y. M. Sverdlov (the future Soviet president) was sent to Petersburg to take over the newspaper. He sacked many of the old staff, including Molotov, and brought a new, more disciplined look to the paper. Lenin was pleased. In a letter to the new board in February 1913, he wrote: 'Let me first of all congratulate you on the vast improvement in the whole conduct of the paper, which has become apparent during the last few days'.[109] But it was not long before Sverdlov too was arrested and exiled, again at the instigation of the artful Malinovsky.

While domestic policies claimed the lion's share of Lenin's attention during this period, he did not entirely neglect the wider international arena. The elections to the fourth Duma happened to coincide with the American presidential election, in which Woodrow Wilson defeated Theodore Roosevelt. Lenin, though an admirer of many aspects of American civilization, was caustic about both Democrats and Republicans. 'The people,' he alleged, 'have been deceived and diverted from their vital interests by spectacular and meaningless *duels* between the two bourgeois parties', duels carefully stage-managed by manipulative and 'astute multimillionaires'.[110]

More absorbing, from the point of view of the Bolshevik leader, were the upheavals in China which, in 1911, led to the collapse of the Manchu Empire and the establishment of Dr Sun-Yat-Sen's republic. The implications for Russia, Lenin argued, were obvious, since 'In very many and very essential respects, Russia is undoubtedly an Asian country and, what is more, one of the most benighted, medieval and shamefully backward of Asian countries.' But he was equally certain of the impact the awakening of the vast Asian continent was bound to have on the Great Powers of Europe. Sooner or later, Western imperialism would become embroiled in a life-and-death struggle with the subjugated peoples of the East and socialism would emerge the victor.[111]

Europe itself was becoming increasingly restless. In the autumn of 1912

Serbia, Bulgaria and their allies, Greece and Montenegro defeated the Ottoman Empire in the first Balkan War. The victors immediately fell out over the division of the spoils, resulting in a second war in which Serbia crushed Bulgaria. For several weeks, it appeared likely that Russia and Austria, at least, would be sucked into the conflict. Lenin remained sceptical, rightly so as it turned out. In December 1912 he wrote to Gorky: 'Probably there will be no war and we shall remain here [in Cracow] for the time being, "taking advantage" of the desperate hatred of the Poles towards tsarism'.[112]

Lenin's remark about the Poles betrays a growing interest in the 'National Question', an issue he had been debating off and on with Rosa Luxemburg since 1908. Too busy himself to devote as much time to its ramifications as he would have liked, Lenin trained a protégé to assist him, J. V. Stalin. Intrigued rather than deterred by Stalin's uncouth manner and unkempt appearance, Lenin got to know the 'wonderful Georgian', when Stalin visited him in Cracow in January 1913. Impressed by his intuitive grasp of the National Question, Lenin invited him to write a paper on the subject for the party's theoretical journal, *Enlightenment*. A professional conspirator with little formal intellectual training, Stalin was flattered by the proposal and immediately assented. The result was 'Marxism and the National Question', a competent though not very original study, carefully worked over by Lenin himself.

Lenin's own 'Theses on the National Question' appeared in June 1913. They reaffirmed his support for national self-determination as the policy most likely to unite the subject peoples of the Russian Empire behind the opponents of autocracy. However, he did not intend self-determination to mean giving *carte-blanche* to every minority within the empire to secede as and when it chose; it would be up to the party to review each case on its merits and in the light of expediency. Former subject peoples remaining within the new post-revolutionary Russia would enjoy wide regional autonomy.[113]

In May 1913 Lenin left Cracow with his wife, his mother-in-law, the Zinovievs and the Bagockis (and their dog Zhulik) to spend the summer in Poronin, a small village near the mountain resort of Zakopane, now close to the frontier with Czechoslovakia. He was concerned about Nadya's health (she was suffering from a goitre, an enlargement of the thyroid gland) and hoped that the mountain air would improve her condition. The Russian party rented a spacious bungalow 2,300 ft (700 m) above sea-level at the foot of the Tatra Mountains. Often shrouded from view by a rainy mist, the snow-capped peaks were resplendent on a fine day, when they were visible from Cracow itself. The lower slopes, interspersed with ornately gabled chalets and translucent waterfalls and streams, opened out on to rich grazing land and fields of wild crocuses. Poronin, at the time, was little more than a long, dusty street lined on either side by picturesque thatched cottages and yawning trees. Traffic was confined to the occasional horse and cart. Lenin, a worshipper of the outdoors, missed no opportunity to explore his new surroundings. Once, on an excursion into the mountains with Bagocki, he became lost in a wood after dark and was on the point of giving up when he noticed a light shining in the distance:

> The light became clearer. Soon we could distinguish two windows. We found the door and entered a large room. On a large stove in the middle a big kettle was boiling, around it all sorts of tourists' crockery. At the table and on plank beds about ten people. On the floor open rucksacks.[114]

They had stumbled on a youth hostel!

Unfortunately, the move brought no improvement in Nadya's condition. She was suffering great distress. Her eyes bulged, her neck swelled and she experienced problems with her breathing. The bromide medication made her feel worse, not better. Bagocki, a neurologist, recommended the Nobel Prize-winning surgeon, Theodor Kocher, who had a clinic in Switzerland. Kocher agreed to operate and in June, Lenin and Krupskaya set out for Berne. They stayed with G. L. Shklovsky and his family while waiting to see Kocher. Lenin passed the time in the local library, working on his notes on the National Question for a mini lecture-tour of Switzerland, which he embarked on once the date for Nadya's operation had been set. In the course of his studies he also became an expert on goitres, consulting numerous medical textbooks on the subject. Her operation took place on 23 July; it was a harrowing experience: 'they tormented Nadya for about three hours without an anaesthetic', Lenin wrote to his mother, 'but she bore it bravely'.[115] She recovered but was never fully cured.

The Ulyanovs returned to Cracow in October 1913. Inessa, who had recently escaped from a tsarist prison, joined them in Galicia, but she did not remain long. Physically weakened by her ordeal, she had lost none of her energy and *joie de vivre*. She accompanied Lenin and Nadya on their walks, assisted them in their party work, played the piano for them in the evenings (Beethoven's 'Pathétique' sonata was Lenin's favourite) and still found time to invite Nadya's mother over to her apartment for a chat and a cigarette. Lenin and his wife felt less lonely and isolated when Inessa was around. Both were disappointed when, tiring of the blinkered provincialism of Cracow, she moved back to Paris.

Lenin now had to deal with the opprobrium he had brought on himself as a result of the Prague conference. The reproaches of his Russian opponents he could cope with; it was more difficult to shrug off the growing international unease. In March 1912 an article highly critical of Lenin appeared in the journal of the German Social Democratic Party, *Vorwarts* (*Forwards*); in July, Luxemburg's Polish and Lithuanian party reacted in similar vein, dismissing Prague as a 'farcical Leninist lark'. Anxious to lower the temperature, the executive committee of the German party proposed bringing all the Russian groups together around the conference table; Lenin would have none of it, refusing point-blank to sit down with

Recallists and Liquidators. Following the formal separation of Bolshevik and Menshevik factions in the Duma, the International Socialist Bureau discussed the Russian situation in London in December 1913. Boycotted by Lenin and Plekhanov (the Bolsheviks sent the future Soviet foreign minister, M. M. Litvinov), the Mensheviks attended 'in droves', according to Luxemburg, who had exerted considerable pressure to get the question on to the agenda. The Bureau resolved to try, once again, to bring the warring factions together, but Lenin was outraged to learn of Kautsky's pronouncement: 'The old [Russian] Party is dead and we can not resurrect it'.[116] On the contrary, Lenin asserted, the Bolshevik-orientated Social Democratic Party was alive and well and in no need of reconstitution.

His relations with fellow socialists abroad were not helped by his obsessive quest to recover the funds entrusted to the Germans Kautsky, Zetkin and Mehring following the Paris meeting of the Central Committee in January 1910. Some of the money had since been returned to the Bolsheviks, but Lenin wanted all of it. He resented having to go cap in hand to the trustees every time he needed money: 'I have the right to the money', he asserted in a letter to Karl Zraggen in February 1912. By June the matter was in the hands of his solicitor, the French lawyer Ducos de la Haille, but little progress was made despite visits to Zetkin in Berlin and several meetings with her friend Rosa Luxemburg. Lenin's truculence soon lost him whatever goodwill he may have had in that quarter. By the end of 1913 he was convinced that the trustees were using their control of the fund to compel the Bolsheviks to unite with their opponents. The issue was never resolved.

In January 1914, Lenin travelled to Brussels to attend a session of the International Socialist Bureau. He was accompanied by Malinovsky as far as Paris, where they both delivered lectures. Inessa was staying at the same hotel. They were now corresponding regularly, Lenin addressing her with the intimate *ty* – no other woman outside his family was so honoured. On arriving in Brussels, he was buttonholed by Emile Vandervelde, Chairman of the Bureau, and asked to submit a report itemizing his differences with the Mensheviks. After complying with this request, he returned to Cracow, via Liège and Leipzig, where he lectured on the national question.

The pressure building from abroad to reunite the party was getting to Lenin. In March he clashed with the secretary of the Bureau, Huysmans:

> The expressions you use in your letter ("tergiversation", "policy of procrastination", etc.) are insulting and you have no right to employ them towards a comrade. I must ask you therefore to take back these expressions without reserve. Unless you do so, this letter to you will be my last.[117]

Huysmans replied with wit and tact but no sooner had this storm blown over than Lenin had antagonized Inessa: 'And again – I'm sorry – I called you the Holy Virgin. Please don't be angry, it was because I'm fond of you, because we're friends, but I can't help being angry when I see "something that recalls the Holy Virgin".'[118]

Lenin could hardly have foreseen the next blow that fate had in store for him. For some time now, the Bolsheviks had been strengthening their influence on the Russian labour movement, wresting control of key trade unions from the Mensheviks, capturing large numbers of seats on the new insurance councils, increasing the circulation of their newspapers and making their presence felt inside the Duma. Even the underground seemed to be on the mend. The Director of Police was only too aware of the secret of their success: 'The faction of Leninists is always better organised than the others, stronger in its singleness of purpose, more resourceful in propagating its ideas among the workers . . .' It was time, the Okhrana decided, to strike a blow at the heart of Lenin's organization. One day in May, during a full session of the Duma, Malinovsky peremptorily resigned his seat, walked out of the chamber and disappeared. Lenin was dumbstruck. It was several days before he confided to Inessa: 'He is not here. It looks like "flight" . . . You can easily imagine how much I am worried'.[119] Shortly afterwards, Malinovsky turned up in Poronin, where Lenin was spending the summer. He was distraught and unable to give a satisfactory account of his behaviour. One of Lenin's other guests, Nikolai Bukharin, recalled the impact Malinovsky's appearance had on the Bolshevik leader:

> The first night I slept in the room upstairs. I slept badly, waking from time to time . . . I distinctly heard Ilyich pacing the room downstairs. He couldn't sleep. He went out onto the balcony, made some tea and again paced up and down the terrace, stopping every now and again. He spent the whole night pacing and thinking. Drowsiness overcame me at times. But as soon as consciousness returned, my ear caught the steady thud below.[120]

Lenin was never able to come to terms with the fact that Malinovsky was a police agent. However, he did allow his former favourite's expulsion from the party for the serious breach of discipline. He attributed the 'false' allegations about Malinovsky to the Liquidators, Martov and Dan, whom he denounced as 'filthy slanderers'. Only after the Revolution was the full extent of Malinovsky's treason revealed.

Lenin had now to prepare for a 'unity conference' of Russian Social Democrats which Vandervelde intended to convene in Brussels in July 1914, anticipating a full congress of the International. Fearing an ambush, Lenin was reluctant to attend in person, but whom could he trust to go in his place? Inessa had all the right credentials: a perfect command of French, a good grasp of the issues and, above all, tact. The pity was that she was in Trieste, enjoying a holiday with her children. Lenin was undeterred. He flattered her, offered to pay her expenses, even to find a baby-sitter to look after her children. Knowing only too well the inordinate burdens Lenin imposed on colleagues in the name of duty to the party,

Inessa was more than a little reluctant to go. 'I am terribly afraid,' Lenin wrote, 'that you will refuse to go to Brussels and thus place us in an *absolutely impossible position* . . . You are the *only suitable person*. So please – I beg you most earnestly – consent, if only for one day.'[121]

Finally, she succumbed to the pressure. Lenin congratulated her on her decision: 'I am extremely grateful to you for giving your agreement. I am positive you will carry off our important role with flying colours and give a fitting answer to Plekhanov, Rosa Luxemburg and Kautsky.'[122] Inessa bravely set off for Brussels, weighed down with reports, assessments, instructions and ultimata, all penned in minute detail by Lenin himself, for example:

> Plekhanov likes to 'disconcert' women comrades with sudden gallantries (in French, and so on). You must be prepared to meet this with a quick repartee – 'I am delighted, Comrade Plekhanov, you are quite an old spark' (or a gallant cavalier) – or something like that in order, politely, to put him in his place.[123]

Once there, she faced a bemusing array of Bogdanovists, Plekhanovites, Mensheviks, Bundists, Poles and Latvians, besides the distinguished European observers. Unperturbed, she stuck to her task of stonewalling the delegates and survived relatively unscathed. Only the Latvian supported Lenin's bleakly uncompromising position. No matter; Lenin was thoroughly satisfied, writing to Inessa on 19 July 1914: 'You handled the matter better than I could have done . . . Language apart I would probably have *gone up in the air*. I would not have been able to stand the hypocrisy and would have called them scoundrels . . . that's what they probably wanted to provoke.' But Inessa had evidently had enough of conferences; later in the same letter Lenin enquired of her, '. . . are you very tired, very angry? Are you wild with me for persuading you to go?'[124] Inessa's reply was conveyed in her refusal to join the Ulyanovs in Galicia. The frontier would probably have been closed to her in any case. On 28 July 1914 Austria-Hungary declared war on Serbia. A week later all Europe was in turmoil.

7

From war to revolution

Lenin was enjoying the summer sunshine at Poronin on that fateful Saturday in August 1914 when Germany declared war on Russia. Overnight he had acquired the status of enemy alien, but there was little he could do but study, with growing concern, the reports coming in from the capitals of the belligerent nations: they made depressing reading. Only a week earlier, Russian workers had been fighting pitched battles with police on the streets of Petersburg; now those same workers, impatient to try on their military uniforms, were prominent among the crowd of one hundred thousand patriots kneeling before the Tsar on Palace Square and singing the national anthem. Brass bands, marching columns of reservists showered with flowers, chock-full recruiting offices, hat-waving, ecstatic crowds – the same, surreal spectacle was repeated everywhere. Already faltering, the voice of the Socialist International was quite drowned out by the jingoistic din. But even Lenin was unprepared for what was to follow. On 5 August, *Vorwarts*, the newspaper of the German Social Democratic Party, informed its readers that the party's deputies had voted unanimously for war credits in the Reichstag. Zinoviev watched in silence as Lenin read and re-read the edition in front of him. He shook his head in disbelief: 'It isn't possible, perhaps this is a forged edition of *Vorwarts*. These miserable German bourgeois have published it to deceive us and to force us to betray the International.' When the news was confirmed, he pronounced a short obituary: 'This is the end of the Socialist International'.[125]

At that moment, he was overtaken by even more pressing concerns. One of the immediate consequences of the war was to whip up a fierce xenophobia. All foreign residents, irrespective of their previous records, were suspected of spying for the enemy. On 7 August the Polish Social Democrat, Jakub Hanecki, heard a knock on his door. It was Lenin with the news that his house had been searched. Fortunately, he explained, the policeman conducting the search was a 'fool'. Seizing on a manuscript which appeared to be full of coded messages, but which was actually a treatise on agrarian relations (the 'ciphers' were statistical tables), the policeman had overlooked Lenin's correspondence, which contained lists of addresses and other party paraphernalia. He did, however, discover a Brauning pistol which Lenin was unable to account for and the following day the Bolshevik leader was taken by train to Nowy Targ (Neumarkt) for questioning. Friends and relatives immediately began working to secure his release. While Hanecki contacted a prominent Polish socialist named Marek who had proved helpful in arranging Lenin's move from Paris to Cracow two years earlier, Krupskaya wrote to the Austrian socialist leader, Victor Adler, asking him to intervene on her husband's behalf. On learning that the Cracow police department had no evidence against him and on Adler's assurance that Lenin was a bona-fide enemy of the tsarist Government, the Austrian Minister of the Interior ordered his release.

Lenin left Cracow on 29 August and waited in Vienna while Adler and the Swiss socialist, Hermann Greulich, made the necessary arrangements for him to travel to neutral Switzerland. He decided to settle in Berne and arrived there on 5 September, conveying to Adler 'Very best regards and deepest gratitude' for his help. Several weeks later, the Ulyanovs moved into a house on Distelweg at the edge of the forest. Their immediate entourage comprised the Shklovskys, who lived about ten minutes' walk away, the Zinovievs (five minutes) and Inessa Armand, just across the road.

Meanwhile, the splits and divisions in the ranks of the socialists continued to multiply. Following the example of the German deputies, their French and Austrian counterparts voted for war credits, the French even accepting cabinet posts. Almost alone, the Russians acted in defiance of their government. On 8 August, after issuing a joint statement condemning the war, the 12 Bolshevik and Menshevik deputies, together with a number of left-wing supporters, walked out of the chamber before the vote on war credits was taken. Some weeks later the Bolshevik deputies were arrested and, in February 1915, put on trial. All were given life sentences in Siberia, despite a demeanour in court which Lenin found positively pusillanimous. He, along with Trotsky, Martov and a group of writers on the Paris-based journal *Golos* (*The Voice*), came out from the beginning with clear anti-war sentiments. Luxemburg, Zetkin, Mehring, Jogiches and the German anti-militarist, Karl Liebknecht, lined up alongside. They were opposed by the 'Defensists', or 'Social Patriots': Plekhanov, Potresov, Alexinsky, the Socialist Revolutionary Rubanovich, the Belgian Emil Vandervelde, and the leading German Social Democrat theorist, Karl Kautsky – the 'renegade' Kautsky as Lenin now insisted on calling him.

Lenin composed his 'Tasks of Revolutionary Social Democracy in the European War' while still living in Galicia. On arriving in Berne, he submitted his views to a group of Bolshevik supporters at a meeting held in a nearby wood. With their approval, the theses were smuggled into Russia by the socialist deputy F. N. Samoilov. Lenin dared not issue them in his own name, for fear they would lead to his expulsion from Switzerland. Instead, they were circulated anonymously as 'an appeal written in Denmark'.

Lenin defined the war as unashamedly 'bourgeois–imperialist and dynastic' in character; it could not, he insisted, be disguised or justified as a response to aggression on the part of the enemy. The 'reformists' and 'opportunists' who had betrayed the International by voting for war credits were, he alleged, responsible for the 'ideological and political collapse of the International'. Against the arguments of the Defensists, he unfurled his own startling slogan: 'for the defeat of one's own government'. It was, he asserted, the duty of all socialists to work tirelessly for revolution, so as to turn the European war into a civil war embroiling all the belligerents. But, if the worst came to the worst, a German victory was 'the lesser evil': 'From the point of view of the working class and the toiling masses of all the people of Russia, the lesser evil would be the defeat of the tsarist monarchy and its army.'

In November 1914 Lenin revived the newspaper *Social Democrat* as a vehicle for propagating his views. He also took every opportunity to publicize them in the lecture hall – during October alone he spoke on the war in Lausanne, Geneva, Berne and Zurich. Plekhanov too gave a lecture in Lausanne which Lenin went out of his way to attend in order to rebut the old man's pro-Defensist views. Plekhanov had only recently been urging Russian *émigrés* living in France to volunteer for the French Army and had boasted to the representative of the Italian socialists, Angelica Balabanov, 'if I were not old and sick I would join the army. To bayonet our German comrades would give me the greatest pleasure'.[126] Now Lenin, his face deathly pale with suppressed indignation, rose to his feet to effect a final break with his erstwhile mentor. While welcoming Plekhanov's denunciation of the German Social Democrats, he dismissed his support for the French as just one more brand of chauvinism. 'Our task,' said Lenin, according to the report on his speech in *Golos*, 'is not to swim with the tide, but to transform the national, the pseudo-national war into a resolute encounter of the proletariat with the ruling classes'. The confrontation ended with Plekhanov receiving the more generous round of applause, but Lenin was undeterred; after all, the hall was packed with Mensheviks.

While there was generally little support for the Bolshevik leader's ultra-left stance in the early part of the war, he was determined to maintain a high profile. The International Socialist Women's Conference, organized in March 1915 by Zetkin in Berne, was almost wrecked by Bolshevik attempts to impose a Leninist resolution on the war. Balabanov was caustic about these tactics:

> For a man like Lenin to sit for days on end in the corner of a coffee house where the women delegates of his faction came to report everything that

happened at the convention and to ask for instructions was, no doubt, ludicrous.[127]

In the end, Lenin agreed to support the majority resolution, providing his own was entered in the minutes.

He and Krupskaya spent the summer of 1915 at the Hotel Marienthal, high in the mountains in the little village of Sorenberg. It was intended to be a rest cure for Nadya (the death of her mother in March had coincided with a recurrence of her own illness). Soon after they arrived, they were joined by Inessa Armand.

Lenin and Inessa had clashed, earlier in the year, over the issue of free love (Inessa was writing a pamphlet on the subject and had sent Lenin a draft for his comments). He was highly critical and the tone of his response was somewhat high-handed and tactless: 'freedom of love . . . is not really a proletarian but a bourgeois demand,' he complained. 'After all, what do you understand by that phrase? What *can* be understood by it?' By freedom of love, he argued, 'the most talkative, noisy, "top" classes' meant nothing more than freedom to indulge in casual affairs, to commit adultery, to avoid having children. Inessa had clouded the issue by asserting that 'even a fleeting passion and intimacy' was purer than the kisses of a loveless married couple. The proper contrast, according to Lenin, should be between 'proletarian, civil marriage with love (adding, *if you absolutely insist* that fleeting intimacy and passion, too, may be dirty and may be clean)' and 'philistine–intellectual–peasant . . . vulgar and dirty marriage without love'. In the end, Inessa gave up the idea of a pamphlet altogether.[128]

Lenin still felt he could take advantage of her good nature. As she was preparing to leave for Sorenberg, he wrote: 'One more request – if you are fed up with all requests (I feel a pang of remorse because you have already had quite a lot of them), don't bother, I can write from here – but if you pass by Kaiser's, ask for a *sample* of large envelopes . . .' This was not the last request. Inessa was also urged to drop in at the offices of the Swiss Alpine Club and find out the price of a stay in their mountain chalets for non-members 'in case we should go for *long* excursions'.[129]

As it turned out, Lenin had less time than he had hoped for mountain-climbing that summer. He was preoccupied with preparations for the forthcoming International Socialist Conference which offered by far the best opportunity to date to promote his views on the war. The conference (exclusively of left-socialists) was organized by the Swiss, Robert Grimm. In an attempt to keep the Press at bay, it was held in the picturesque village of Zimmerwald, a comparatively remote spot in the uplands south of Berne. Thirty-eight delegates attended from eleven countries, including Russia and Poland. Among the Russian delegation were Trotsky, Martov, Axelrod, Lenin and Zinoviev. They arrived on the afternoon of Sunday 4 September 1915, after a two-hour drive up a steep mountain pass. The gathering was incommunicado throughout the next four days, and had to rely for entertainment on the yodelling talents of Grimm and the vocal dexterity of the Socialist Revolutionary leader, Victor Chernov, with his extensive repertoire of Russian folk-songs.

On the third day of the conference, Lenin introduced his resolution on the war. In uncompromising terms, it called for 'revolutionary struggle against capitalist governments' and proclaimed the need for 'civil war, not civil peace'.

As Lenin expected, the detailed implications of his resolution were too radical even for the majority of left socialists to swallow. (According to Trotsky, Lenin was 'in a minority of one' on many issues at Zimmerwald.) On the war, his supporters – about eight strong – were opposed by a substantially larger group of moderates, led by the German, Georg Ledebour, who called for an immediate peace without annexations and indemnities. In the end, Grimm succeeded in framing a compromise resolution which won the unanimous support of the delegates, but only after a good deal of arm-twisting. They concluded their deliberations at 2.30 a.m. on 9 September by singing 'The Internationale'. Eventually, news of Zimmerwald found its way on to the pages of most Western newspapers. The proprietor of the hotel was delighted with the publicity and promised to make a donation to the cause. 'I suspect, however, that he soon changed his mind,' Trotsky remarked sceptically.[130]

The day after Lenin arrived back in Sorenberg, he and Nadya went on a climbing expedition to the Rothorn. On reaching the summit, 'Ilyich suddenly lay down on the ground, in an uncomfortable position almost in the snow, and fell asleep . . .'[131]

Towards the end of 1915, Lenin began to work on a book about imperialism and his researches took him to Zurich. Initially intending to stay only a few weeks, he eventually decided to make his home there. He and Krupskaya rented a flat on the Spiegelgasse from a shoemaker named Kammerer. The stench from the neighbouring sausage factory was insufferable but the sound proletarian instincts of Herr Kammerer and his family more than made up for the inconvenience. On one occasion Krupskaya claims to have overheard his wife exclaim: 'The soldiers ought to turn their weapons on their governments.' 'After that,' Krupskaya recalled, 'Ilyich would not listen to any suggestions about changing quarters'.

Zurich's attractions were not confined to its libraries. There were a number of lively discussion clubs, including the Eintracht Society and, Lenin's favourite, the Bowling Club. Shortly after he arrived, in February 1916, a group of artists, calling themselves the Cabaret Voltaire, organized a riotous evening at the Café Meier. Among the audience were some Russians who contributed to the festivities by improvising on the balalaika. It was the beginning of the Dada movement.

Lenin could hardly afford a lively social life; never, in fact, had he found it so difficult to make ends meet. Things would have been even worse had it not been for the 2,000 roubles left them by Elizaveta Vasilyevna in her will. By the end of 1915 this source of income was almost exhausted and they began exploring other avenues, with a growing sense of desperation. Early in 1916, Lenin approached the secretary of the Russian *Great Encyclopedia* with a view to writing articles, frankly admitting that he was 'in an extraordinarily bad situation with regard to my own literary employment'. He received no reply. Throughout the year his letters are full of complaints about the exchange rate, about rising prices and about the difficulty of finding work. The party could do little to help. For the first time he found himself exposed to the full rigours of *émigré* poverty.[132]

The following April, 44 anti-war socialists gathered in Berne for a second international conference. Lenin arrived, spiritually fortified perhaps by a performance of Wagner's *Die Walkure* which he had attended earlier in the month. The other members of the Bolshevik delegation were Zinoviev and Inessa Armand. Anxious about the security situation in the Swiss capital, Grimm arranged for the various representatives to travel by train to Kienthal, an isolated village on the shores of Lake Thun. The conference lasted six, gruelling days. As usual, Lenin came ready to do battle, armed with draft resolutions, a manifesto and notebooks full of calculations on the likely affiliation of each and every delegate on every conceivable issue. No effort was spared in the quest to win over supporters – he was capable of spending as much as eight hours attempting to convert a single delegate to his point of view. He was equally energetic in dealing with his opponents, querying the credentials of Martov and Axelrod and threatening a walk-out when Grimm objected to his bludgeoning tactics. In the end, Lenin secured only 12 votes for his platform, but both the mood of the conference and the sources of his support suggested a leftward shift among anti-war socialists in the months since Zimmerwald. The final statement called on the proletariat of all countries to 'Lay down your weapons. You should turn them only against the common foe – the capitalist governments.' Lenin left Kienthal moderately satisfied.

In July 1916 he completed one of his most significant works: *Imperialism, the Highest Stage of Capitalism*. This was only the latest in a series of investigations into the nature of modern imperialism. J. A. Hobson's book, *Imperialism*, which first appeared in 1902, was followed by Rudolph Hilferding's *Finance Capital* (1910) and Nikolai Bukharin's *Imperialism and the World Economy*, published just a few months before the completion of Lenin's own study. (Lenin wrote a highly complimentary introduction to Bukharin's work.)

Lenin set out to explain why imperialism, the 'monopoly stage of capitalism' must be regarded as its 'highest' or ultimate manifestation. But he was equally concerned to expose the causal relationship between capitalism and war. Wars, both among the advanced capitalist States of the West and between those States and the societies of the developing world which they were systematically exploiting, were inevitable, he argued, for as long as capitalism survived.

His starting-point was that capitalism was no longer a progressive force. The free competition of the *laissez-faire* era described by Marx had been followed by a new one in which production was concentrated in Leviathan-like syndicates and trusts which aimed at nothing less than monopoly control. Monopoly had brought about 'immense progress in the socialis-ation of production' but had simultaneously created disparities between some branches of industry and others. Equally retrogressive was the tendency for giant cartels and business corporations to use their monopoly power systematically to freeze out competition and to forestall indepen-dent technological innovation. At the same time, financial control was passing from the industrialists themselves to a handful of banking con-glomerates. Using Lenin's terminology, this implied 'The merging of bank capital with industrial capital, and the creation, on the basis of this "finance capital", of a financial oligarchy'.

In the more advanced sectors of industry, these monopolistic conditions lead, however, to the creation of surplus or excess capital which can find no outlet in the metropolitan countries. Instead, capital is exported like any other commodity and invested in colonies or semi-dependencies where factors such as cheap raw materials and low labour costs ensure profits on a hitherto unheard-of scale. To protect these investments, the metropolitan countries are eventually compelled to annexe the territories themselves. 'It is beyond doubt,' concluded Lenin, 'that capitalism's transition to the stage of monopoly capital, to finance capital, is *connected* with the intensification of the struggle for the partition of the world.'

Lenin used this analysis to explain why, in defiance of the predictions of Marx and Engels, there had been a noticeable improvement in the economic condition of workers in the more advanced countries. Capitalism had found a new proletariat to exploit in the form of the backward colonial peoples. Some of the profits accrued in the process had been used to bribe a privileged stratum of workers, which Lenin termed the 'labour aristoc-racy'. However, this could not, he argued, prevent the relentless pauperiz-ation of the mass of workers which was intrinsic to capitalism itself: 'So long as capitalism remains capitalism, surplus capital will not be used to raise the standard of living of the masses in a given country, for this would mean a decrease in profits for the capitalists. Rather, it will be used to raise profits by the export of capital abroad to the backward countries'. And there was a further contradiction inherent in imperialism as the highest stage of capitalism. The partitioning of the world to secure new markets had taken place at a time when advanced industrial powers, like Britain, had been at their height. By the early twentieth century, however, other great powers (Germany and the USA, for example) were arriving on the scene, but there was little territory left over for them to exploit. They had no alternative, therefore, but to resort to militarization and war. This, in itself, imposed a great strain on the powers concerned, but the exploitation of the underdeveloped territories had other unwelcome consequences. As Lenin put it:

> Capitalism itself gradually provides the subjugated with the means and resources for their emancipation and they set out to achieve the goal which once seemed highest to the European nations: the creation of a united national state as a means to economic and cultural freedom. This movement for national independence threatens European capital in its most valuable and most promising fields of exploitation, and European capital can maintain its dominance only by continually increasing its military forces.

The result is a merging of the movement for national liberation awakening in the colonies with the impetus for social revolution in the advanced countries of the West, in both cases aggravated and fuelled by the fundamental instability of the capitalist system.

After completing *Imperialism*, Lenin left Zurich with his ailing wife and headed south for Mount Flums, high in the Alps and close to the Austrian frontier. They remained here for six weeks. The only drawbacks of the place were the infrequency of the post (deliveries once a day, by donkey), the milk diet imposed by the Chudivise rest home – milk soup for lunch! – and the following lamentable ritual:

> almost every morning about six o'clock a bell would ring, the public would gather to see the hikers off, and they would sing a farewell song about a cuckoo . . . Vladimir Ilyich, who liked to sleep in the morning, would grumble and bury his head under the quilt.[133]

The remainder of 1916 was best forgotten so far as Lenin was concerned. His mother had died in Petrograd (Petersburg was renamed during the First World War) in July; two months later his brother-in-law, Mark Elizarov, wrote to tell him that Anyuta had been arrested yet again. His financial situation was worse than ever and he was alienating almost everyone with his spluttering irritability and intolerance. He was at war, not only with the Great Powers but with those on his own side as well – with Rosa Luxemburg on the future of the German Social Democratic Party, with Radek on relations with the Poles, with Bukharin on the nature of the State and with Bukharin and Pyatakov jointly on national self-determination. When Gorky wrote asking him to soften the tone of his remarks about Kautsky in *Imperialism*, he hit the roof. However much he bemoaned the situation, he was basically unrepentant. To Inessa he wrote:

> Look at my fate. One militant campaign after another – against political stupidities, banalities, opportunism, etc. This since 1893. And the hatred of the vulgar people in payment. But I still would not exchange this fate for 'peace' with the vulgarizers.

By the beginning of 1917 he was physically and emotionally exhausted, telling Inessa: 'I am tired of meetings; my nerves are weak, my head aches; I am absolutely tired.'[134]

He derived some consolation from the fact that at 46 his uncomprising views on the war and revolution were striking a responsive chord among Swiss Social Democrats more than 20 years his junior. The older generation, he believed, was past saving: 'It is only worth working with youth,' he confided to Inessa. And so it was the young socialists of Zurich that he chose to address on 22 January 1917, the twelfth anniversary of Bloody Sunday. He told them that although

> We of the older generation may not live to see the decisive battle of the coming revolution . . . I can, I believe, express the hope that the youth which is working so splendidly in the socialist movement of Switzerland, and of the whole world, will be fortunate enough not only to fight, but also to win, in the coming proletarian revolution.[135]

It was an unduly pessimistic forecast. One day, six weeks later, just after Nadya had finished washing up and Lenin was getting ready to return to the library after lunch, there was a frantic knocking at the door. It was a Polish friend of his with some startling news – revolution had broken out in Russia!

8

The road to power

Petrograd, 8 March 1917, 3.00 p.m. A queue has formed outside the
Filippov bakery on Bolshoi Prospekt, to the rear of the Peter–Paul
Fortress. In the queue are some 200 people, mostly women, anonymous
figures in drab, worn coats and tightly bound headscarves. The temperature is several degrees below zero. In a few hours the women will be
starting a new shift in one of the Vyborg textile mills. Some have not tasted
bread for two days. The war is going badly. The women's conversation is a
patchwork of news, hearsay and prejudice, delivered *sotto voce*. They
blame Jewish speculators for high prices and the lack of bread, milk and
other basic foodstuffs. The wife of a waiter at the Astoria swears that the
maître d'hôtel can still get hold of bread on the black market; her
companion curses the 'Germans' at court and rasps an obscenity coupling
the Tsarina with Rasputin. Refugees pouring into Petrograd from the front
are accused of taking 'Russian' jobs and of making the housing situation
even worse. The women are vaguely surprised by the wild excesses of their
talk, by the tears welling up in their eyes and by the surfacing of a raw
anger which they had previously been able to subdue. A cry of disbelief,
tinged with despair, escapes from the women pressing at the gates. No
flour has been delivered. The back of the queue surges forward and one or
two in the crowd begin screaming hysterically. Shouts of 'bread', 'bread'
are heard as a youth picks up a blackened piece of ice and hurls it at the
bakery, shattering a ground-floor window. The women shake the gates
with a rhythmic frenzy. They give way. Pandemonium ensues.

Near by, in the Vyborg district, hundreds of workers from the steel and
textile mills are already marching down Bolshoi Sampsonievsky Prospekt
towards the River Neva, singing the 'Marseillaise'. As they pass a
succession of factories – Russian Renault, Old Parviainen, Erikson, Nobel
– they call out to the workers inside 'Down tools', 'Join us'. If the response
is not immediate, they begin flinging stones, iron bolts, anything to hand
into the yards. Invariably, the men leave work, though some slink home

rather than join the demonstrators. On reaching the river, the crowd finds its passage across the Liteiny Bridge blocked by mounted police. The more determined find an alternative route across the ice. Confronted by another police cordon, they overturn a tramcar and break a few windows before returning home.

The following day began cold and misty, with a light drizzle. By 9 a.m. 40,000 workers had taken to the streets, chanting 'Down with war' and 'Down with the government'. Armed with stones and pieces of ice, they forced their way across the Neva and into the city centre. The shops and restaurants on the fashionable Nevsky Prospekt had closed, anticipating trouble, but curious onlookers watched the entertainment from the upper storeys. A demonstration materialized around the 'hippo', the grotesque statue of Alexander III on Znamenskaya Square, but when Cossack troops received orders to disperse the crowd, they hesitated. One soldier was seen to wink at the demonstrators.

By Saturday 10 March, the strike was general. Red banners appeared at meetings and the workers were joined by students and members of the public. When a colonel of police attacked the crowd with his whip on the Liteiny Bridge, he was dragged from his horse and beaten to death. A girl presented a Cossack with a bouquet of red roses and the women shouted 'Comrades, lower your bayonets, join us'. Some soldiers shouldered their rifles, but shooting was reported near the city duma and the Gostinny Dvor shopping precinct.

More than 500 miles (800 km) away, at army headquarters in Mogilev, Tsar Nicholas II wired General S. S. Khabalov, commander of the Petrograd Military District, with the order to suppress the disorders 'by tomorrow'.

In response to the Tsar's command, Petrograd was transformed into an armed camp. All public buildings were guarded and the bridges across the Neva were raised. Again the workers thwarted this action by marching across the ice and proceeding directly to Znamenskaya Square. There, a bloody confrontation ensued as troops opened fire. When some showed reluctance, their commander seized a rifle and began firing at the demonstrators himself. It was this and similar shows of brutality which decided the issue. By the evening there were rumblings of discontent among units of the Pavlovsky Regiment stationed on Mars Field, near the Winter Palace. Early the following morning, soldiers of the Volhynia Regiment, disturbed by the previous day's violence, rebelled with cries of 'enough blood'. When their commanding officer refused to join them, they killed him. The rebellion spread like wildfire to other units. On that same day, the Kresty Prison was burned down and a huge bonfire made of police files. The police themselves had long since disappeared from the streets and were being gradually replaced by a citizen's militia, whose members, sporting red armbands, patrolled the streets in cars and trucks requisitioned from the military.

The government, meanwhile, was in total disarray. On Sunday 11 March, the President of the Duma, M. V. Rodzyanko, wired the Tsar to report 'Anarchy in the capital . . . shooting in the streets . . . supplies of food and fuel completely disrupted . . . universal dissatisfaction growing . . . there must be no delay in forming a new government enjoying the confidence of the country. Any hesitation would mean death'. When the Tsar ignored this advice and instead ordered the prorogation of the Duma, Rodzyanko sensed a parting of the ways.

The following day a 'Temporary Committee of the Duma' installed itself in the Tauride Palace with the object of restoring order to the streets of Petrograd. Later that same evening, in another part of the palace, a gathering of moderate socialists (predominantly Mensheviks and labour leaders recently released from prison) decided to organize elections to a Soviet of Workers' Deputies to ensure the permanence of the revolution. A provisional executive was appointed, with N. S. Chkheidze as chairman and A. F. Kerensky and M. D. Skobelev as vice-chairmen. Rodzyanko, driven to distraction by the incessant ringing of the telephones in his office, again wired Mogilev. The Tsar's reaction was contemptuous: 'That fat Rodzyanko has again sent me some nonsense to which I will not even reply'. He decided to set out for Tsarskoe Selo but communications were so disrupted that he was unable to proceed beyond Pskov.

By now, the Temporary Committee of the Duma was forming a Provisional Government. Two members of the committee, A. I. Guchkov and V. V. Shulgin, set out for Pskov to inform the Tsar of these developments and to urge him to abdicate. Nicholas, resplendently attired in full Cossack uniform, received them at 9 p.m. on Thursday 15 March. He was calm and composed. He had, in fact, already made up his mind after consulting the Army High Command. Nicholas agreed to abdicate but elected to transfer the crown not to his young son, Alexei, who suffered from haemophilia, but to his brother, the Grand Duke Mikhail. The necessary papers were signed at 11 p.m. The following day, Grand Duke Mikhail himself renounced the throne, so bringing the 300-year-old Romanov dynasty to an end.

Lenin's state of mind can readily be imagined. Only two days after learning of the Revolution he and Zinoviev published their first response, the 'Draft Theses, March 17, 1917'. Over the following weeks, in lecture notes, in correspondence and in more considered pronouncements, like the 'Letters from Afar' and the 'April Theses', Lenin began charting his party's route to power.

While others were heralding the arrival of the bourgeois–democratic revolution, he was giving it its marching orders. The Russian bourgeoisie, he insisted, was quite incapable of giving the people 'peace, bread and freedom', so its representative, the Provisional Government, must be immediately overthrown. Lenin called instead for a second, proletarian revolution which would bring the workers and poor peasants to power in a new, Soviet Government. In this context the call to end the imperialist war and transform it into a civil war would be enough, he believed, to incite the workers of Europe to unleash socialist revolutions everywhere. Thus, the immediate task of the Bolshevik Party was to oppose the Provisional Government, arm the masses and prepare them for the seizure of power. Lenin was adamant that this was a matter for the Bolsheviks alone: there must be '*No rapprochement with other Parties*', he underlined in a letter to Lunacharsky in March 1917.[136]

His initial elation on hearing of the overthrow of tsarism soon gave way to the sober realization that returning to Russia would be far more difficult than it had been in 1905. Britain and France were, after all, unlikely to allow such a brazen defeatist as Lenin to pass through their territories – and in any case he could not be sure of his reception in Petrograd. Determined, none the less, to 'go at any cost – even through hell', he explored every kind of possibility, no matter how outlandish, in his feverish yearning to return home. He would travel to England on papers procured by Karpinsky (Lenin would alter his appearance by wearing a wig); he would fly over Germany; or perhaps he could assume the guise of a deaf-and-dumb Swedish sailor? It was left to Martov to come up with a more practicable, if controversial, scheme. What if the Provisional Government could be persuaded to allow an exchange of Russian *émigrés* for German civilian internees?

The German Government at least, was likely to be sympathetic to such an idea. They were more anxious than ever to remove Russia from the war as their troops in the east were urgently required for redeployment on the western front. The Foreign Ministry had already invested several million marks in various schemes aimed at promoting social unrest in Russia. Two freelance agents, the Estonian, Alexander Keskulla, and the Russian-born Alexander Helphand ('Parvus') had attempted to recruit Lenin to the cause and Keskulla, at least, had channelled German monies into Bolshevik organizations in Switzerland, in all probability, anonymously. When the Swiss socialist, Robert Grimm, put out some initial feelers on the *émigrés*' behalf, therefore, he received encouragement. At first, Lenin allowed Grimm a free hand but he quickly became impatient with the apparent lack of progress. On the last day of March he decided to accept the German offer, irrespective of the attitude of the government in Petrograd. A more 'reliable' Swiss socialist, Fritz Platten, now agreed to take responsibility for the transit arrangements across Germany, while Lenin made direct contact with the German Ambassador to Switzerland, von Romberg. By 3 p.m. on Wednesday 4 April, Lenin and Krupskaya were on their way to Berne for the final round of negotiations. Lenin had already cabled Jakub Hanecki in Stockholm with a request to set aside funds for the second leg of the journey from Sweden into Russia. As Hanecki was a close business associate of Parvus, the provenance of this money remains a matter of controversy.

The conditions for the journey were now finalized. Platten would accompany the *émigrés* through Germany and act as their intermediary. The train on which they were to travel would have extra-territorial rights and would remain sealed until the passengers left Germany. As a *quid pro quo*, Lenin gave an assurance that he and his associates would attempt to secure the release of German civilians presently detained in Russia. Every passenger was obliged to sign a typed statement, reminding them of the conditions of transit and of the risks involved. (A French newspaper had recently reported that the new Russian Foreign Minister, Pavel Milyukov, was threatening to charge anyone travelling through Germany with high treason.) Apart from Lenin and Krupskaya, the party included Zinoviev, his wife and son, Inessa Armand, Karl Radek (a deserter from the Austrian Army), the Georgian, Mikha Tskhakaya (veteran of the 1905 London congress), and Grigori Sokolnikov, a former collaborator with Martov on the journal *Nashe Slovo* (*Our Word*).

Before leaving, Lenin tried to win over fellow socialists to his highly controversial plan of action. He did not have much success. To make matters worse, the arch-Defensist, G. A. Alexinsky, was making great capital out of his relations with the Germans, making the journey a major talking-point with the *habitués* of the Zurich cafés, among them Stefan Zweig, James Joyce and the composer, Ferruccio Busoni.

Early on the morning of Monday 9 April, the travellers began to assemble at the Volkshaus in Berne. For Lenin, the experience was somewhat akin to leading a party of school children. They were loud, high-spirited and giddy with excitement, and he regarded them with a paternalistic tolerance which would soon begin to wear thin. Krupskaya was checking their baggage for the umpteenth time: the books, newspapers, Press cuttings and party documents were all there, neatly packaged – there was little room for clothes and other personal items. Lenin shook his head incredulously at the late arrivals as Platten made a head-count and beckoned them in the direction of the station. They were in Zurich in time for lunch at the Zahringerhof Hotel, in the course of which Lenin read out his 'Farewell letter to Swiss Workers'. Then, at about 2.30 p.m., they left for the station where they were greeted by an irate and vocal band of demonstrators waving banners and hurling insults: '*provocateurs*!', 'traitors', 'German spies'. Just before they were due to depart, one of Lenin's companions rushed to him with the news that Blum was on the train. Dr Oscar Blum had asked to have his name added to the passenger-list but he had been refused after Lenin raised doubts about his bona fides. Infuriated by this act of defiance, he hunted down the offending doctor, grabbed him by the collar and flung him out on to the platform.

At 3.10 p.m. precisely, the train left Zurich and headed for the Swiss frontier. The 'sealed' train, comprising an engine, a single, green carriage and a baggage wagon, was waiting at Gottmadingen, on the German side

LENIN'S RETURN FROM EXILE,
APRIL 1917

Tornio

FINLAND

Gulf of Bothnia

NORWAY

SWEDEN

Turku

Vyborg

PETROGRAD

STOCKHOLM

DENMARK

RUSSIA

MALMO

Trelleborg

Sassnitz

HOLLAND   GERMANY

BERLIN

BELGIUM

FRANKFURT

POLAND

Mannheim

Karlsruhe

STUTTGART

FRANCE

Ulm

Gottmadingen

AUSTRIA-HUNGARY

ZURICH

BERNE

+++++ Train Route (between Gottmadingen and Sassnitz
        in the sealed train)

SWITZERLAND

····· Sea Crossing

of the border. After a short delay, all 32 passengers were allowed to proceed on their hazardous journey through 'enemy' territory.

For the next six days, Lenin shepherded his flock like Moses leading the chosen people to the promised land. And, like Moses, he was a stern and exacting travelling companion. Annoyed by the tobacco fumes creeping insidiously into his compartment, he banished smokers to the toilets. When this led to a queue, discomforting the genuine users, he issued passes to regulate the flow. He was equally uncompromising where noise was concerned. The gusts of uncontrollable laughter coming from next door were disturbing his concentration. Identifying the culprit as Olga Ravich, he took her by the hand and deposited her in a more remote part of the train.

Olga's high spirits were soon dissipated by the sheer monotony of the journey. The train was no better than a mobile prison. She and her companions preyed on one another's nerves; like caged animals, they yearned to break out and run free. At night, sometimes during the day, they hallucinated about a Russia which seemed ever more remote, lost in a maze of railway sidings and meandering track. Would they, in the end, reach their destination, they wondered anxiously, or were they fated never to return home? It was late Wednesday evening before they reached the port of Sassnitz on the Baltic coast, only to find that they had missed their connection. They caught the next ferry to Sweden, arriving at Trelleborg late at night, following a rough crossing. Hanecki was at the quayside to meet them. They reached Stockholm on the morning of 13 April.

Lenin had much to do in the Swedish capital and little time to do it in, as he had decided to leave for Finland by the evening train. Leaving his bags with the porters of the Hotel Regina, he went shopping at the insistence of his companions, who did not want him to be seen in Petrograd wearing his worn derby hat, shabby suit and crude, hobnailed boots. He obliged them with the greatest reluctance, being too exhausted to offer much resistance. He had spent most of the previous night cross-examining Hanecki on the situation in Russia and fending off newspapermen who had boarded the train *en route* in the hope of an interview – an early intimation of his newly acquired celebrity status. Nevertheless, he had good reason to feel satisfied as he wandered the streets of Stockholm. The German leg of the journey had gone more or less as planned; most importantly, the conditions stipulated by himself and Platten had been scrupulously observed by the German Government. It was, therefore, annoying, to say the least, to learn that Parvus was in Stockholm seeking a meeting. Clearly, there was still a danger of his being compromised. Lenin took the possibility so seriously that he rejected these overtures in the most forthright terms and called on witnesses to attest to the fact.

Immediately on boarding the train that evening, he began studying the Russian newspapers he had picked up in Stockholm. His blood-pressure rose as he scanned the *Pravda* editorials composed by Stalin and Kamenev, both recently returned from exile. Why were they indulging in this love affair with the Provisional Government? Why were they compromising on the war? Nadya, who had grown used to these rhetorical flourishes, shook her head sympathetically. The 500-odd miles (800 km) around the Gulf of Bothnia would soon pass!

At Haparanda they disembarked and crossed the River Torniojoki by sledge. On the far side was the Tornio customs post, gateway to Finland and the Russian Empire. They were nearly home. Then, as they approached the wooden hut with its chevroned sentry post, Lenin suddenly became aware of the presence of British as well as Russian soldiers. Would they be sent back now, or even arrested? The British insisted on interviewing each passenger individually and on examining their baggage. The Russian officials then gave them a brief questionnaire to fill out. Asked to give a forwarding address, Lenin wrote: Shirokaya Street 48/9, Apartment 24, Petrograd [Anyuta's flat]. Everyone except Platten, who was not a Russian citizen, was allowed through. The tension broke and they all began laughing like children. Lenin embraced Tskhakaya in a bear hug before rushing off to the telegraph office to wire his sisters: ARRIVING MONDAY ELEVEN P.M. TELL *PRAVDA*. ULYANOV.

The train waiting to take them from Tornio to Petrograd was a familiar Russian one. Nadya recalled 'the shabby third-class carriages, the Russian soldiers; everything was terribly good'. It also happened to be Easter Sunday so there was a festive atmosphere on board. One of the soldiers shared his *paskha* (a type of cheesecake eaten in Russia at Easter) with the son of one of the exiles. 'Our people were glued to the windows,' remembered Krupskaya. 'On the platforms of the stations through which we passed, soldiers stood about in groups. Ussievich put his head out of the window and yelled: "Long live the world revolution!".' The troops looked on in amazement.[137]

Meanwhile, Lenin was chatting to the soldiers who had crowded his compartment. They were Defensists to a man. Summoning up his old skills as a propagandist, he encouraged them to talk before introducing some gently probing questions of his own. Generally, he got a good reception, though few of the soldiers, if any, were persuaded that the war could be ended in the way he suggested.

Terijoki . . . Kuokkala . . . The train was slowing down again. Lenin knew the stations of the Finland line by heart. The next stop was Beloostrov – they were now in Russia proper and the passengers disembarked to have their papers checked. As he jumped down from his carriage, Lenin was surrounded by scores of cheering workers from the local munitions plant. He recognized Kamenev among them, then the handsome, moustachioed Alexander Shlyapnikov, one of the few leading Bolsheviks to witness the revolution in Petrograd. Looming from the darkness was another figure whom Lenin did not recognize. As the man gripped him in a bear hug, he was introduced as Fedor Raskolnikov, a

Bolshevik agitator at the Kronstadt naval base. Before Lenin knew it, he
was being carried into the waiting-room on the shoulders of a group of
workers. Embarrassed and a little put out, he gave a hurried speech before
presenting himself to customs officials.

Back in Petrograd, the Finland Station was vibrant with expectation.
The Bolshevik organizers had left nothing to chance in the welcome they
had prepared for their leader. There were no newspapers because of the
Easter holiday, but the party had blitzed the working-class districts with
handbills: 'Lenin arrives today. Meet him'. The station interior was a sea of
red. Banners hung from the pillars. Triumphal arches had been erected.
Women clasped bunches of flowers. Sailors from the Baltic fleet had
formed a guard of honour. There was even a band. But where was Ilyich?
The train was due at 11 p.m. The officials consulted their watches
anxiously. Then, at ten past, the powerful headlights of a locomotive
loomed into view. The crowd surged forward and the cheering began. As
the steam hissed about the wheels of the engine and the first carriage doors
swung open, the band gave a routine performance of the 'Marseillaise'. A
small figure in a dark, flapping overcoat walked briskly towards the station
concourse. Lenin, preoccupied with the problem of finding a cab at such a
late hour, gave a smile more akin to a grimace as Alexandra Kollontai,
feminist and former Menshevik, rushed forward and presented him with a
bouquet of flowers. Lenin clutched them to his chest as if for protection as
he inspected the naval guard of honour. Next, a young man whom he
recognized as Ivan Chugurin, a former student at the Longjumeau party
school, stepped forward, his eyes streaming with tears, and presented
Lenin with an honorary party card, designating him a member of the
Vyborg district organization. Lenin beamed and nodded his approval of
this honour before being led into the ornate splendour of what had been
the imperial waiting-room, where a sullen Chkeidze pronounced this
speech of welcome:

> Comrade Lenin, in the name of the Petrograd Soviet of Workers' and
> Soldiers' Deputies and the whole revolution we welcome you to Russia
> . . . but we believe that the principal task of the revolutionary democracy
> at present is to defend our revolution from every kind of attack both
> from within and from without. We believe that what is needed is not
> disunity but the closing of the ranks of the entire democracy. We hope
> you will pursue these aims together with us.[138]

Lenin was glancing distractedly at the ceiling and fidgeting with his
bouquet. As soon as Chkeidze had finished, he turned his back and
addressed the onlookers in a quite different key: 'The sun of the world
socialist revolution has already risen. In Germany there is a seething
ferment. Any day now we shall see the collapse of European imperialism . . . Long live the world socialist revolution!'[139] The Soviet representa-

4 Street barricades during the Moscow uprising, December 1905.

5 Burning a farm. Russian troops carry out a punitive expedition in the Baltic provinces, 1906. From *L'Illustration*.

26 Ceremonial opening of first Duma by Tsar Nicholas II, 10 May 1906. (*opposite above*)

27 Inessa Armand. (*opposite below*)

28 Lenin in 1910. He lived in exile in Paris in the rue Marie-Rose from 1909 to 1912. (*above*)

29 Lenin's mother in 1912, four years before she died.

30 Lenin in Poronin, August 1914.

31 Two years later. Lenin in Zurich, 1916.

32 The Tauride Palace, Petrograd.

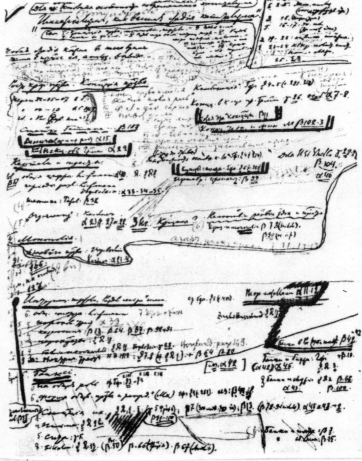

Н. ЛЕНИНЪ (ВЛ. ИЛЬИНЪ).

ИМПЕРІАЛИЗМЪ,

КАКЪ НОВѢЙШІЙ ЭТАПЪ

КАПИТАЛИЗМА.

(Популярный очеркъ)

———

СКЛАДЪ ИЗДАНІЯ:
Книжный складъ и магазинъ „Жизнь и Знаніе"
Петроградъ, Поварской пер., 2, кв. 9 и 10. Тел. 227—42
1917 г.

33 *Imperialism, the Highest Stage of Capitalism* (title page, 1917, and handwritten draft).

34 Lenin in disguise on his way to Finland, August 1917.

35 Lenin's false passport for Finland.

Къ Гражданамъ Россіи.

Временное Правительство низложено. Государственная власть перешла въ руки органа Петроградскаго Совѣта Рабочихъ и Солдатскихъ Депутатовъ Военно - Революціоннаго Комитета, стоящаго во главѣ Петроградскаго пролетаріата и гарнизона.

Дѣло, за которое боролся народъ, немедленное предложеніе демократическаго мира, отмѣна помѣщичьей собственности на землю, рабочій контроль надъ производствомъ, созданіе Совѣтскаго Правительства — это дѣло обезпечено.

ДА ЗДРАВСТВУЕТЪ РЕВОЛЮЦІЯ РАБОЧИХЪ, СОЛДАТЪ И КРЕСТЬЯНЪ!

Военно-Революціонный Комитетъ
при Петроградскомъ Совѣтѣ
Рабочихъ и Солдатскихъ Депутатовъ

25 октября 1917 г 10 ч. утра

36 Proclamation declaring the overthrow of the Provisional Government.

37 Bolsheviks canvassing for the Constituent Assembly, October 1917. The banner denounces capitalism and calls for the confiscation of land and a democratic republic.

38 Barricades in Liteiny Prospekt, Petrograd, 1917. (*opposite above*)

39 The Hotel Metropole, Moscow, showing damage sustained during the Revolution. Fighting was much fiercer here than in Petrograd. (*opposite below*)

40 Members of the Soviet delegation of Brest-Litovsk, 1918. Sitting (left to right): L. B. Kamenev, A. A. Ioffe, Madame A. A. Bitsenko; standing (left to right): Captain of the General Staff, W. W. Zopski, unknown, L. D. Trotsky, L. M. Karakhan.

41 Demonstration on the opening day of the Constituent Assembly, 5 January 1918. (*opposite*)

42 Lenin reviews
troops during the
Universal Military
Training drive, Red
Square, Moscow, 1919.
(*opposite above*)

43 The artist I. I.
Brodsky painting Lenin
during a session of the
Comintern
(Communist
International) in 1921.
(*opposite below*)

44 Lenin at his desk in
the Kremlin. (*above*)

45 Lenin and
Krupskaya at Gorki,
1922. (*right*)

46 Lenin, confined to a
wheelchair, during his
last illness, 1923.
(*overleaf*)

tives looked on in stunned silence as Lenin was carried out in triumph on the shoulders of soldiers and sailors, too buoyed up with emotion to worry about the implications of his address. To the cheers of the waiting crowd, Lenin was hoisted on to the turret of an armoured car, a searchlight illuminating his diminutive frame against the backdrop of the starry night sky. After another short speech, the procession moved off across the Sampsonievsky Bridge to the Kshesinskaya Mansion, once the residence of a prima ballerina of the Marinsky Ballet and now headquarters of the Bolshevik Party. Here the speech-making and festivities went on late into the night and it was already getting light when Lenin and Krupskaya left for Shirokaya Street. Later, as they were preparing for bed, they burst simultaneously into laughter. Anyuta's adopted son, Gora, had framed the bed with a banner inscribed: 'Workers of the world unite!'

The following morning, after visiting the graves of his mother and sister, Olga, at the Volkov Cemetery, Lenin made his way to Room 13 of the Tauride Palace, where he addressed Bolshevik delegates to the All-Russian Conference of Soviets. He was warmly received as he walked briskly to the podium. His speech began in a manner that was studiedly matter of fact: 'I've sketched out a number of theses which I intend to expand on,' he explained, glancing at his notes. 'Lack of time has prevented me from delivering a more detailed report.' A hush fell on his listeners as they rehearsed the anticipated line of argument . . . watchful tolerance of the Provisional Government . . . conditional support for the war effort, pending a negotiated peace – the conciliatory platform advocated by Stalin and Kamenev in *Pravda*. Instead, Lenin bombarded them with one combative slogan after another: 'not the slightest concession to "revolutionary defencism"', 'No support for the Provisional Government', 'Not a parliamentary republic . . . but a Soviet republic of Workers', Farm Workers' and Peasants' Deputies'. There was not a trace of compromise in his demands for: 'Nationalisation of all land', 'social production and distribution to be under the *control* of the Soviets of Workers' Deputies', 'Abolition of the police, the army and the bureaucracy. The salaries of officials, all of whom are to be elected and subject to replacement at any time, are not to exceed the average wage of a competent worker'.[140]

While this kind of impetuous talk alienated Mensheviks, Socialist Revolutionaries and not a few Bolsheviks (not to speak of the Kadets), it turned out that Lenin was closer to the mood of his party than many suspected. At the seventh conference, held in the second week of May, the delegates voted for motions opposing both the war and the Provisional Government and calling for the arming of the proletariat. The fact that five out of the nine members of the newly elected Central Committee, including Kamenev, V. P. Nogin and V. P. Milyutin, were moderates was less important to Lenin than the fact that rank-and-file Bolsheviks appeared to be moving in his direction.

The Provisional Government's honeymoon period was already at an end. The economy was deteriorating rapidly: inflation was rampant, food and clothing were becoming scarcer, the transport system was grinding to a halt, agriculture was bordering on anarchy. The ten million men under arms (the 'peasants in grey greatcoats') were becoming increasingly restive. In Petrograd, the majority of the 300,000-strong garrison were raw recruits, ill-disciplined and poorly trained. Their attitude to officers had changed dramatically following the promulgation of the famous Order No. 1 which provided for elected committees in all army units and absolved soldiers from obeying any order not conforming with Soviet policy. In May, the Minister for Foreign Affairs, P. N. Milyukov, was dismissed at the behest of the Soviet, which objected to his increasingly aggressive stance on the war. The cabinet shake-up which followed produced a coalition that included Mensheviks and Socialist Revolutionaries for the first time, but the broadening of its base did little to improve the government's popularity. More and more political meetings in the capital were producing resolutions calling for 'All power to the soviets'.

For Lenin, these were hectic days. The *Pravda* offices on the Moika Embankment had become a second home. When he was not there, rattling off articles at the rate of one a day, he could most likely be found at Kshesinskaya's Mansion across the Neva, or attending a meeting of the Soviet at the Tauride Palace, or perhaps delivering a speech to workers at one of the city's major factories. There was so much work to be done. The Revolution had taken the Bolsheviks as much by surprise as had Bloody Sunday in 1905. Their support in the capital had increased eight-fold since March; even so, the Mensheviks and Socialist Revolutionaries were much more strongly represented in the soviets and the latter were infinitely more popular in the country as a whole.

Nevertheless, the tide was beginning to turn. Alexander Kerensky, the Minister of War in the new coalition government (and, incidentally, the son of Lenin's former headmaster), had ordered a new offensive to begin on 1 July. As preparations went ahead and the troops of the Petrograd garrison began leaving for the front, 1,000 delegates were arriving in the capital for the first Congress of Soviets. The scene in the Military Academy, where the sessions took place, was one of utter chaos. Soldiers, sailors and workers milled about the corridors, talking, smoking and drinking tea. Chairs and benches were scattered everywhere and cigarette ends littered the floors. At night, the school became a gigantic dormitory, laid out with hundreds of camp-beds covered by red blankets.

Lenin joined the Bolshevik contingent at the back of the hall, a small figure lost in a vast crowd. His first intervention restored him to prominence. The Menshevik Minister of Posts and Telegraphs, I. G. Tsereteli, was arguing that there was no party in Russia prepared to assume sole power. At once, Lenin was on his feet, 'Yes, there is such a Party! No Party can refuse and our Party certainly doesn't. We are ready to take power at any moment'.[141] Catcalls and hoots of derisive laughter greeted this impudent assertion, but Lenin had revealed his hand.

Behind the scenes, meanwhile, the Bolsheviks were making preparations to stage an anti-war demonstration timed to coincide with the launching of Kerensky's much publicized offensive. Lenin's contribution was a blistering attack on the war, delivered to a session of the congress on 22 June. The government was forewarned and with the co-operation of the Soviet, a ban was imposed on all demonstrations for a period of three days.

Lenin soon had his revenge. On 1 July the Soviet staged its own demonstration, intended to serve as a grand affirmation of its policies. Some 400,000 workers, soldiers and citizens paraded down the majestic Nevsky Prospekt in bright sunshine. To the chagrin of the government's Socialist Revolutionary and Menshevik supporters, however, most of the banners proclaimed Bolshevik slogans: 'Down with the war!', 'Down with the ten capitalist ministers!' and 'All power to the soviets!'

The offensive on the south-western front began on the same day. Thirty-one divisions were thrown into the fray and 1,300 guns pounded enemy positions, but the Russians won only the initial skirmishes. The Germans rushed to the assistance of their Austrian allies and within three weeks the Russian Army had endured 60,000 casualties. It was slowly bleeding to death.

Shortly after the 1 July demonstration, Lenin left the capital to recoup for a few days at Bonch-Bruevich's summer home at Neivola, in Finland. Just over two weeks later, in the early hours of 17 July, he was awoken by an emissary from the Central Committee, Maximilian Saveliev, with an urgent message to return to Petrograd at once. They took the first available train and were back at the Finland Station in a matter of hours.

They found the Kshesinskaya Mansion in turmoil. The previous day, troops belonging to the First Machine Gun Regiment, anxiously awaiting transfer to the front, had taken to the streets demanding 'All power to the soviets'. Within hours, the government had an insurrection on its hands, as soldiers and workers converged on the city centre, demonstrating *en masse* outside the Marinsky and Tauride Palaces. It was clear from the somewhat garbled information Lenin was receiving that the Bolshevik Military Organization was deeply implicated in the revolt. The situation was alarming. As he pondered the various courses of action open to him, he became aware of a commotion in the street. Outside, thousands of sailors from the Kronstadt naval base were gathering expectantly. Bolshevik supporters to a man, they were champing at the bit to go into action. Lenin could not find the words to address them. Instead, he turned on his military specialists, Nevsky and Podvoisky, for encouraging the rebellion without properly weighing up the consequences: 'You should be thrashed for this,' he snarled. Then, recovering his composure, he ventured out on to the balcony. His statesmanlike appeal for calm, for peaceful protest, disappointed the sailors who had armed themselves to the teeth. But Lenin reckoned that it was too early for the Soviet to part company with the Provisional Government and that the Bolsheviks were not yet strong enough to insist. As he returned indoors to continue his deliberations, the frustrated, angry columns of sailors headed into the city centre and became caught up in a gun battle with snipers concealed among the roof-tops of the Nevsky Prospekt. Later they ambushed the Socialist Revolutionary leader, Viktor Chernov, outside the Tauride Palace; had Trotsky, who happened to witness the incident, not intervened, the minister of agriculture would certainly have been lynched.

Apparently helpless, the government turned to the Soviet which reluctantly came to its defence, summoning units from the front and supporting other measures aimed at restoring order. There was enough circumstantial evidence to pin the blame for the insurrection on the Bolsheviks and, by a happy coincidence, intelligence officers now revealed that they could substantiate the charge that Lenin was an agent of Germany. Although the investigations were still incomplete, the Minister of Justice, P. N. Pereverzev, decided to leak to the Press some of the purportedly incriminating documents (mostly telegrams from Hanecki to Bolsheviks in Petrograd). The results were dramatic. 'Lenin, Hanecki and Kozlovsky German Spies!', screamed a newspaper headline of 18 July. 'Horrors!' sensationalized another, 'Petrograd was seized by the Germans'. Even *Izvestiya*, the newspaper of the Soviet, charged the Bolsheviks with the deaths of 400 workers, soldiers, sailors, women and children. Vengeance was the order of the day. Krupskaya recalls overhearing a housewife in her own neighbourhood jeering: 'And what's to be done with this Lenin who's come from Germany? Should he be drowned in a well, or what?'[142]

The party was outlawed. On 18 July, cadets from the Military Academy raided the offices of *Pravda*, hurling the latest edition of the newspaper into the Moika Canal. The following day, the Bolsheviks were forced to vacate the Kshesinskaya Mansion after soldiers threatened to blow it up with heavy artillery. Simultaneously, orders went out to the front to ban all Bolshevik newspapers and organizations and to prohibit all political meetings within the battle zone. There were also sweeping arrests. Kamenev, Lunacharsky and the naval agitators, Fedor Raskolnikov and Pavel Dybenko were all captured. Trotsky, who had only just joined the party, gave himself up, while Kollontai was arrested in Finland and taken back to Petrograd, where her interrogators demanded to know: 'Have you brought in any spies, Bolshevik?' Lenin and Zinoviev, however, managed to evade their pursuers.[143]

It had been a close shave. Lenin had chanced to leave the *Pravda* building only moments before it was raided. Shortly afterwards, Sverdlov arrived at Shirokaya Street to help him escape. 'Yakov Mikhailovich threw his waterproof around my brother and they left the house at once, completely unobserved,' Manyasha remembered. They walked the short distance to Mariya Sulimova's apartment, overlooking the grimy and polluted Karpovka Canal, but Lenin knew he could not stay there for long. The following day, he and Nadya crossed into Vyborg, spending the night with a factory worker named Kaurov. Soon they were on the move again. The reason? 'Kaurov's son was an anarchist,' Nadya recalled; 'the young men messed around with bombs, so it wasn't a very suitable safe house'. At this critical juncture in his life, Lenin's thoughts turned to posterity. He rushed off a note to Kamenev, which was in fact never delivered: '*Entre nous*, if they do me in, please publish my notebook: "Marxism and the State" (the book with the blue binding). I consider it important, because Plekhanov and Kautsky have both got it wrong.'[144]

His next hiding-place was the home of Stalin's future father-in-law, S. Ya. Alliluyev. Safely ensconced on the fifth floor, Lenin received a steady stream of news from visiting comrades, like Ordzhonikidze, Nogin, Stasova and Stalin himself. From his sister, he learned that Anyuta's apartment on Shirokaya Street had been raided and searched – and that local residents had signed a petition demanding the family's eviction for its alleged pro-German sympathies. There was a heated discussion about whether he should give himself up and face his accusers in open court. He was anxious to clear his name but as his safety could not be guaranteed, even by the Soviet, a more secure hiding-place had to be found.

Late on the night of 23 July, after embracing Nadya and telling her: 'We may not see each other again', he left the Alliluyev's and threaded his way through the back streets of northern Petrograd to Sestroretsk Station, where his party contact, Nikolai Emelyanov, was waiting for him. On Emelyanov's advice, they waited for the 2 a.m. "boozers'" train (favoured by revellers returning from a night on the town) which took them as far as Razliv, a scattering of cottages and holiday homes about 20 miles (32 km) away. At first, Lenin hid in the hayloft of Emelyanov's barn; later, he moved with Zinoviev to a small clearing in the forest, which could be reached only by rowing across a nearby lake. They spent the daylight hours in the open, discussing party business in the warm summer sunshine, bothered only by the mosquitoes which thrived on the marshy surroundings; at night they slept in a straw hut, shaped like a haystack.

Lenin was deeply immersed in a new theoretical treatise, *State and Revolution*, in which he returned to the theory of proletarian dictatorship. He argued that the coming revolution would entail smashing the bourgeois State machine altogether and replacing it with a State of a new type, modelled on the Paris Commune. Every proletarian and poor peasant would become an active participant in government, at the expense of the bourgeoisie who would be rooted out from all positions of power and disenfranchized. Lenin's workers' democracy would be policed by armed workers and administered by a bureaucracy reconstructed from top to bottom and comprising elected officials, paid workmen's wages and serving in rotation. Lenin could foresee no problem whatever in getting capitalism to work for its new masters:

Capitalist culture has *created* large scale production, factories, railways, the postal service, telephones, etc., and *on this basis* most of the functions of the old 'state power' have become so simplified and can be reduced to such exceedingly simple operations of registration, recording and checking that they can easily be performed by every literate person for ordinary 'workmen's wages'.

When all opposition had been eliminated, the need for even this modified form of State would disappear, leaving it to 'wither away'.

Towards the end of August, Lenin left Razliv for the relative safety of Finland. This entailed a change of identity and appearance: Vladimir Ilyich Lenin became Konstantin Petrovich Ivanov, metalworker from Sestroretsk. He shaved off his moustache and beard and put on a wig, giving him a surprisingly youthful appearance; a worker's cap and blouse completed the disguise. Zinoviev, Emelyanov, Eino Rahja (a Finnish Social Democrat) and the Petrograd Bolshevik, Shotman, accompanied him as far as Levashovo, where Emelyanov and Shotman, who had gone on ahead, were arrested. The others slipped the police net and caught a train to Udelnaya, where they stayed the night. The following evening, Lenin and Rahja (Zinoviev was holed up in a safe house) returned to the local railway crossing and waited. After a while, locomotive number 293 loomed into view. The driver, a friend of Rahja's, stopped the train and helped Lenin aboard. They crossed the frontier undetected, Lenin playing the part of fireman with gusto.

He arrived in Helsingfors on 23 August. On the same day in Petrograd, Alexander Kerensky, now prime minister, was trying to placate his new commander-in-chief, General Kornilov. While Kerensky agreed with the general that measures were needed to restore discipline at the front and strengthen the defences of the capital against a possible German advance, he was not prepared to impose martial law on the railways, as Kornilov insisted was necessary, or to transfer factories producing defence equipment to military control. Their parting was acrimonious. It would have been soured further had Kerensky been able to overhear some of Kornilov's private utterances. It was 'high time to hang the German agents and spies with Lenin at their head,' he confided to his chief of staff; time also 'to disperse the Soviet of Workers' and Soldiers' Deputies and scatter them far and wide'.[145] Buoyed up by widespread conservative support, he began making his own preparations for a show-down with the revolutionaries, moving troops up from the front to within striking distance of Petrograd and talking darkly of the Bolshevik–German threat. Kornilov reckoned he had Kerensky in his pocket and anticipated being brought into the government; Kerensky, on the other hand, suspected Kornilov of plotting to introduce a military dictatorship and, on 9 September, demanded his resignation. Kornilov replied by staging a rebellion.

Unable to consult Lenin for lack of time, the Bolshevik leaders still at large resolved to play a direct role in the Soviet-organized resistance. And despite the set-backs of the July Days, the party proved more effective than any other in rallying forces loyal to the revolution.

In the end, Kornilov's mutiny was put down with ease. The trains carrying his troops from the front were halted some 40 miles (64 km) from the capital by railwaymen pulling up track and refusing to operate signals. Many of the 'rebel' soldiers changed sides on learning the true purpose of Kornilov's mission. The general himself was arrested on 1 September and imprisoned in a monastery near Mogilev.

It was difficult to argue any more that the Bolsheviks were the aiders and abetters of counter-revolution and, in the wake of the mutiny, many of their activists were released from prison and the party's newspapers were allowed to appear again. Lenin's advice arrived too late to make any difference to the outcome, but his supporters took it to heart: 'We are fighting against Kornilov, even *as Kerensky's troops do*, but we do not support Kerensky. *On the contrary*, we expose his weakness . . .'[146]

The events of the summer of 1917 provided Lenin with much food for thought. In the wake of the July Days he had turned his back on the slogan 'All power to the soviets', denounced the Socialist Revolutionaries and Mensheviks as counter-revolutionaries and called for an armed uprising to transfer power directly into the hands of the workers and poor peasants. The Central Committee had debated his theses and decisively rejected them. The Kornilov mutiny induced in him a brief change of mind. He argued that it might still be possible to persuade the other left-wing parties to break with Kerensky's 'bourgeois' government in favour of an exclusively socialist administration responsible to the soviets. This line was much more satisfactory to his colleagues and they endorsed it enthusiastically (and with not a little relief). Their contentment, however, was short-lived. On 28 September, the leader of the Bolsheviks in Finland, Ivar Smilga, arrived in Petrograd with two letters from Lenin. Their contents were disclosed at a Central Committee meeting shortly afterwards. 'We were all aghast', Bukharin later recalled. The voice of moderation had suddenly but irrevocably been discarded; Lenin was breathing fire: 'History will not forgive us if we do not assume power now,' he pleaded. 'Take power at once in Moscow and Petrograd' and 'we will win *absolutely* and *unquestionably* . . . All the objective conditions exist for a successful insurrection'.[147]

At first, the Central Committee wanted to burn both letters; second thoughts prevailed, however, and the originals were retained, though not circulated as Lenin had intended. The majority voted to continue seeking an agreement with the other left-wing parties and to put all talk of insurrection aside.

What had induced Lenin's sudden change of mind? Perhaps the most persuasive factor was undeniable evidence of a strong surge of support for Bolshevik policies, especially among workers and soldiers. On 12 September the Petrograd Soviet had adopted a Bolshevik resolution for the first time; shortly afterwards, the party's brightest new recruit, Leon Trotsky, was elected Chairman of the new Presidium, alongside Rykov and Kamenev. From now on, the Soviet was irreconcilably opposed to the Provisional Government. Bolshevik resolutions were also passed in the Soviets of Moscow and Kiev while the party made substantial gains in municipal elections held about the same time.

Lenin was now living in Helsingfors where his host, the local police chief, Gustav Rovio, provided the perfect cover. Rovio was a Social Democrat who owed his appointment to the March revolution. He used his influence to ensure that Lenin's correspondence reached its destination without resorting to the post office. So far, so good; but Helsingfors was a long way from Petrograd and Lenin needed to keep a close eye on his colleagues. So, on 6 October, disobeying a Central Committee ruling that he should stay put for his own safety, he moved to Vyborg, still in Finland but within striking distance of the Russian capital.

Lenin's letters became increasingly abrasive as he sensed now defiance ('treason'), now evasion ('cowardice') on the part of his colleagues. He tried everything in his attempts to persuade them: reassurance – 'the victory of the insurrection is "now *guaranteed*"; revolutionary sentiment – '*De l'audace, encore de l'audace, et toujours de l'audace!*' [Danton]; threats – 'I am compelled to tender my resignation from the Central Committee'; all to no effect. Their attention was stubbornly focused on the second Congress of Soviets, due to meet on 2 November (later postponed to the 7th). It appeared reasonable to assume, in the light of recent events, that here the Bolsheviks would command a majority. Why not then, revive the slogan 'All power to the soviets' to legitimize their assumption of power? But Lenin would have none of this. In the letter containing his resignation (dated 10 October) he wrote:

> 'To wait' for the Congress of Soviets is idiocy, for the congress *will give nothing* and can give nothing . . . We have thousands of armed workers and soldiers in Petrograd who could immediately seize the Winter Palace, the General Staff Building, the telephone exchange and the large printing presses. If we were to attack at once, suddenly, from three points, Petrograd, Moscow, and the Baltic fleet, the chances are a hundred to one that we would succeed with smaller sacrifices than on July 3–5.[148]

In this scenario, the role of the Congress of Soviets would be simply to confirm the Bolsheviks in power.

Of course, Lenin did not intend his resignation to be taken seriously; nor was it. But he had to open his colleagues' eyes to what they evidently could not see – that the moment they had been waiting for all their lives really had arrived and that to delay, even for an instant, would be fatal.

On 20 October, therefore, 'Konstantin Petrovich Ivanov' materialized in Petrograd at the home of Margarita Fofanova, 1 Serdobolskaya Street. She lived on the fringes of the city, virtually in open country, close to the Finland railway line. Her apartment was on the fifth floor of a perfectly anonymous tenement block. Fofanova, a long-time party member and friend of Nadya's, could be trusted with his life. After a perfunctory greeting, Lenin began issuing instructions. She was to address him as Ivanov. She must remind him to wear his wig whenever he left the privacy of his own room. He must have the newspapers brought to him daily so that he could read them over breakfast. Going over to the window, he inspected the exterior of the building. There was a balcony, with a drain-pipe close by – a possible escape route in an emergency. He expressed himself satisfied.

Lenin now pressed for an early meeting of the Central Committee to hammer out an agreed strategy. Sverdlov, his organizer-in-chief, obliged, summoning the 12 available members to an address on the Karpovka Canal on the evening of 23 October. Shortly before 10 p.m. Lenin arrived in his now-customary disguise, much to the amusement of Kollontai who observed how 'clean-shaven and wearing a wig, he looked every inch the Lutheran minister'. He was received by one of Sverdlov's administrative assistants, Galina Flakserman, who shared the apartment with her husband, the great Menshevik diarist, N. N. Sukhanov. (Sukhanov was spending the night at the office after his wife had solicitously advised him against coming home on account of the bad weather.) On any other occasion, Lenin might have permitted himself a wry smile, but not tonight. Glancing around the table at those keenly attentive faces lit by the single hanging lamp, he sensed that this was going to be a difficult moment. Sverdlov, he could rely on. Stalin? Probably. The 'Muscovites' (Dzerzhinsky, Lomov, Bubnov, Sokolnikov, Iakovleva) were an unknown quantity. How *did* things stand in Moscow? Uritsky, of course, was a former Menshevik. As for Trotsky . . . but Trotsky loved a scrap and, by all accounts, was raring to go. Bravo, comrade Trotsky! His eyes searched the faces of Kamenev and Zinoviev for clues – the latter, shorn of his curly locks and sporting an unaccustomed beard, a disguise that Lenin, at least, had grown used to, looked sheepish. Kamenev, on the other hand, would be a difficult nut to crack . . .

Lenin spoke for an hour, quietly but forcefully putting the case for insurrection. He upbraided his colleagues for their 'indifference' at a time when (according to rumour) the government was intending to surrender Petrograd to the Germans without a fight. Even the possibility that the cradle of the revolution might fall into the hands of imperialists was unthinkable; they must act at once. To wait for the Constituent Assembly, as some comrades were advocating, was, in Lenin's opinion, suicidal – the voting will 'obviously not be with us'. The cards, he argued, were stacked in their favour. The international situation had never looked brighter (there had been one or two small-scale mutinies in the German fleet), while Bolshevik support at home had grown in leaps and bounds. He urged them, pleaded with them to direct every ounce of their energies towards insurgency and nothing but insurgency. In a final effort to jolt them out of their complacency, he suggested that the springboard for the uprising should – *must* – be the Northern Region Congress of Soviets, due to meet the following day!

Lomov was the first to respond, with some background information on the situation in Moscow; Yakovleva and Uritsky followed. Suddenly, there was a knock at the door. Twelve revolutionary hearts simultaneously skipped a beat, but it was only Sukhanova's brother with the samovar. The debate dragged on until well after dawn, Kamenev and Zinoviev alone voicing principled opposition to Lenin. As the tide of opinion seemed to be going his way, he tore a page from a school exercise-book and began scribbling out a resolution in pencil. It was put to the vote and adopted 10–2. Insurrection was now the order of the day. After a hearty breakfast of black bread, sausage and cheese, the bleary-eyed delegates wandered out into the cold drizzle. With decorous chivalry, Dzerzhinsky offered Lenin his overcoat; the latter was forced to accept as a matter of party discipline: 'It's an order of the Central Committee, Comrade!'[149]

A week passed. The Northern Region Congress of Soviets came and went, but no insurrection was set in train. Then, on the night of 29 October, Lenin was summoned to the premises of the Lesnoi district duma, on the outskirts of Petrograd, for a second meeting of senior Bolsheviks and made to go through the whole performance again. He reiterated, in even more forceful terms, that 'Power must be seized immediately, at once'. But it emerged from the discussion which followed that both workers' and soldiers' leaders were sceptical about their ability to mobilize the masses for street action. Everyone was pinning their hopes on the second Congress of Soviets. The reports of the rank-and-file activists gave Kamenev and Zinoviev additional ammunition to hurl at Lenin. Kamenev even tried to have the previous resolution overturned. However, in the end the original decision was endorsed, though without committing the party to a specific tactical plan or timetable. Kamenev immediately resigned from the Central Committee.

Lenin left the meeting in a blind rage. Eino Rakhia, who accompanied him everywhere at that time, recalled: 'The wind tore Lenin's hat from his head but he didn't even notice because he was so upset by Zinoviev's and Kamenev's stand against him'.[150]

Two days later, Lenin was called to the telephone and told that the two renegades, having been unable to get their views published in the Bolshevik Press, had turned to Gorky's newspaper, *Novaya Zhizn*. The terms of the statement brought to public attention the kind of action the party was contemplating. The cat had been let out of the bag.

Lenin's response was swift. He demanded their immediate expulsion from the party. At the same time, he summoned his military experts, Vladimir Nevsky, Nikolai Podvoisky and Vladimir Antonov-Ovseenko, to a secret meeting in an apartment on Serdobolskaya Street, only a stone's throw from his own hide-out. With scarcely suppressed impatience, he heard out their excuses: the Petrograd garrison could not be counted on; only 3,000 sailors were immediately available; the Red Guard units had more or less evaporated . . . All three agreed that they would need more time, at least another ten days to two weeks, if there was to be a realistic hope of success. Lenin brushed their objections aside. The insurrection must begin tomorrow or the next day, he insisted. His lieutenants left the meeting encouraged but not a little bewildered by their leader's supreme self-assurance; it was difficult to see what could be done in the space of just two or three days.

In fact, Lenin was no longer relying on the Military Organization to carry out his plans. At the end of October, the government suddenly announced its intention to move the greater part of the garrison to the front, seeming to confirm rumours about the imminent surrender of Petrograd. The Soviet responded by forming its own organization to defend the revolution, the Military Revolutionary Committee. Charged with the task of arming workers and arranging the deployment of troops to guard the city, its members included three prominent Bolsheviks: Trotsky, Antonov-Ovseenko and Podvoisky. The committee did carry out genuine defensive functions but it had simultaneously been hijacked by the Bolsheviks for their own purposes: its premises on the third floor of the Smolny Institute now became the insurrectionists' headquarters.

The threat to remove the garrison troops to the front had the effect of turning them decisively against the government; this was crucial in strengthening the authority of the Military Revolutionary Committee and, by association, the Bolsheviks. On the night of 3 November a deputation of committee members went to see the Commander of the Petrograd Military District, General Polkovnikov, to inform him that in future all orders would require their approval. Two days later, after much deliberation, units stationed at the Peter–Paul Fortress voted overwhelmingly to place themselves and their weapons at the disposal of the committee. With the city's major arsenal now in their hands and the fortress guns aimed directly across the Neva at the Winter Palace, the would-be insurgents had made a critical advance.

Tuesday 6 November was cold, damp and grey; a fine drizzle moistened and muddied the streets and back alleys of the capital. Everyone went about their business more or less as usual, stopping only to pick up the latest edition of the newspaper or to read the notices which appeared on every available wall and hoarding. To the ordinary inhabitant, the situation was confusing but, at the same time, strangely fascinating. As the American journalist, John Reed, recalled:

At the corner of the Morskaya and the Nevsky, squads of soldiers with fixed bayonets were stopping all private automobiles, turning out the

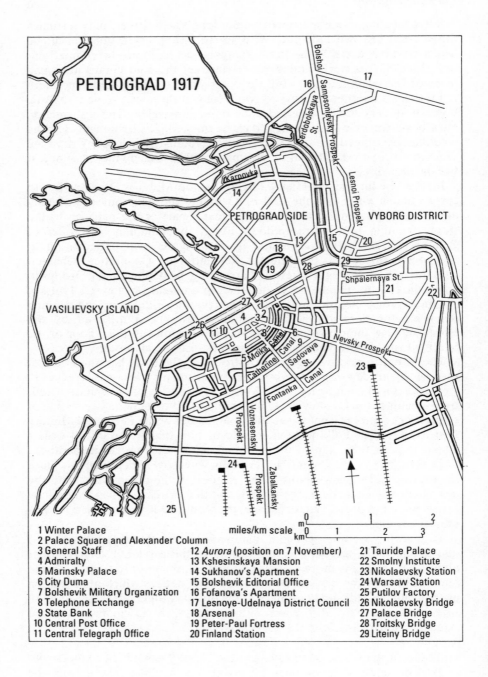

PETROGRAD 1917

Bolshoi

Sampsonievsky Prospekt

16

17

Serdobolskaya St.

Lesnoi Prospekt

Karpovka

14

PETROGRAD SIDE

VYBORG DISTRICT

13

15

20

18

28

29

19

Shpalernaya St.

21

22

VASILIEVSKY ISLAND

27

7

26

4

3

2

12

11 10

8

6

5 Moika

9

Sadovaya St.

Nevsky Prospekt

23

Catherine Canal

Fontanka Canal

Voznesensky Prospekt

Zabalkansky Prospekt

N

24

25

miles/km scale

0   1   2
m
0   1   2   3
km

1 Winter Palace
2 Palace Square and Alexander Column
3 General Staff
4 Admiralty
5 Marinsky Palace
6 City Duma
7 Bolshevik Military Organization
8 Telephone Exchange
9 State Bank
10 Central Post Office
11 Central Telegraph Office

12 *Aurora* (position on 7 November)
13 Kshesinskaya Mansion
14 Sukhanov's Apartment
15 Bolshevik Editorial Office
16 Fofanova's Apartment
17 Lesnoye-Udelnaya District Council
18 Arsenal
19 Peter-Paul Fortress
20 Finland Station

21 Tauride Palace
22 Smolny Institute
23 Nikolaevsky Station
24 Warsaw Station
25 Putilov Factory
26 Nikolaevsky Bridge
27 Palace Bridge
28 Troitsky Bridge
29 Liteiny Bridge

occupants, and ordering them towards the Winter Palace. A large crowd had gathered to watch them. Nobody knew whether the soldiers belonged to the Government or the Military Revolutionary Committee. Up in front of the Kazan Cathedral the same thing was happening, machines being directed back up the Nevsky. Five or six sailors with rifles came along, laughing excitedly, and fell into conversation with two of the soldiers. On the sailors' hat bands were *Aurora* and *Zaria Svobody* – the names of the leading Bolshevik cruisers of the Baltic Fleet. One of them said, 'Kronstadt is coming!'[151]

Yet the population was so used to the military comings and goings that the more important developments passed almost unnoticed. At about noon, 200 greatcoated figures, wearing grey fur hats and carrying rifles on their shoulders, filed into Palace Square. They were members of the Women's Shock battalion, sent to reinforce the regular guard. During the afternoon they were joined by cadets, dragging artillery pieces into the huge forecourt. This was all part of Kerensky's belated attempts to win back the initiative. Pale, thin and nervous, his bristled hair standing on end, the prime minister hardly cut a reassuring figure as he rushed backwards and forwards between the General Staff Building and the Marinsky Palace, dispatching urgent telephone messages to the front, addressing parliamentary delegates; issuing orders to close down the Bolshevik newspapers, to arrest the members of the Military Revolutionary Committee, to have the bridges across the Neva raised to prevent workers crossing over from the industrial districts. It was all so much sound and fury . . .

Late in the afternoon, the Military Revolutionary Committee went into action, taking control of the Central Telegraph Office, the Baltic Station and the Petrograd News Agency. Earlier, cadets sent to guard the Palace Bridge had been surrounded by an angry crowd and marched back to barracks.

At about 4 p.m. it began to get dark and the temperature dropped sharply. As the street lights came on, banks, shops and offices closed and streams of workers went home early, packing the grimy, red-liveried trams as they trundled their way up and down the Nevsky Prospekt. Later on, the city streets filled up again with their regular evening traffic. Elegantly dressed men and women began arriving at the Alexandrinsky Theatre, eager to see Meyerhold's production of Alexei Tolstoy's play, *The Death of Ivan the Terrible*. Music lovers made their way to the Marinsky to see Chaliapin in *Boris Godunov*. The Restaurant de Paris and A l'Ours began serving dinner. Cinemas, cafés, bars, night-clubs, all opened at the customary hour. Everything was unremarkable.

In the living-room of Fofanova's apartment meanwhile, Lenin was pacing up and down like a caged tiger. All day long he had been pleading with his colleagues to allow him to go to the Smolny Institute, but to no avail. He began to suspect their motives for ordering him to stay at home.

Were they really concerned about his safety or had they lost their nerve? At about 6 p.m. he grabbed a notepad and scribbled a final message to anyone who would listen:

> We must at all costs, this very evening, this very night, arrest the government . . . We must not wait! We may lose everything! . . . History will not forgive revolutionaries for delays, when they could be victorious today (and will certainly be victorious today) while they risk losing much tomorrow, while they risk losing everything. If we seize power today, we seize it not against the soviets but for them.

He folded the note and asked Fofanova to take it to Krupskaya 'and no one else'.[152]

Shortly after 10 p.m., Eino Rakhia arrived with the news that the bridges had been raised. Lenin took this to be the signal that the insurrection was under way and decided to go to Smolny in person. Seeing that all protests were in vain, Rakhia insisted on accompanying him. The two of them then slipped quietly out of the house. They were just in time to catch the last tram returning to the depot. There were no other passengers but, to Rakhia's horror, Lenin immediately began chatting to the conductress. Despite his heavy disguise, his voice was *bound* to give him away. As luck would have it, the woman turned out to be a Bolshevik supporter who proudly informed Lenin that there was a revolution in progress. As the tramcar began to fork away from the Finland Station, her two curious passengers alighted and disappeared into the night.

They crossed the Liteiny Bridge unchallenged and proceeded along Shpalernaya Street, past the House of Preliminary Detention where Lenin had been imprisoned 20 years earlier. It was a clear, moonlit night but ice cold. A sharp wind swept across the Neva, numbing the upper half of Lenin's face (the lower half was covered by a bandage – part of the disguise) and making his eyes water. Suddenly, they were stopped by two cadets on horseback who demanded to see their papers. Rakhia pretended not to understand, digging deep into his pockets for the revolvers he had hidden there, while Lenin began to walk on ahead. The soldiers took them for drunks and, spurring their horses, rode off into the night. At last, the two revolutionaries approached the front entrance of the institute. Pushing past the crowd, they showed their passes to the sentries who looked nonplussed. The passes were out of date and, not recognizing Lenin, they refused to let him through. Rakhia had to create a diversion to enable both of them to slip past. The forecourt was cluttered with trucks, armoured cars and motorcycles. There was a machine-gun placement on either side of the front entrance.

Lenin went directly upstairs. The dimly lit corridors were crowded with men and women in a hurry: unshaven, dishevelled men in collars and ties shouting instructions, secretaries delivering messages, bearded soldiers with rifles slung over their shoulders, Red Guards leaving at the double on a special assignment. No one had time to notice the little man in the strange garb as he walked straight into the offices of the Military Revolutionary Committee. Rakhia was dispatched at once to fetch Trotsky, while Lenin sized up the situation. He began to take over immediately, poking his head round one door after another to check on how things were going.

The news became more encouraging as the night progressed. At 2 a.m. an engineer battalion occupied the Nikolaevsky Station, thus securing the route to Moscow. The power station was taken shortly afterwards. At about 3.30 a.m. the cruiser *Aurora* anchored alongside the Palace Bridge. The State Bank was occupied at about 6 a.m. and the telephone exchange an hour later. At 8 a.m. the Warsaw Station fell to the insurgents, cutting off the route to army headquarters at Pskov. Later that morning, political detainees were released from the Kresty Prison and, at about 2 p.m., the fleet sailed in from Kronstadt. There had been remarkably little fighting throughout the night and relatively few casualties.

The first meeting of the Bolshevik Central Committee to take place after the Revolution was held early on the morning of 7 November in Room 36 on the first floor of the Smolny Institute. The proceedings were constantly interrupted by couriers bringing updates on the situation, but Lenin was immune to every distraction. Now he wanted to know why no action had yet been taken to seize the Winter Palace and to arrest the members of the Provisional Government. At the end of the discussion, he began matching names to ministerial responsibilities. 'Minister', everyone felt, had a decidedly bourgeois flavour.

'What about "People's Commissar"?' Trotsky suggested. Lenin was delighted.

'Yes, that's *very* good, it smells of revolution. And we can call the government itself "the Council of People's Commissars".'[153]

Shortly after the meeting dispersed, Lenin drafted his first manifesto: 'To the Citizens of Russia', informing the population, in the name of the Military Revolutionary Committee, that the Provisional Government had been overthrown. A few hours later, Trotsky opened an emergency session of the Petrograd Soviet with an account of the events of the previous night. He was followed by Lenin himself, who was greeted by cheers and a thundering ovation. Bleary-eyed and unshaven, his voice almost hoarse, he told the enthusiastic delegates what they wanted to hear. The war would end immediately. The landlords' estates would be broken up. Workers would be given control over production. There was more cheering as he departed, anxious to get down to the business of drafting decrees.

The opening session of the Congress of Soviets was due to begin at 2 p.m., but Lenin argued for its postponement until the Winter Palace had fallen and the members of the Provisional Government were safely under lock and key. He had been assured by Podvoisky that the palace would fall at noon, then 3 p.m., then 6 p.m. By 10.30 p.m. it was clear that the congress would have to go ahead with the Winter Palace still under siege.

John Reed was with the delegates waiting in the Assembly Hall of the Smolny Institute:

> In the row of seats, under the white chandeliers, packed immovably in the aisles and on the sides, the representatives of the workers and soldiers of all Russia waited in anxious silence or wild exultation the ringing of the chairman's bell. There was no heat in the hall but the stifling heat of unwashed human bodies. A foul blue cloud of cigarette smoke rose from the mass and hung in the air. Occasionally someone in authority mounted the tribune and asked the comrades not to smoke; then everybody, smokers and all, took up the cry 'Don't smoke, comrades!' and went on smoking . . . It was 10.40 p.m. Dan, a mild-faced, baldish figure in a shapeless military surgeon's uniform, was ringing the ball. Silence fell sharply, intense, broken by the scuffling and disputing of the people at the door.[154]

After causing an uproar by making a pointed reference to the fate of party comrades under bombardment in the Winter Palace, Dan formally opened the Congress and passed on to the first item on the agenda – the election of the Presidium. The majority of the delegates (300 out of 670) were Bolsheviks, and this was reflected in the composition of the new Presidium. Thunderous applause now broke out as Trotsky, Lunacharsky, Kollontai, Rykov, Nogin, Ryazanov, Krylenko, Kamenev and Zinoviev took their positions on the platform. Kamenev (whose treason to the party had been forgiven but not forgotten by Lenin) was elected chairman to replace Dan.

Suddenly, a hoarse, almost hysterical voice could be heard above the general din. It was Martov.

> What are they doing there, what are they doing there? [he shouted pointing at the Bolshevik-dominated Presidium] The civil war is beginning, comrades! The first question must be a peaceful settlement of the crisis. On principle and from a political standpoint we must urgently discuss a means of averting civil war. Our brothers are being shot down in the streets! At this moment, when before the opening of the Congress of Soviets the question of power is being settled by means of a military plot organised by one of the revolutionary Parties.[155]

He went on to demand an all-socialist coalition as the only means of ending the bloodshed – a proposal warmly received, even by the Bolsheviks. But now the atmosphere began to change as one after another of Martov's more moderate colleagues rose to denounce the Bolsheviks' 'criminal political venture' and to demand mobilization against it. Uproar ensued. To the accompaniment of jeers, catcalls and whistles, the majority of Menshevik and Socialist Revolutionary delegates walked out of the hall, strengthening the position of the Bolsheviks in the process. Soon afterwards, Trotsky rose to speak. He thundered against those who had criticized the actions of his newly adopted party:

What has happened is an insurrection, and not a conspiracy . . . The masses of the people followed our banner, and our insurrection was victorious. And now we are told: renounce your victory, make concessions, compromise. With whom? I ask: with whom ought we to compromise? With those wretched groups who have left us? . . . No, here no compromise is possible. To those who have left and to those who tell us to do this we must say: you are miserable bankrupts, your role is played out; go where you ought to go: into the dustbin of history![156]

'Then we'll leave!' rejoindered Martov and there was a second walk-out.

By now it was the early hours of the morning and Kamenev called a brief adjournment. When the delegates reassembled, they were told that the members of the Provisional Government had been arrested and imprisoned. There was general dismay when they heard that Kerensky had already left for the front. Lunacharsky then rose to present Lenin's political programme:

To All Workers Soldiers and Peasants

The Soviet authority will at once propose a democratic peace to all nations and an immediate armistice on all fronts. It will safeguard the transfer without compensation of all land – landlord, imperial and monastery – to the peasants' committees; it will defend the soldiers' rights, introducing a complete democratisation of the army; it will establish workers' control over industry; it will ensure the convocation of the Constituent Assembly on the date set; it will supply the cities with bread and the villages with articles of first necessity; and it will secure to all nationalities inhabiting Russia the right of self-determination . . . Long live the revolution![157]

Lenin had retired to Bonch-Bruevich's apartment near Smolny to catch up on some sleep. Sometime later Bonch awoke to find the light still on. Lenin was sitting at the desk, hand on head, writing furiously. There was so much to be done.

9

Dictatorship of the proletariat

Shortly after 9.30 on the morning of 7 November 1918, Lenin left his office
in the Kremlin to attend the celebrations marking the first anniversary of
the Bolshevik Revolution. He was joined in the short walk across Red
Square to the Bolshoi Theatre by a bearded and bespectacled figure
wearing the brown leather jacket of a party activist. This was Sverdlov,
now at 32, President of the infant Soviet republic. Outside the theatre, they
were met by a delegation from the All-Russian Congress of Soviets which
accompanied them to an adjoining square, where Lenin was to unveil a
temporary monument to Marx and Engels. The rather coarse-looking
statue, which sharp-witted Muscovites would later nickname 'Cyril and
Methodius' after the founding fathers of the Russian Orthodox Church,
was the outcome of a fierce directive sent by Lenin to the Commissar for
Enlightenment, Lunacharsky, only three weeks previously:

> I heard today Vinogradov's report on the busts and monuments, and am
> utterly outraged; nothing has been done for months; to this day there is
> not a single bust; the disappearance of the bust of Radishchev is a farce.
> There is no bust of Marx on public display, nothing has been done in the
> way of propaganda by putting up inscriptions in the streets. I reprimand
> you for this criminal and lackadaisical attitude, and demand that the
> names of all responsible persons should be sent to me for prosecution.
> Shame on the saboteurs and thoughtless loafers![158]

Fortunately for Lunacharsky, the unveiling went off without a hitch. After
a short address, the procession moved off in the direction of Red Square to
the accompaniment of the 'Marseillaise', 'The Internationale' and the
'Funeral March'. At the Kremlin wall, Lenin unveiled another memorial, a
bas-relief dedicated to 'the fallen in the struggle for peace and the
brotherhood of peoples' before mounting the rostrum to deliver his major
speech of the day. His voice, tremulous and slightly hoarse, his hands now
thrust into the pockets of his overcoat, now released to grip the rim of the

podium, his feet shuffling back and forth, driving him forward like a piston, Lenin warmed to his theme:

Let us honour the memory of the October fighters by taking an oath before their monument, to follow in their footsteps and imitate their fearlessness and heroism. Let their rallying cry be our rallying cry, the cry of the rebel workers of all countries. The cry of: 'victory or death!'

Then followed the first 7 November parade of the Soviet regime. Columns of workers, chanting slogans and carrying portraits of Marx or red banners with gold-lettered inscriptions, alternated with soldiers of the newly formed Red Army which Lenin promised to turn into an awesome military machine some three million strong.

The formalities concluded, the Revolution's greatest son left his place on the reviewing stand and returned with studied unobtrusiveness to his office in the Kremlin.

He entered a room which was remarkable only for its modesty. In the centre was a plain wooden desk and a conference table with a green baize cloth, around which were stationed three or four leather armchairs. The floor was only partly, and rather shamefacedly, covered by a worn carpet. The walls were lined with bookcases, a large map, several portraits (Marx of course being the most prominent) and a clock which kept bad time. A notice warned 'No Smoking'. Everything here was as neat and well-ordered as the rooms of his childhood. His desk was another matter. Lenin sighed and shook his head as his eyes fell on the pile of ribbon-bound folders which had materialized in the course of his brief absence. The desk top was cluttered: the current edition of *Pravda* rested precariously on a pile of books he had marked for his attention, partly obscuring the official papers, classified according to various degrees of urgency; pens; stiletto-sharp pencils which he habitually used to fire off memos and instructions to colleagues ('Read through, grasp, follow through *speedily* and let me know the result'); calendars; scissors; a mother-of-pearl paper knife; an inkstand; glue . . . Pushed to the edge was his favourite piece of bric-à-brac: the iron figure of an ape studying an oversized human skull. Sitting down, Lenin grabbed the folders, placed them at his feet and began sifting through the ream of teletype messages which had just been brought to him. Presently, the closest to hand of five telephones began ringing with a jarring sound he was coming increasingly to dislike. He answered the call, shouting and gesticulating at the disembodied voice as though its owner were standing next to him. Then, setting down the receiver, he began writing. From time to time his secretaries entered the room, speaking only if they were spoken to. He asked one of them, Lydia Fotieva perhaps, to send off a message on the Hughes telegraph to Trotsky, asking for the latest on the military situation in Astrakhan. Once more he took up his pen, but the words simply would not come. He summoned up one final effort at concentration before surrendering. Leaning back in his chair, he allowed his mind to wander back to those first frenzied weeks in power.

It was 5 January and the Constituent Assembly had finally gathered in Petrograd. Life in the capital had become intolerable, even grotesque. There was cake and chocolate to eat (for those who could afford it) but no bread. People sat around in hats and overcoats because of the lack of fuel. There was scarcely enough electricity to keep even Smolny in business. There was no public transport. Snow had been piling up in the streets for weeks and the bodies of dead horses froze where they had fallen, emaciated and exhausted. Only crime flourished.

From day one there had been stubborn opposition to Soviet power: some of it open, some of it insidious. A strike by Civil Servants. A threatened strike by railwaymen. Menshevik- and Socialist-Revolutionary sponsored committees of public safety springing up everywhere. Then there were the saboteurs, the speculators, the priests, the landlords and the capitalists to contend with. Then the military threat: Krasnov about to attack Petrograd; Dutov poised to invade the Urals; Kaledin's Cossacks encamped on the Don; Kornilov, Denikin, Alekseev and the other tsarist generals on the loose in the south; nationalist forces in the Ukraine; White forces in Finland; Romanian forces threatening Bessarabia; German forces consolidating in the Baltic. In this context, the Constituent Assembly was just one more fortress to storm.

He had been expecting trouble ever since the elections when the Socialist Revolutionaries had won a landslide victory – 400 seats against the Bolsheviks' 175. To intimidate the opposition, he ordered the arrest of the Kadets (and one or two right-wing Socialist Revolutionaries for good measure) and closed down their newspapers. Then, on the eve of the Assembly's opening, he summoned reinforcements from Helsingfors and Vyborg and assigned his ever-dependable Latvian riflemen to patrol the approaches to the Tauride Palace.

Late in the morning of the 5th, Bonch-Bruevich called with the news that Red Guards had opened fire on demonstrators trying to pass down the Liteiny Prospekt. (Another Bloody Sunday, Gorky would later call it). Lenin asked to be kept informed, before leaving Smolny by car with Nadya and Manyasha. There was little sign of trouble when he arrived at the Tauride Palace, but he was advised all the same to enter by a back door.

At 4 p.m. the Bolshevik delegation finally entered the hall. From his place in the government box, Lenin kept a weather-eye on the debates but took no part in them. He recalled being amused by the sailors in the gallery taking imaginary pot-shots at the delegates below. And why not? They were showing their contempt for an anachronism, a bourgeois parliament. In the soviets they had found something better, a higher, more perfect form of democracy. Good for them!

Lenin left the box at regular intervals to communicate with his officials.

There had been another matter on his mind that day – the whereabouts of two goods trains bringing desperately needed provisions of bread and coal up to Petrograd from Kharkov. He spoke to Skrypnik about it. He remembered meeting some other people in the corridors: Petrovsky and the American comrades, Reed and Williams (they had discussed the best way of learning foreign languages). Petrovsky (an old hand from the fourth Duma) asked him what he thought of the performance: 'Boring!'

At 10 p.m. the Central Committee met to review the situation. About an hour later, someone brought the news that the assembly had refused to endorse the 'Declaration of the Rights of the Toiling and Exploited Peoples', a formulation of the Bolshevik programme which had been presented earlier in the day by Sverdlov. That decided it. Lenin immediately wrote out a draft resolution stating his party's intention to withdraw from the assembly forthwith. Then, at about 1 a.m., he called an emergency meeting of Sovnarkom, the Council of People's Commissars. After some argument, he succeeded in convincing his colleagues that a Bolshevik walk-out would not be enough; it was necessary to send all the delegates packing – preferably without resorting to violence – on the grounds that they were conducting 'the most rabid struggle against Soviet power'. He gave the necessary orders to the commander of the guard, Zheleznyakov.

They told him later that the delegates had refused to leave the building, even after two 'requests'. Zheleznyakov had responded by turning off the lights. By 5.30 a.m. the building was empty. When the deputies returned that morning, they found all the entrances to the palace barred by troops . . .

There was a knock at the door. It was one of his secretaries with a telegram just received from the front. Her face was wreathed in smiles – it *must* be good news. Taking it from her hand, he began reading: VALIANT TROOPS OF SECOND ARMY SEND HEARTY CONGRATULATIONS ON GREAT ANNIVERSARY AND REPORT: IZHEVSK TAKEN BY STORM TODAY 17.40 PM SHORIN GUSEV SHTERNBERG.

Lenin dictated his reply before leaving his desk to study the map on the wall.

The military situation had deteriorated further since the time of the Constituent Assembly. General Krasnov's Cossack forces had recaptured the Don from the Reds and were making incursions into the neighbouring provinces. The Volunteer Army of General Denikin occupied the entire Kuban, severing communications between the Caucasus and the Soviet heartland. The Urals and part of the Volga were controlled by Komuch (Committee of Members of the Constituent Assembly), a Socialist Revolutionary alternative government whose forces included former Czech prisoners of war from the Austro-Hungarian Army. Siberia was another hotbed of opposition to Soviet rule, with Japanese and British forces in Vladivostok, a Provisional All-Russian Government, backed by

Cossacks and the (White) Siberian Army, in Omsk and an anti-Soviet administration in Tomsk.

Despite all this, Lenin was in an optimistic frame of mind on that Friday in November 1918. Central Europe was in turmoil following the defeat of Germany and Austria-Hungary, offering the best prospect yet of international socialist revolution. Only the previous day, Lenin had told the Soviet delegates meeting in the Bolshoi Theatre: 'Germany has caught fire and Austria is burning out of control'. More immediately, the end of the war meant the withdrawal of German forces from Russian soil.

One of his first actions on coming to power had been to offer *all* the combatants a 'just' and 'democratic' peace, based on the right of all nations to self-determination. The Allies had reacted scornfully, but the Germans, anxious to release their troops for redeployment on the western front, agreed to open negotiations and an armistice was signed in December 1917. The Russians did not intend the negotiations to be taken seriously; they were expecting revolution to break out in Western Europe at any moment, following their own example. However, by January, when the Germans presented their terms, no more than rumblings were discernible. To the consternation of most of his colleagues, Lenin recommended acceptance, even though this entailed the loss of Poland, Lithuania and western Latvia. He was overruled. Instead, Trotsky, who as Foreign Commissar headed the Soviet delegation, returned to Brest-Litovsk with a startling reply: Russia rejected the terms but was unilaterally declaring an end to the war. The response of the German Commander-in-Chief, General Hoffmann, was predictable – '*unerhort!*' (unheard of). On 18 February hostilities were renewed and the Germans marched, virtually unopposed, deep into Soviet territory. Within five days they had covered 125 miles (200 km), capturing Pskov, Narva, Minsk and Mogilev. The Soviets relented but the Germans now wanted more. Russia would lose Poland, Lithuania and western Latvia outright. Her troops were to withdraw from Estonia, Finland and the southern Transcaucasus (opening the way to secession) and the entire Ukraine was to become autonomous. This added up to one-third of all her arable land (most importantly the huge grain reserves of the Ukraine), one-third of her factories, three-quarters of her iron and coal deposits and more than 60 million of her citizens. To cap it all, Germany demanded a huge indemnity.

At 10.30 a.m. on 23 February 1918, the Central Committee met to discuss the new terms. A faction of 'Left Communists', led by Bukharin, argued passionately against signing the treaty. They called instead for a war of revolutionary defence, believing that a show of heroism in the face of overwhelming odds would be enough to provoke an uprising by German workers. Lenin was unmoved. He acknowledged that the peace was 'shameful' but begged his comrades to face up to reality: 'Stop the policy of revolutionary phrasemongering,' he urged, 'or you will be signing the death warrant of Soviet power within three weeks.' He denied losing faith in proletarian internationalism but insisted on the need to 'concede space in order to win time'. The debate dragged on for three-and-a-half hours with tempers and emotions running high (Bukharin was close to tears). Sensing that the tide of opinion was going against him and fearing that this would mean the end of the revolution in Russia, Lenin played his last card. He threatened to resign – and this time he was serious. It was enough; the terms were accepted by seven votes to four.

As soon as the meeting was over, Lenin remembered hurrying out to instruct the operators of the radio station at Tsarskoe Selo to be ready to transmit messages between the German and Soviet Governments throughout the night. The Peace of Brest-Litovsk was eventually signed on 3 March 1918 and ratified by the party and by the Congress of Soviets several days later. Late on the night of the 12th, the government left Petrograd for the comparative safety of Moscow.

The telephone had begun ringing again. It was Bonch-Bruevich, reminding him about the concert-meeting he had promised to attend at the Lubyanka that evening, organized by employees of the Cheka, the security police. He looked at his watch.– yes, it was time to be going. After tidying his papers, he went to collect his overcoat and to say goodnight to the office staff. His chauffeur, Stepan Gil, was waiting for him by the car. He gave an involuntary start as Gil swung open the door, a reaction that was now habitual with him. As he settled into the back seat, the memories of that terrible day in August came flooding back . . .

The atmosphere in Moscow had been tense. It was only a few weeks since the Left Socialist Revolutionaries had assassinated the German Ambassador, Count Mirbach, and then tried to seize power. The revolt had been put down but it was a close run thing and a chilling reminder of the government's vulnerability, even in its own capital.

The 30 August too began with an assassination. This time the victim was Moisei Uritsky, Chairman of the Petrograd Cheka. Everyone around Lenin panicked, fearing this might be the signal for yet another coup attempt, but he was far too busy to give the matter much thought. He spent the morning dealing with the mound of paperwork awaiting his signature – the minutes of the previous day's cabinet meeting, a request from the military to authorize the requisitioning of cars for the front, something about the reorganization of the Commissariat for Health, a decree calling up doctors for military service, another repudiating agreements between the Tsar's Government and Germany. He also had to send a telegram reprimanding a junior officer for requisitioning a writing-desk from a station-master on the Ryazan-Urals railway without the necessary authorization. Did they really need to bother him with this kind of thing?

Manyasha joined him for lunch and pleaded with him to cancel his engagements for the rest of the day, but he brushed her concerns aside. His first appointment was at the Corn Exchange in the Basmannaya district. This was followed by a long drive across the city to the Michelson armaments plant, where he arrived at about 6.30 p.m. He addressed the workers for an hour on the theme 'Two powers: the workers' dictatorship and the dictatorship of the bourgeoisie'. The place was packed and he had difficulty finding his way out through the crowd. Every few steps someone would stop him with a greeting, or question, or complaint (there were many complaints). Finally he reached the car. Even now they would not let him get away; two women began arguing with him about food requisitioning. He spoke to them for some minutes, trying to calm them down. Then he turned away. He watched as Gil leaned across the passenger seat to open the car door. Suddenly there was an ear-splitting explosion behind him. Then another . . . then another. He felt a searing pain in his chest as he began to stagger, then fall. Lying on the ground, gasping for breath, he could hear them shouting and screaming: 'They've killed him', 'They've shot Lenin.' As Gil helped him into the car, he asked who had shot him, but no one stood still long enough to answer. Gil too was close to panic, waving his gun wildly with his free hand. He asked to be taken home. He remembered refusing to allow them to carry him up the stairs, feeling that if he surrendered now he would surely die. When Manyasha saw the blood on his shirt, she began to weep. They laid him on the bed. There were people rushing about everywhere, looking for bandages and medicines. Fortunately, Bonch's wife was there to give him a morphine injection. Sverdlov came in, then Lunacharsky, whom he told off for gawping. He was still conscious when they brought Nadya into him. She was grief-stricken and he felt sorry for her. 'You must be tired,' he told her. 'Go and lie down.' Then the surgeon Mints and his team began to operate.

Lenin had been shot three times. One bullet tore through his jacket and hit a bystander, a second lodged in his shoulder. The third entered his left arm, skirted his lung and just failed to penetrate the arteries in his neck. His heart was displaced in the process, causing severe internal bleeding and giving him persistent difficulties with breathing. For some time his condition was critical, but he eventually pulled through. Lenin's assassin, Fanya Kaplan-Roid, was executed almost immediately. Her death was followed by a campaign of 'Red Terror' in which hundreds, possibly thousands, died. Civil war had arrived with a vengeance.

In January 1919 Lenin left Moscow for a short holiday in the Sokolniki Woods to the north of the city. Krupskaya, now Deputy Commissar for Enlightenment, was visiting a school there and Lenin was to join her. As he was driving through the suburbs, several men ran out into the road and, brandishing revolvers, ordered the car to stop. Gil himself takes up the story:

Vladimir Ilyich opened the door:
  'What's the matter?', he asked.
  One of the attackers bellowed:
  'Get out! Shut up!'

He grabbed Vladimir Ilyich by his sleeve and pulled him out. Completely baffled, Ilyich repeated:

'What's the matter, comrades? Who are you?' and he reached to get out his pass.

Maria Ilychna [Manyasha] and Com. Chebanov also got out of the car, without understanding what was going on. Two robbers stood on either side of Vladimir Ilyich pointing their revolvers at his forehead.

'Don't move!'

Another man, facing Vladimir Ilyich, grabbed the lapels of his coat drawing them aside with a swift professional gesture, pulled out of the pocket of his jacket a wallet with documents and a small Browning.

The attackers then ordered Gil out of the car, climbed in themselves and drove off. Gil and his three passengers (Chebanov still clutching the jug of milk he had been carrying) made their way on foot to the local House of Soviets which was, fortunately, just up the road. The night watchman at first refused to allow them in but quickly changed his tune when Gil produced his papers. They were ushered past a dozing telephonist and introduced to the deputy in charge, who immediately phoned the Lubyanka for another car. Gil again:

Those at the other end of the line must have been wondering whether the whole affair had a political meaning, since Lenin added:

'No, no, no, certainly not political . . . if it had been, they would have shot me immediately. It was robbery, pure and simple.'[159]

The Chairman of the Council of People's Commissars held up by criminals on the streets of his own capital – and right under the nose of the local soviet! Alas, such incidents were all too typical of life inside 'Sovdepia' (a derogatory term coined by the Whites for the territory remaining under Bolshevik control). At the end of 1918, Sovdepia contained about 30 of the former Russian Empire's 50 provinces, an area of approximately one million square miles (2.6 million sq km) and 60 million inhabitants. But Soviet authority was precarious even here. The frontiers of Sovdepia fluctuated with the ebb and flow of the civil war. Communications between Moscow and the periphery were continually breaking down. Transport was paralysed. Key agricultural and industrial regions had either been lost to the enemy or were still being hotly contested. In the cities, essential services had virtually ceased to exist and diseases such as typhoid, cholera and scarlet fever were endemic. Nor was there any hope of succour from a universally hostile outside world. Life had descended to the most primitive level, as this extract from Pasternak's *Doctor Zhivago* makes abundantly clear:

Train after train, abandoned by the Whites, stood idle, stopped by the defeat of Kolchak, by running out of fuel and by snow drifts. Immobilised for good and buried in the snow, they stretched almost uninterruptedly for miles on end. Some of them served as fortresses for armed bands of robbers or as hideouts for escaping criminals or political fugitives – the involuntary vagrants of those days – but most of them were communal mortuaries, mass graves of the victims of the cold and typhus raging all along the railway line and mowing down whole villages in its neighbourhood.[160]

In these harrowing circumstances, Lenin was preoccupied not with building socialism but with feeding a starving population. The Decree on Land, introduced the day after the Bolshevik insurrection, had given *ex post facto* recognition to the peasant land seizures which had been going on for some time. In February 1918, the land was nationalized and the Bolsheviks began a half-hearted attempt to promote collectivized farming, but this had foundered on the rock of peasant individualism. The food-supply system, already in a parlous state after the four years of European war, now broke down entirely. The situation was exacerbated by the loss of the Ukraine and other grain-producing areas. To make matters worse, the lack of manufactured goods, and any other incentive to trade, led the peasants to consume more and more of their own produce. By the beginning of 1918, Lenin was forced to fall back on coercion. 'Food supply detachments', consisting of hungry and unemployed workers accompanied by armed Chekists, went into the countryside to take the food for themselves. This, at first *ad hoc*, measure was systematized in May 1918 in what became known as the 'Food Dictatorship'. Simultaneously, 'Committees of the Village Poor' were formed to help the detachments uncover the whereabouts of grain hoards supposedly hidden by kulaks (wealthy peasant farmers). In this way, food requisitioning was converted by Lenin into a weapon of class struggle. The effect of these draconian measures, however, was to unite the peasantry, not to divide them. During 1919 even less grain was produced than in the previous year and at the eighth Party Congress in March, Lenin indirectly admitted his mistake:

> Owing to the inexperience of our Soviet officials and the difficulties of the problem, the blows which were intended for the kulaks very frequently fell on the middle peasants. In this respect we have sinned a great deal but the experience we have gained will enable us to do everything to avoid this in future.[161]

It would be some time, however, before the policy of food requisitioning was finally abandoned.

The food crisis had terrible consequences for those living in the towns. Factory production had already fallen dramatically during 1917; Lenin supplied the *coup de grâce* with the Decree on Workers' Control, which gave workers enormous scope to interfere in the running of their enterprises. He saw the resulting chaos as a useful means of waging class warfare against the industrial bourgeoisie. During 1918–19, hundreds of factories were forced to close, owing to the lack of raw materials and fuel, while those which survived produced solely for the defence sector. Money wages, rendered meaningless by inflation, were replaced by wages in kind (eggs, flour, etc.), but even these payments were rarely met in full: the bread ration in Petrograd, for example, fell at one point to 2 oz (57 g) per day. The starvation would have been even worse were it not for the *mesochniki* ('bagmen'), the black marketeers from the villages who carried sacks of grain and other produce to town for sale at vastly inflated prices. Workers with relatives in the countryside fled the cities *en masse*: the population of Petrograd fell from about 2.5 million in 1917 to nearer 600,000 two years later.

Much of Lenin's day-to-day administration was involved with the practicalities of food supply. On 6 January 1919, he wired the Food Commissar of the Simbirsk region:

A committee representing 42 organisations of starving Petrograd and Moscow workers is complaining about your inefficiency . . . You are obliged to receive grain from the peasants day and night. If it is confirmed that you have not been accepting grain after 4 p.m., compelling the peasants to wait until morning, you will be shot.

It was not just Petrograd and Moscow that were affected by the food shortages:

11 November 1919. To the Chairman, Special Food Commission, Eastern Front.

Supplies for the starving workers of the Urals are urgently needed. Report what you have done, how much you have provided and whether these workers can be sent out to collect grain beyond Kurgan.

When grain did arrive, it was a cause for major rejoicing. In March 1919, Lenin sent a message to Kamenev:

The bearers are comrades from Sarapul district, Vyatka province. They have brought us and Petrograd 40,000 poods of grain each. This is such a remarkable feat that it fully deserves quite special congratulations . . . A paragraph about it should also be given to the press.

Even members of Lenin's own administration often went hungry. In May 1919 he felt compelled to write to the new Soviet president, Mikhail Kalinin, on behalf of one of his own officials, A.D. Tsyurupa:

Tsyurupa receives 2,000 rubles, a family of 7, dinners at 12 rubles each (and supper) 84 per day × 30=2,520 rubles. They are underfed! . . . The children are adolescents, they need *more* than an adult. Please increase his salary to 4,000 rubles and give, in addition, a grant of 5,000 rubles in a lump sum to the family, which arrived from Ufa *without clothing*.[162]

Lenin's centre of operations was the third floor of the Kremlin. A long corridor separated his private apartment, consisting of four small rooms, shared
with his wife and younger sister, from his office and the adjoining cabinet
room. Leading off from the corridor were the offices of his secretariat.

The most important government work was dealt with by Sovnarkom,
the Council of People's Commissars. Here Lenin ruled with a rod of iron.
Sovnarkom met two or three times a week, usually in the evenings.
Sometimes 30 or 40 people squeezed into the cabinet room, by no means
all of them commissars or their deputies. This overcrowding infuriated
Lenin so much that on one occasion he wrote to his secretary, Lydia
Fotieva:

> There are evidently people sitting here who were invited to attend for
> *other* items. I don't want to chase them out. However, I hereby
> reprimand you and the other secretaries: you have been told a hundred
> times that people are to be invited in *solely* for the item in question.[163]

As there were up to 60 items on the agenda, people were often kept
waiting quite a long time in the ante-room. To reduce the length of the
meetings, Lenin drew up a series of standing orders stipulating the amount
of time to be allocated to each spokesman, usually five or ten minutes. At
the end of the allotted time, he would consult his stop-watch and cut the
speaker off, in mid-sentence if necessary.

Throughout these meetings, Lenin would be conducting all kinds of
government business, as his sister, Anyuta, recalled:

> Vladimir Ilyich was never satisfied just with the meeting alone: now he
> would be turning to the secretary, while still listening to the report or
> discussion, to ask for some information or documents, now he would be
> sending notes to some comrade or other present in the room, on some
> question having nothing to do with the matter under discussion, or reply
> to such notes from others. Some people who had no business affecting
> them on the agenda for a particular night's meeting, would nevertheless
> come along solely for the opportunity of exchanging a word on some
> matter or other with Ilyich.[164]

Lenin expected a high standard of self-discipline from his ministers. He
insisted on punctuality, to the extent of laying down a series of penalties for
latecomers: a reprimand inserted into the minutes for a first offence, the
loss of a day's pay for a second and a rebuke in the government newspaper
for a third. He disliked smoking in cabinet (there was a notice to that
effect, but his colleagues needed constant reminders); he also expected
people to keep to their seats and to refrain from slovenly behaviour
(putting feet up on the chair, and so on). He was ever mindful of the need
to overcome the Russian 'disease' of 'Oblomovism':

> Organisation [he reminded the delegates at the eighth congress] was

never a strong point with the Russians in general, nor with the Bolsheviks in particular; nevertheless the chief problem of the proletarian revolution *is that of organisation.*

By the time of the eighth congress (in March 1919), the civil war had entered a new, more deadly phase. Soviet attempts to capitalize on the departure of the Germans by launching an offensive in the vacated Baltic, Belorussian and Ukrainian Provinces ran quickly into the sand. While their backs were turned, a new front opened up in the east. In November 1918 the former commander of the Black Sea fleet, Admiral A.V. Kolchak, began marching along the route of the Trans-Siberian railway towards Chelyabinsk. In March 1919 his forces captured Ufa and in April, Chistopol: in just eight weeks, Kolchak had advanced more than 250 miles (400 km). The Soviet Government was caught unawares with the bulk of its forces concentrated against the Don Cossacks in the south. On 26 April, Lenin belatedly sent a telegram to S.V. Gusev: 'Urgent measures must be taken to help Chistopol. Have you given this sufficient thought? Have you exhausted all possibilities? Wire!'

Meanwhile, Denikin's Volunteer Army, after routing the soviets in the northern Caucasus and joining up with the Don Cossacks, was pressing northwards from its base in Ekaterinodar (Kuban). In May, the combined forces swept through the Don region and into the southern Ukraine, capturing Tsaritsyn on 30 June, Poltava on 29 July and Kiev and Odessa on 23 August. Emboldened by these and other victories, Denikin now set himself a new goal – the occupation of Moscow itself.

Lenin had convinced himself that both White offensives were part of a grand strategy devised by the 'imperialists' to throttle the Soviet regime and stamp out Communism before it could spread. As he put it in a speech to the Moscow Soviet on 3 April 1919: 'The imperialists of the whole world have got us by the throat, they are trying to defeat us by means of a mighty armed offensive and we must take them on in a life and death struggle.' According to this logic, the salvation of the revolution in Russia depended less on the performance of the Red Army than on the ability of the European proletariats to overthrow their governments and come to the assistance of the Soviet republic. There were some encouraging signs of this during the early part of 1919. Although a coup staged in Berlin by the newly formed German Communist Party, the Spartakusbund, ended in ignominious failure (and in the murder of its two most distinguished leaders, Karl Liebknecht and Rosa Luxemburg), Soviet republics were successfully established in Hungary and Bavaria shortly afterwards. Simultaneously a rash of strikes, nationalist demonstrations, riots and mutinies broke out across the face of Europe from the Danube to the Clyde. Lenin was exhilarated: 'The victory of the world-wide proletarian revolution is assured', he proclaimed to an international audience in March. A few days later, he spoke in similar vein to the government of the new Hungarian

Republic: 'the time is not far away when communism will triumph all over the world . . . Long live the world communist republic!' And on May Day he ended his address with the slogans 'Long live the international republic of Soviets! Long live Communism!'[165]

Lenin dated the foundations of the new Communist order to January 1919: 'When the German *spartakusbund* with its world-famous and world-renowned leaders, such faithful champions of the working class as Liebknecht, Rosa Luxemburg, Klara Zetkin and Franz Mehring . . . called itself the "Communist Party of Germany", then the *foundation* of a really proletarian, really international, really revolutionary Third International, a *Communist International*, became a fact'.[166] The next step was to transform this 'fact' into an organizational reality. On 2 March 1919, 52 delegates, purporting to represent 30 countries around the world, assembled in the Kremlin's Mitranovsky Hall for the founding congress of the Third International. It was an historic occasion but, for all the fine speeches and bold resolutions, the congress amounted in substance to little more than a show-piece, a propaganda extravaganza. Only the German delegation arrived with a proper mandate, while Holland, America and Japan were all represented by the same person! Of course, Lenin was not one to fuss over the constitutional niceties. Finding the Italian socialists unrepresented, he turned to Angelica Balabanov, who was acting as secretary and translator, and told her: 'You have so many mandates from the Italian Socialist Party, you are more than authorised to vote for it; and then, you read *Avanti!* [the party newspaper], you are informed'. She was not to be convinced.[167] The paucity of credible delegates was not the only problem. The German representative, Hugo Eberlein (known by the *nom de guerre* 'Albert' – he was on the run from the German police) calmly informed the assembly that he had been instructed to oppose any attempt to create a new International as premature. This was a grave blow to the Russians. They were let off the hook by the Austrian delegate, Steinhardt, who, after making a dramatic late entrance, managed to convince the gathering that a European-wide revolution was imminent and that to deprive it of coherent leadership might be fatal.

So, thanks to Steinhardt, Lenin had his Third International after all; but, despite all the prognostications, the 'world' revolution failed to materialize. The Bavarian republic collapsed, by a cruel irony, on May Day, the Hungarian republic limped on for a little while longer, but by August, Soviet Russia stood alone.

Given the military situation, this was a chilling prospect. One can sense Lenin's growing anxiety in his correspondence. On 5 May he wired two of his commanders on the southern front, Antonov-Ovseenko and Podvoisky:

The Central Committee of the Party imposes a stern reprimand on Antonov and Podvoisky for having done absolutely nothing serious to liberate the Donets Basin, despite their promises and repeated insistent demands. The CC orders that the most strenuous efforts be made and warns that otherwise it will bring them before a Party court.

As the crisis deepened, Lenin's tone became even more desperate: 'Concentrate all forces in the Donets Basin [he ordered Rakovsky on 28 May], take all you can from the Western Front, reducing to a minimum all active operations on your Western Front'.

A day later, he wired Ioffe: 'Not a single promise is being fulfilled: the Donets Basin has no reinforcements, the mobilisation of workers is proceeding at a disgracefully sluggish pace. You are personally responsible for the inevitable catastrophe'.

It was not only the southern front that was causing concern. On 29 May, he made this sombre prediction: 'If we do not win the Urals before the winter, I consider that the revolution will inevitably perish'.

In an effort to shake up the high command, the Central Committee replaced the Commander-in-Chief, Vatsetis, with another former Tsarist officer, General S. S. Kamenev. This action was taken against the advice of Trotsky, who saw his influence diminish as a result. Trotsky took umbrage and, on 17 June, Lenin felt compelled to send his Commissar for War this sarcastic message:

> Comrade Trotsky is mistaken: here there are neither whims, nor mischief, nor caprice, nor confusion, nor desperation, nor any 'element' of these pleasant qualities (which Trotsky castigates with such terrible irony). What there is, what Trotsky overlooked, namely, that the majority of the Central Committee is convinced that General Head-quarters is a 'den' and that *all is not well* at headquarters, and *in seeking a serious improvement*, in seeking ways for a *radical change* it has taken a definite *step*. That is all![168]

The civil war reached its climax in the autumn. By then, Kolchak's advance had run out of steam but Denikin pressed forward relentlessly, taking Kursk in September and Orel (186 miles/300 km from Moscow) the following month. The Red Army's arsenal at Tula was now in the direct line of the advance. The situation was dire and there was worse to come. In October, General N. N. Iudenich, having crossed the frontier into Russia from neighbouring Estonia, launched a direct assault on Petrograd. Within ten days, the former imperial palaces of Pavlovsk and Tsarskoe Selo had fallen and the advance guard had reached the Pulkovo Heights, overlooking the city. One of the soldiers recalled seeing 'the dome of St Isaac's and the gilt spire of the Admiralty – one could even see trains pulling out of the Nicolai station, and the white plumes of their steam trailing across the brown landscape as they hurried towards Moscow'.[169]

In fact, October marked the end of the White advance. Iudenich's forces, small in number, exhausted after months of campaigning and short of supplies were halted at the last minute by Red Army units licked into

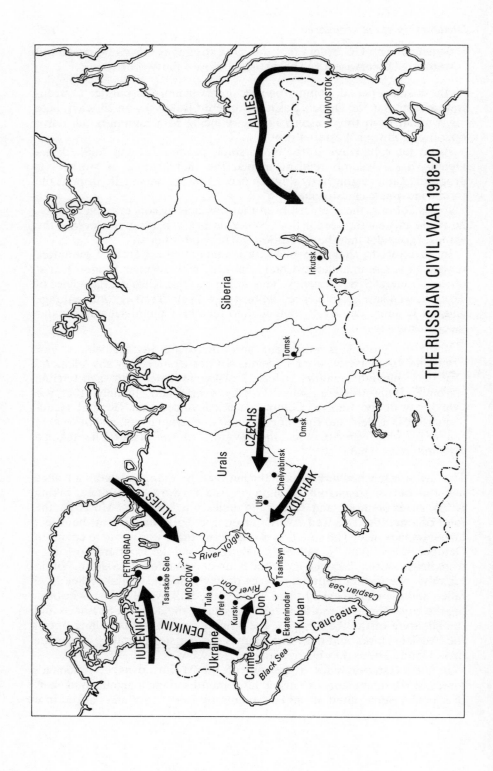

THE RUSSIAN CIVIL WAR 1918-20

ALLIES

VLADIVOSTOK

Siberia

Irkutsk

Tomsk

CZECHS

Omsk

Urals

Chelyabinsk

KOLCHAK

Ufa

ALLIES

PETROGRAD

Tsarskoe Selo

River Volga

Tsaritsyn

MOSCOW

River Don

Caspian Sea

Tula

IUDENICH

Orel

DENIKIN

Don

Kursk

Ekaterinodar

Kuban

Ukraine

Caucasus

Crimea

Black Sea

shape by Trotsky. Meanwhile, on the southern front, Denikin's march towards Tula was abruptly halted by the arrival of Red reservists, stiffened by veteran Latvian riflemen, on his left flank. As this group pounced from one direction, Semen Budenny's Red cavalry attacked from the other, threatening the Volunteer Army with encirclement. There was no alternative but to beat a hasty retreat. Within six weeks, Denikin had already been forced back to the Don. He was subseqeuently chased through the Kuban to the Black Sea by Red units under the command of M. N. Tukhachevsky until, in January 1920, he departed with the battered remnants of his demoralized army for the Crimea. Kolchak was overcome just as conclusively. Hopelessly over-extended, his Siberian army had been driven out of the Urals by the end of the summer. By November he was back in Omsk, where he had started. Separated from the remainder of his forces, he was captured and executed at Irkutsk in January 1920. It was not the end of civil war but it was the turning-point. The Revolution had been saved.

The 22 April 1920 was Lenin's fiftieth birthday. The celebrations were unprecedented. Congratulatory telegrams and letters flooded in to his office; *Pravda* and *Izvestiya*, as well as the local Press, were full of articles applauding his personal and political qualities; there were posters, portraits, postcards, badges, two official biographies produced with the popular consumer in mind, even poems. Vladimir Mayakovsky, the uncrowned bard of the Revolution (whose verse, incidentally, Lenin could not abide) wrote this paean of praise:

> But who can restrain himself
> and not sing
> of the glory of Ilich? . . .
> Kindling the lands with fire everywhere,
> where people are imprisoned,
> like a bomb
> the name
> explodes:
> Lenin!
> Lenin!
> Lenin! . . .
> I glorify
> in Lenin
> world faith
> and glorify
> my faith.[170]

There was talk of publishing a complete edition of Lenin's works, even of establishing a Lenin Institute and a Museum in Moscow (although this was kept quiet at the time).

He was simultaneously horrified and embarrassed by all this adulation.
When Kamenev broached the matter of the collected works, Lenin's
response was

> 'Why? Completely superfluous. Everything possible was written thirty
> years ago. It's not worth it.' Only my remark that youth must learn and
> that it was better when they learned from his works, instead of from the
> writings of Martov and Tugan-Baranovsky, caused him to hesitate. And
> he confessed subsequently to M. S. Olminsky 'You have no idea how
> unpleasant I find the promotion of my person'.[171]

The party honoured the occasion by holding a commemorative meeting in
Moscow the following day. One after another, Lenin's old comrades-in-
arms, Kamenev, Zinoviev, Bukharin, Lunacharsky and Stalin, testified to
his greatness. But Lenin himself was not there. Only when all the tributes
were over did he appear briefly and make a speech – not a personal
reminiscence but some brief remarks on the history of the revolutionary
movement. He concluded by warning the party against complacency
and conceit which would turn it into something 'stupid, shameful and
ridiculous'.

A number of foreign writers and journalists met Lenin at this time and
some of them have left their impressions. The American, Lincoln Eyre,
saw a man in

> a slightly soiled soft white collar, a black tie and dark brown business
> suit, the trousers stuffed into knee-high boots of thick felt, the warmest
> kind of foot covering . . . There was about him that mental alertness, that
> intellectual electricity which is perhaps the most salient characteristic.

H.G. Wells recalled 'a pleasant, quick-changing brownish face, with a
lively smile and a habit . . . of screwing up one eye as he pauses in his talk.'
In Wells's view, Lenin was 'not very like the photographs you see of him
because he is one of those people whose change of expression is more
important than their features'. The sculptress Clare Sheridan observed
how, when he received a telephone call, 'his face lost all the dullness of
repose and became animated and interesting'. Lenin conversed with his
Anglo-Saxon guests in English, resorting only occasionally to an interpre-
ter. Eyre describes his English as 'slow' but 'very pure'; Wells says Lenin
spoke 'excellent English', but according to Bertrand Russell he knew the
language only 'fairly well'. Russell was struck by his laughter: 'He laughs a
great deal; at first his laugh seems merely friendly and jolly, but gradually I
came to feel it rather grim'. Wells's overall impression was mixed. He was
fascinated by the socialist experiment going on in Russia but the scale of
the devastation caused by civil war appalled him. Set against this, Lenin's
apparent obsession with such long-term goals as electrification seemed to
assume an unreal quality. Russell's overall impression was decidedly
negative. While acknowledging Lenin's absolute lack of self-importance,

as well as his 'honesty, courage, and unwavering faith – religious faith in the Marxian gospel', he went on to remark that 'He has as little love of liberty as the Christians who suffered under Diocletian'. The anarchist, Emma Goldman, also came away with Lenin's contempt for traditional notions of Western democracy ringing in her ears: 'Free speech is a bourgeois prejudice, a soothing plaster for social ills' [he is alleged to have told her]. 'In the workers' republic economic well-being talks louder than speech'.[172]

Freedom of speech was an issue which loomed large in Lenin's renewed correspondence with Maxim Gorky. His warm but stormy relationship with Russia's leading proletarian writer had taken a downward spiral following the Bolshevik seizure of power, which Gorky had denounced as promoting violence and extremism. Shortly after the Revolution, Gorky wrote, in the Menshevik-leaning newspaper *Novaya Zhizn*:

> The working class cannot fail to understand that Lenin is only perform-
> ing a certain experiment on their skin and on their blood . . . Lenin is
> not an omnipotent magician but a cold-blooded trickster who spares
> neither the honour nor the life of the proletariat.[173]

Gorky continued to write in this vein until the Soviet Government closed the paper down on 16 July 1918 (incidentally, the same day as the murder of the Tsar's family in Ekaterinburg). When he learned of the attempt on Lenin's life, however, Gorky rushed to see him. The subsequent reunion was not all sweetness and light, but a reconciliation of sorts was patched together. Gorky took advantage of this to urge Lenin to do what he could to protect Russia's writers and intellectuals, who were generally having a hard time. This was not a cause for which Lenin had much sympathy. Lunacharsky recalled a meeting between them in 1919 in the course of which Gorky reminded Lenin of his personal debt to the intelligentsia:

> 'But they are the same people', went on the writer, 'who assisted you
> personally, hid you in their homes, etc.'
> Smiling, Vladimir Ilyich answered:
> 'Yes, of course they are excellent, good people and that is precisely
> why their homes have to be searched. Of course they are excellent and
> good, of course their sympathy goes always to the oppressed, of course
> they are always against persecution. And what do they see now around
> them? The persecutor – our Cheka; the oppressed – the Cadets and the
> SRs who flee from it. Obviously, their duty, as they conceive it, tells
> them to ally themselves with the Cadets and the SRs against us. And we
> must catch active counter-revolutionaries and render them harmless.
> The rest is clear.'
> And Vladimir Ilyich laughed, quite without malice.[174]

Gorky's apparent obsession with the fate of intellectuals alternately infuriated and nonplussed Lenin. He argued that, by surrounding himself with such people, Gorky was inevitably getting a distorted picture of what

was going on in the Soviet republic. He tried to explain what he meant in
two long letters written in the summer of 1919, but his impatience
constantly got the better of him. In the first, written in the middle of July,
he writes:

> You are engaged, not in politics and not in observing the *work* of political
> construction, but in a particular profession, which surrounds you with
> embittered bourgeois intellectuals, who have understood nothing, for-
> gotten nothing, learnt nothing and *at best* – have lost their bearings, are
> in despair, moaning, repeating old prejudices, have been frightened to
> death or are frightening themselves to death . . . You have put yourself
> in a position in which you *cannot* directly observe the new features in the
> life of the workers and peasants, that is, nine-tenths of the population of
> Russia; in which you are compelled to observe the fragments of life of a
> former capital [Gorky was then living in Petrograd], from where the
> flower of the workers has gone to the fronts and to the countryside, and
> where there remain a disproportionately large number of intellectuals
> without a place in life and without jobs, who *specially 'besiege'* you.
> Counsels to go away you stubbornly reject.[175]

In spite of this discouragement, Gorky persisted in taking up the cases of a
number of Kadet politicians, petitioning for their release from prison.
Exasperated, Lenin replied to his letter in September 1919:

> Why do you speak in such an angry, ill-tempered manner? Just because
> some tens (albeit even some hundreds) of Cadet and near-Cadet little
> gentlemen will spend a few days in prison in order to *forestall conspir-
> acies* . . . conspiracies which threaten the lives of *tens* of thousands of
> workers and peasants.
>   Think only, what calamity, what injustice! A few days or even weeks
> of prison for intellectuals in order to prevent the slaughter of tens of
> thousands of workers and peasants![176]

In fact, Lenin did intervene in particular cases. On 12 April 1919, for
example, he wired officials of the Orel Soviet: 'Writer Ivan Volny has been
arrested. His friend Gorky earnestly requests the greatest caution and
impartiality in the investigation. Can he be set free under strict surveillance? Wire.' (Volny was released.) And in March 1920 he informed
Gorky that the chemist, A. V. Sapozhnikov, had been freed and assured
him that scientists in general would be better provided for.[177]

Gorky frequently deplored the actions of the Soviet Government and
was not afraid to say so. But in criticizing Lenin, he also recognized his
greatness. In a highly idiosyncratic piece written for the journal of the
Communist International in July 1920, Gorky wrote:

> Lenin's mistakes are the mistakes of an honest person, and no reformer
> in the world has ever operated without making mistakes . . . He always

speaks of one thing – getting rid of social inequality. His faith in this is the faith of a fanatic – but an educated fanatic, not a metaphysical or mystical one . . . In a religious era, Lenin would have been considered a saint . . . A stern realist, a shrewd politician, Lenin is gradually becoming a legendary figure. This is good.

Lenin's reaction can readily be imagined. He presented the Politburo with a resolution which concluded: 'In the future *such* articles must *on no* account be published in *Kommunisticheskii internatsional*'.[178]

Becoming increasingly disillusioned with the socialist experiment, Gorky left Soviet Russia in August 1921, ostensibly to recover his ailing health. By the time he returned seven years later, he had got his way. Lenin had indeed become a 'legendary figure'.

The year 1920 also marked the closing chapter in Lenin's relationship with Inessa Armand. After returning to Russia in the sealed train, she had settled in Moscow, to become an important figure on the city Soviet. Lenin's relationship with her (now necessarily more distant) continued to have its ups and downs. Inessa disappointed him by siding with her Left-Communist Moscow colleagues at the time of Brest-Litovsk but after the attempt on his life, she was the first person outside his family whom he asked for. Subsequently, she and her children were frequent visitors to the Kremlin apartment and they were among a select number able to phone Lenin direct in the Kremlin. Inessa probably saw more of Krupskaya than Lenin himself at this time, but his affection for her never diminished. He helped Inessa's son, who had served with the Tsarist flying corps during the war, over the political obstacles he encountered in wanting to train as a Red aviator and was equally fond of her daughters, Varvara and 'little' Inessa. Early in 1919, Inessa visited France with the Red Cross on a mission to repatriate Russian prisoners-of-war. On her return, she threw herself into improving the working conditions of factory women in Moscow, a cause which had always been close to her heart. The following year, she was the motivating force behind the first International Conference of Communist Women. But her health had never been good and in February 1920 she fell ill with pneumonia. Lenin wrote, expressing his concern and demanding that her son call him 'every day between 12 and 4' to report on her condition. At the same time, he began to make arrangements for her to visit a sanatorium at Kislovodsk in the Caucasus. In August he wrote to the authorities there, requesting them to 'do everything' to help her and 'to provide the best accommodation and treatment'. He also contacted Ordzhonikidze, instructing him that Inessa was to be moved to another resort should Kislovodsk fall to the Whites: 'Please reply by letter and, if possible, also by telegram'. The move turned out to be necessary. In September, she and her son were evacuated to the comparative safety of Nalchik, but on the way she contracted cholera and died. Her body was brought back to Moscow for burial and Lenin was one of the principal mourners. Angelica Balabanov was also there and was shocked by his appearance:

> Not only his face but his whole body expressed so much sorrow that I dared not greet him, not even with the slightest gesture. It was clear he wanted to be alone with his grief. He seemed to have shrunk; his cap almost covered his face, his eyes seemed drowned in tears held back with effort. As our circle moved, following the movement of the people, he too moved, without offering resistance, as if he were grateful for being brought nearer to the dead comrade.[179]

Permanently tired from overwork and now tortured by personal anguish, Lenin cut a disturbingly worn figure when the German Communist, Clara Zetkin, visited him in November 1920:

> As Lenin spoke, his face before me was all shrivelled up. Countless wrinkles, great and small, furrowed deep into it. And every wrinkle spoke of a heavy sorrow or a gnawing pain. A picture of inexpressible suffering was visible on Lenin's face.[180]

Unfortunately, Zetkin was unable to bring him the news he most wanted to hear, the news he had been waiting for now for three long years – the outbreak of revolution in Europe. As he remarked ruefully to Bolshevik delegates at the eighth Congress of Soviets shortly afterwards: 'vanquishing all the imperial powers would, of course, be a most pleasant thing, but for a fairly long time we shall not be in a position to do so'. This was a far cry from the Lenin of November 1918 or the spring of 1919.

The final opportunity, and a quite unexpected one, had come earlier in 1920, following the invasion of Soviet territory by the Polish leader, Jozef Pilsudski. Poland had become independent in November 1918 and had already taken advantage of Soviet weakness by seizing part of Belorussia. In April 1920 the Polish Army launched an offensive in the Ukraine, capturing Kiev with little resistance. It was unable to consolidate, however, and in June the Reds retook Kiev (the sixteenth time the city had changed hands in the course of the civil war) before driving the poles back the 400 miles (644 km) to Brest-Litovsk. The question now arose: should the Red Army call a halt to its advance or should it press on to Warsaw? Lenin favoured the second alternative. He was convinced that the 'liberating' Soviet forces would be greeted enthusiastically by Polish workers, who would revolt and establish their own Polish Soviet republic. This might even be enough, Lenin hoped, to fan the flames of revolution in neighbouring Germany. Overriding Trotsky's vehement opposition, he ordered Tukhachevsky to resume his offensive. A provisional revolutionary committee proceeded from Moscow to Bialystok, ready to take over the government. Hopes also rose in Petrograd, where the second congress of the Comintern was then in session. 'A great map hung in the congress hall on which was marked the daily movement of our armies,' Zinoviev later recalled,

> And every morning the delegates stood with breathless interest before this map. It was a sort of symbol: the best representatives of the international proletariat with consuming interest, with palpitating heart, followed every advance of our armies, and everyone realized perfectly that, if the military aim set by our army was achieved, it would mean an immense acceleration of the international proletarian revolution.[181]

Alas, it was not to be. Tukhachevsky was stopped and defeated at the River Vistula and the workers of Warsaw, far from welcoming the prospect of a Soviet liberating army, rushed to volunteer for their own. Lenin concluded bitterly:

> The Poles thought and acted, not in a social, revolutionary manner, but as nationalists, as imperialists. The revolution in Poland which we counted on did not take place. The workers and peasants, deceived by Pilsudski . . . defended their class enemy, let our brave Red soldiers starve, ambushed them and beat them to death.[182]

Hostilities ceased in October 1920 and a peace favouring the Poles was signed at Riga in March 1921. Trotsky acknowledged that Lenin had made 'very grave mistakes' in the Polish campaign.

He was allowed little time to reflect on them. With the defeat of General P. N. Wrangel's Crimean-based army in the autumn of 1920, the civil war finally came to an end, giving Lenin's opponents within the Communist Party the first opportunity for more than two years to express their views, without being accused of disloyalty. The most important group to emerge was christened by Lenin the 'Workers' Opposition'. Led by two of his closest associates during the war, the former metalworker, Alexander Shlyapnikov and the Bolsheviks' most outspoken feminist, Alexandra Kollontai, the Workers' Opposition was widely supported by rank-and-file trade unionists, both inside and outside the party. Its demands included a return to the industrial policies of 1917: workers' control, the end of one-man management and the practice of encouraging 'bourgeois specialists' to stay in industry by offering them higher wages. The Opposition also wanted a more active role for the trade unions and a return to genuine democracy.

The 'Democratic Centralists', consisting largely of former Left Communists (with the significant exception of Bukharin) concentrated on reforming the party, which they felt had become too authoritarian, too heavily bureaucratized and corrupt. They demanded proper elections, more open debate and less centralization. They also wanted to see a revival of the soviets, whose powers had diminished drastically in the course of the civil war.

At the end of 1920, the Workers' Opposition clashed head-on with

Trotsky, who had been appointed Commissar for Transport earlier in the year. Trotsky wanted draconian measures to get industry on its feet again, measures which amounted to putting all workers under military discipline. He was supported by a number of senior figures in the party, including Dzerzhinsky, Krestinsky and a leading economist, E. A. Preobrazhensky.

Lenin attacked Trotsky's demand for the nationalization of the trade unions in his speech 'The Trade Unions, the Present Situation and Trotsky's Mistakes' delivered to the eighth Congress of Soviets at the end of December 1920. But his own policies were extreme enough at this time. He does not seem to have opposed the militarization of labour in principle; indeed, the Labour Code already in force sanctioned longer working hours, stipulated heavy penalties for absenteeism and forbade movement from one factory to another. Nor were there any compensating factors for the workers – the food situation was as bad as ever. Lenin's policy towards the peasants was undergoing a gradual change, but this did not come in time to prevent another requisitioning drive in February 1921.

Once, in conversation with Angelica Balabanov, Lenin observed that none but the Russian people could have endured the almost inconceivable hardships of the civil war. But there was a limit to what even the Russian people were prepared to put up with. In February 1921, food procurement led to full-scale rebellion which began in the province of Tambov before spreading eastwards to engulf the Urals and parts of western Siberia. Everywhere, villages united to resist all attempts at requisitioning, rejected every manifestation of Soviet power and even interfered with the transportation of wheat bound for Moscow and other towns.

The workers of Petrograd were also on strike in February, demanding an immediate improvement in the food ration and the distribution of shoes and winter clothing. When the President of the Trade Union Council came to negotiate, the workers killed him. On 28 February the unrest spread to Kronstadt, where sailors on the battleship *Petropavlovsk*, under the slogan 'All power to soviets, not to parties', joined with workers in demanding the return of elections, freedom of the Press and of assembly, the end of requisitioning, the payment of wages 'in gold and not in paper trash' and the abolition of all party privileges. The government refused to negotiate, insisting on unconditional surrender. This produced out-and-out rebellion. A 'Provisional Revolutionary Committee', formed under the influence of anarchists and Left Socialist Revolutionaries, began to administer Kronstadt as an independent territory. Many Kronstadt Communists tore up their party cards and joined the rebels.

This was the atmosphere in which the tenth Party Congress opened on 8 March. On that very day, in fact, preparations were begun to put down the rebellion. The commanders, Tukhachevsky and Kamenev, were sent to Kronstadt with a Red Army task force of 50,000 troops. When the soldiers appeared reluctant to fire on their own people, a huge phalanx of Communist Party members, including some 300 delegates from the congress, were dispatched to stiffen their resolve. They let it be known that Lenin was proposing an end to requisitioning (which was indeed the case) and this seems to have induced a change of mind in at least some of the soldiers; others had to be marched across the ice at gunpoint. It was 18 March before the Kronstadt fortress was finally stormed. The defenders resisted to the last man, inflicting 10,000 casualties on the Red Army (including ten of the congress delegates). The Red forces wreaked a terrible revenge: thousands of rebels were subsequently massacred, executed or imprisoned. The 'pride and glory of the revolution' as Lenin and Trotsky liked to refer to the Kronstadt sailors, had been consumed by its own.

Kronstadt cast a terrible shadow over the proceedings of the congress and, while it is true that Lenin had for several weeks been considering a change in economic policy, the rebellion certainly removed any lingering doubts and helped him carry his ideas to the anxious and shaken delegates. The *ad hoc* economic experimentation of the previous three years, including the ban on private manufacturing, the wholesale programme of nationalization, the seizure of peasant surpluses, the replacement of private trade with barter and the partial attempt to abolish money, were all now swept away. Lenin proposed, or rather insisted upon, a 'temporary retreat', to become known as the New Economic Policy (NEP). Requisitioning was to be replaced by a tax in kind, soon to be substituted by a money tax. The peasants were to be free to dispose of any surpluses, implying the return of private trade and the market. Only the 'commanding heights' of the economy (banking, foreign trade, large-scale industry) were to remain in the hands of the State; the remaining small firms and artisanal enterprises could be leased and run as co-operatives. Money made a return. Wages were to be paid in cash, public services and utilities would cease to be free, even investment by foreign capitalists was to be encouraged. But it was the concessions to the peasantry that were the *raison d'être* of NEP.

As he watched the Soviet regime, which had withstood enemy occupation, intervention by foreign governments, the onslaught of the combined White forces and subversion from within, come perilously close to going under at the hands of those sections of society in whose name it had taken power in the first place, Lenin swallowed the bitter pill, as he had at Brest-Litovsk, and, in the process, pulled back the Revolution from the edge of the precipice.

But, in the short term at least, the new policy of conciliation towards the peasants came too late. In 1921, the harvest, which amounted to less than half the pre-war average, was accompanied by a terrible drought. Three million peasants died of starvation or disease on top of the millions more who had perished in the course of the civil war. The government was helpless and appealed to the International Red Cross, the American Relief Administration and other agencies for help. It was the worst famine since

1891, when the young Vladimir Ulyanov had advocated witholding support from the government relief effort on the grounds that this was standing in the way of progress. Now his own government was grateful for all the help it could get.

The tenth congress also marked the end of attempts to democratize the party. 'Comrades,' Lenin told the delegates, 'this is no time for an opposition'. The subsequent resolution 'On Party Unity', sponsored by Lenin himself, stated:

> The congress orders the immediate dissolution, without exception, of all groups that have been formed on the basis of some platform or other, and instructs all organisations to be very strict in ensuring that no manifestations of factionalism of any sort be tolerated. Failure to comply with this resolution of the congress is to entail immediate expulsion from the party.

Karl Radek's response was typical:

> In voting for this resolution I feel that it can well be turned against us, and nevertheless I support it . . . Let the Central Committee in a moment of danger take the severest measures against the best party comrades, if it finds this necessary . . . Let the Central Committee even be mistaken![183]

10
Leninu kaput

During the summer of 1921, Lenin's health began to deteriorate. The headaches and insomnia, which had been plaguing him for some time now, became more frequent. He complained of feeling 'very tired and ill' and of being unable to concentrate. In July, he developed hyperacusis, a sensitivity to loud noises, and the telephone bells in his office had to be replaced with flashing lights. Most untypically, he asked for a month's leave of absence and on 13 July left Moscow for his summer retreat at Gorki. This elegant and imposing stately home had formerly belonged to a mayor of Moscow; it was made available to Lenin following the attempt on his life. He was never really comfortable in the opulent surroundings and insisted on occupying the smallest rooms. He did, however, enjoy strolling through the grounds, either alone or in the company of family and friends.

But the insomnia persisted. On 9 August, he wrote to Gorky, 'I am so tired that I am unable to do a thing'. A week or so later he returned to Moscow. In December, he asked for another leave of absence which was later extended by the Politburo to the end of March. His headaches were now more severe and he could obtain relief only by resorting to cold compresses. He considered taking a long vacation in the Caucasus (something he was always recommending to others), but nothing came of it. In March 1922 he was examined by two German specialists, Professor Felix Klemperer and the neurologist, Otfrid Foerster, but they could find nothing seriously wrong with him. In an interview given to the *New York Times*, Klemperer reported only that Lenin was suffering from 'moderate neurasthenia' caused by overwork. Another Berlin specialist suggested that the headaches might be caused by lead poisoning from the bullets still lodged in Lenin's shoulder and neck. Both Klemperer and the Soviet Minister of Health, N. A. Semashko, were highly sceptical about this diagnosis, but on 23 April Lenin was admitted to the Soldatenkovo (now Botkin) Hospital for an operation to remove the bullet in his neck.

Everything went off without a hitch and he was allowed to leave the
following day.

There was no obvious improvement in his condition, however, and on 23
May he had to leave Moscow for another period of rest. Three days later,
on the morning of 26 May, he 'felt dizzy as he got out of bed and had to
grab hold of a nearby cupboard'. Later, he began to experience acute
abdominal pains and nausea. At first, the doctors suspected food poisoning
but it soon became clear that Lenin was seriously ill. He was, in fact,
suffering from arteriosclerosis of the brain, the disease which had killed his
father at the age of 54. This first stroke deprived him temporarily of the use
of his right arm and leg and left his speech impaired. It was 'the first
warning bell', as he himself recognized. The specialists, however, were still
unsure of their diagnosis and the public was informed only that Lenin was
suffering from gastro-enteritis. 'I thought the best diplomats were at the
Hague, but it seems they are in Moscow,' he observed tartly.[184]

By the summer, he felt a little better. His symptoms eased and he felt
able to read books and newspapers and to receive visitors. Apart from
members of his family, several political colleagues came to see him,
including Stalin. In an up-beat account intended for readers of *Pravda*, the
newly appointed General Secretary of the Party reported that Lenin
appeared 'fresh and invigorated . . . We laugh over the doctors who
cannot understand that professional politicians cannot refrain from talking
about politics when they meet'. This was on 13 July. On 5 August, Stalin
made another trip to Gorki: 'This time I found Comrade Lenin surrounded
by a mountain of books and newspapers. There was no trace of overtired-
ness and overstrain . . . It is our old Lenin who looks craftily, one eye
closed, at his interlocutor'. They joked about reports in the foreign Press
that Lenin was dying. 'Let them lie and rejoice,' Stalin reported Lenin as
saying. 'One should not deprive the dying of their last consolation.'[185] By
the end of the summer Lenin was writing again and on 2 October he
returned to his desk at the Kremlin. He had given his doctors an assurance
that he would rest completely for at least two days in every week, but this
soon went by the board. Between October and December, in fact, Lenin
wrote 224 letters, saw 171 people and chaired 32 meetings. This was hardly
taking it easy. Those who saw him during this period differ in their
recollections. The American journalist, Louis Fischer, watched him deliver
a speech to the Central Executive Committee of the Soviet on 31 October
and was amazed at his apparent fitness: [Lenin] 'walked so fast it seemed to
me he was running on tiptoe to the stage . . .' However, when Balabanov saw
him speak two weeks later to delegates of the Communist International,
she noticed that he appeared occasionally to lose his train of thought
and had to keep referring to Karl Radek for German words and phrases
which had slipped his memory. On 20 November, he spoke for what turned
out to be the last time in public to members of the Moscow Soviet. Once
again, his remarks were uncharacteristically vague and disjointed. Three

weeks later, he suffered a second stroke. This time the paralysis of the right side was permanent, though his speech remained unaffected. He informed the Politburo of his intention to 'retire'. Most of his colleagues continued to hope (and perhaps believe) that one day Lenin would return to public life, but Stalin had no such illusions: '*Leninu kaput*' was his alleged remark – 'Lenin is finished'.

For much of 1922 illness had prevented Lenin from exercising his customary political authority. However, he was not so incapacitated as to be unable to keep in touch with what was going on both inside and outside the party. As time progressed, he became increasingly convinced that things were going wrong, that the Soviet ship of state was badly off course and heading for treacherous waters. Overshadowing everything was the dead hand of bureaucratism which seemed to stifle initiative and proliferate attitudes and mores which Lenin found intolerable in Communists: rudeness, arrogance, dishonesty, servility, deviousness, disloyalty. Even more disturbing, he began to recognize these qualities in the behaviour of some of those occupying positions of the highest trust.

Lenin had long been aware of Stalin's personal shortcomings, his coarseness, his intolerance, his occasional acts of insubordination, but had turned a blind eye to them in view of his outstanding abilities. Stalin commended himself as someone who could get things done without being afraid of getting his hands dirty. At the time of the Revolution he had been one of the least known of the leading Bolsheviks, but by 1919 he was not only Commissar for Nationalities but also a member of the Politburo and the Central Committee. In the same year, he was appointed head of Rabkrin, the Workers' and Peasants' Inspectorate, a new watchdog agency charged with reducing bureaucracy, improving efficiency and rooting out corruption from the Soviet administration. When Preobrazhensky, a close ally of Trotsky, took exception to Stalin's appointment, Lenin rejoindered:

> We must have someone to whom any national representative can appeal . . . Where is such a man to be found? I do not think that Preobrazhensky can point to anyone but Stalin. It is the same with the Workers' and Peasants' Inspectorate. The job is enormous. To cope with it there must be a man with authority at its head.[186]

The same argument was, doubtless, used to justify Stalin's next appointment, that of General Secretary of the Communist Party, another newly created post giving him control over all party personnel. Strange to say, no one at the time thought the job particularly important.

The two major issues with which Lenin was concerned in the months leading up to his second stroke – the future of the foreign-trade monopoly and Soviet Russia's relations with the other republics – brought him up against Stalin.

Lenin had been determined that, despite the relaxations of NEP, foreign trade should remain the exclusive preserve of the State. He was particularly concerned about the possibility of Russia's more entrepreneurial-minded peasants coming into direct contact with the corrupting influence of the foreign capitalist. Few of his colleagues shared these concerns to anything like the same degree and only one of them, Trotsky, was prepared to fight his corner in the Politburo. When the matter came up for discussion in May 1922, Lenin's view prevailed, but his opponents (including Stalin) took advantage of his illness to revive the issue in the Central Committee, where they succeeded in considerably diluting his proposals. When Lenin returned to work in October and discovered just what had been going on, he was furious and insisted on the decision being reversed. After much deliberation, it was agreed to put the matter again to the Central Committee, though Stalin attached a note to Lenin's letter making his own views clear: 'Comrade Lenin's letter has not made me change my mind as to the correctness of the decision . . .' Lenin became seriously ill again on 12 December, but he was still able to solicit Trotsky's support on the foreign-trade issue: on 15 December he wrote (with great difficulty, Lydia Fotieva recalled), 'Comrade Trotsky, I think we have arrived at a full agreement. I ask you to announce our solidarity in the [Central Committee] plenum'.[187] When the meeting took place three days later, Lenin's theses were adopted. He then persuaded Krupskaya to ignore doctor's orders and dictated a note of congratulation to Trotsky. Somehow Stalin managed to find out about the letter. He telephoned Krupskaya and subjected her to a torrent of insult and abuse, culminating in a threat to bring her before a party court. Not wishing to distress Lenin, she told only Kamenev and Zinoviev about the incident. Apparently, Stalin apologized.

By 1922 the territorial boundaries of Soviet Russia were more or less established and Moscow was anxious to formalize relations between ethnic Russia, known as the Russian Soviet Federal Socialist Republic (RSFSR) and the contiguous Soviet republics of the Ukraine, Belorussia, Armenia, Azerbaijan and Georgia. Of these, Georgia was the last to be incorporated following an invasion by Soviet troops, in February 1921, which deposed the Menshevik Government of Noi Zhordania. Lenin was aware of Zhordania's support among the Georgian peasantry and advocated a softly, softly approach towards the new Soviet territory. But his advice was ignored and within a month or two Stalin and Ordzhonikidze, the party's chief representative in the Caucasus, had clashed with local Communists over a proposal to integrate Georgia into a Transcaucasian Federation with Armenia and Azerbaijan. The Georgians resented this demotion in their status and feared (with ample justification) that Stalin's real goal was a unitary Soviet State under Russian domination. They resolved to fight the proposals tooth and nail.

Lenin supported the idea of a federation but he deplored Stalin's high-handedness towards what were, after all, his own people. In September 1922 he urged Kamenev and Zinoviev to take up the issue, opining that,

'Stalin is in rather too much of a hurry'. At the same time, he introduced some modifications to the proposals in an attempt to make them more palatable to the Georgians. He wrote again, on 6 October:

> Comrade Kamenev! I declare war to the death on dominant-nation chauvinism. I shall eat it with all my healthy teeth as soon as I get rid of this accursed bad tooth. It must be *absolutely* insisted that the Union Central Executive Committee should be *presided* over in turn by a Russian, Ukrainian, Georgian, etc. *Absolutely!*[188]

But Stalin and Ordzhonikidze were laws unto themselves. Shortly after Lenin had written this letter, they summoned the members of the Georgian Central Committee to Moscow and subjected them to threats and insults. The committee resigned in protest. Complaints were now landing on Lenin's desk thick and fast and a commission of inquiry had been appointed to investigate what was going on. On 12 December Lenin interviewed one of its members, the head of the Cheka, Felix Dzerzhinsky, and despite evasions on his part, managed to discover that on one occasion Ordzonikidze had actually struck a Georgian party official. Lenin was 'deeply upset' by this revelation and ordered that Ordzhonikidze be removed from office and suspended from party membership. The following day, he suffered the onset of his second stroke.

Now Stalin was responsible for Lenin's medical supervision. On 24 December he convened a meeting of the doctors and, together with Kamenev and Bukharin, laid down a regimen which Lenin was to follow. He was to receive no visitors. He was to be allowed to dictate for no more than ten minutes daily. He was to receive no political news of any kind, nobody was to 'communicate to Vladimir Ilyich anything from political life, so as not to give him cause for reflection and anxiety.' The permission to dictate was a concession – Lenin had threatened to refuse all treatment if he were not allowed to express his thoughts on paper.

Immediately, he began his 'Letter to the Congress', now known as his 'Testament'. His headaches were unbearable and he was able to proceed only with a cold compress on his head. He dictated slowly and with great difficulty. The sight of the stenographer waiting for his next thought made him frustrated and bad tempered, so he occasionally resorted to the telephone.

Concerned first and foremost with the future of the party, he presented an assessment of each of the leaders:

> Comrade Stalin, having become General Secretary, has unlimited authority concentrated in his hands and I am not sure that he will always be capable of using that authority with sufficient caution. Comrade Trotsky is distinguished not only by outstanding ability. He is personally perhaps the most capable man in the present Central Committee but he has displayed excessive self-assurance and shown excessive preoccupa-

tion with the purely administrative side of things. These two qualities of
the two outstanding leaders of the present can inadvertently lead to a
split . . . the October episode with Zinoviev and Kamenev was, of
course, no accident; but neither can the blame for it be laid upon them
personally any more than now separation from Bolshevism can upon
Trotsky. . . . Bukharin . . . the favourite of the Party . . . has never
made a study of dialectics and, I think, never fully understood it. . . .
Pyatakov . . . a man of outstanding will and outstanding ability . . .
shows too much zeal for the administrative side of work to be relied on in
a serious political matter.[189]

To these evenly balanced judgements Lenin added this postscript on 4
January 1923:

> Stalin is too rude and this defect, though quite tolerable in our midst and
> in dealings among us Communists, becomes intolerable in a General
> Secretary. Therefore I propose to the comrades to find a way of
> removing Stalin from that position and appointing in his place another
> man who in all other respects differs from Comrade Stalin . . . being
> more tolerant, more loyal, more polite and more considerate to com-
> rades, less capricious, etc.[190]

Five copies were made of the document. Lenin kept one, his secretaries
another and the remainder were entrusted to Krupskaya, who was
empowered to open them in the event of his death. All five were then
placed in envelopes and sealed with wax.

Lenin completed his Testament on 31 December 1922. During January
and February he dictated five more articles in the same laborious way:
'Pages from a Journal', 'On Cooperation', 'Our Revolution', 'On the
Workers' and Peasants' Inspectorate' and 'Better Fewer But Better'. He
hoped they might influence delegates attending the forthcoming party
congress which, for the first time, he was unable to attend. He had already
given his notes on the National Question, which contained more damning
judgements on Stalin, to Trotsky but the latter unaccountably failed to
make use of them. Most of his other observations concerned bureaucratism, an issue which had now become almost an obsession with him. He had
some harsh things to say about current Soviet administrative practices and
was particularly scathing about the Workers' and Peasants' Inspectorate:
'Everybody knows that no other institutions are worse organised than
those of our Workers' and Peasants' Inspectorate and that under present
conditions nothing can be expected from this People's Commissariat'.

Lenin's cure for the disease of bureaucratism was re-education: 'We
must at all costs set out, first, to learn, secondly, to learn, and thirdly, to
learn'. It was possible to learn even from the bourgeoisie: 'we hear people
dilating at too great length and too flippantly on "proletarian" culture. For
a start we should be satisfied with real bourgeois culture'. Soviet adminis-

trative attitudes, according to Lenin, were still steeped in the old tsarist ways. What was needed was a complete overhaul of the existing system and the wholesale retraining of a new generation of officials. This would take time and would require patience, honesty and humility.

The tone of these articles is less that of a headmaster addressing his errant pupils than of a benign father warning his children of the dangers which lay ahead. Just occasionally, the old optimism shines through:

> In the final analysis, the outcome of the struggle will be determined by the fact that Russia, India, China, etc., account for the overwhelming majority of the population of the globe. And during the last few years it is this majority that has been drawn into the struggle for emancipation with extraordinary rapidity, so that in this respect there cannot be the slightest doubt what the final outcome of the world struggle will be. In this sense, the complete victory of socialism is fully and absolutely assured.[191]

One day early in March 1923, Lenin found out about Stalin's abusive telephone call to Krupskaya. He was already feeling ill again but insisted on dictating a letter to one of his secretaries, M. A. Volodicheva. It read:

> To Comrade Stalin,
> highly secret, personal,
> copies to Comrades Kamenev and Zinoviev
>
> Esteemed Comrade Stalin,
> You allowed yourself to be so ill-mannered as to call my wife on the telephone and to abuse her. She has agreed to forget what was said. Nevertheless, she has told Zinoviev and Kamenev about the incident. I have no intention of forgetting what has been done against me, and it goes without saying that what was done against my wife I consider also to have been directed against myself. Consequently, I must ask you to consider whether you are willing to withdraw what you said and apologise, or whether you prefer to break off relations between us.
> Respectfully yours,
> LENIN[192]

Five days later, on 10 March, Lenin suffered a third stroke. The paralysis of his right side now returned and he lost the power of speech. He became feverish and experienced difficulty with his breathing. The Politburo finally decided to tell the truth about his illness and *Izvestiya* began issuing daily medical bulletins.

On 15 May, he was taken by ambulance to Gorki, where he was examined by a new team of specialists. Gradually, his health began to show modest signs of improvement. In June, Krupskaya wrote to Clara Zetkin, 'there are days when I begin to hope that recovery is not impossible'. Lenin learned to walk again using a stick or by leaning on the arm of a medical orderly or guard. Krupskaya tried teaching him to speak (he had refused to see a therapist), but he got no further than a few barely intelligible monosyllables. He was equally unsuccessful in his attempts to write with his left hand.

His moods now became more extreme and unpredictable. He was easily depressed, even tearful on occasions. At other times he would fly into a rage because someone failed to understand a word or a gesture. On top of his other afflictions, he now discovered that he was more or less completely word blind. At first, he was kept ignorant of all political news but Krupskaya was eventually allowed to read him the newspapers. She read selectively, in an attempt to keep him calm. He was curious to hear news of old friends (Martov too was ill and was to die later in 1923).

He continued to receive visitors. Anyuta's adopted son, Gora, came to see him during the summer and found him in the garden:

> Vladimir Ilyich was sitting in his wheelchair in a white summer shirt with an open collar . . . A rather old cap covered his head and the right arm lay somewhat unnaturally on his lap. Vladimir Ilyich hardly noticed me even though I stood quite plainly in the middle of the clearing.[193]

If the weather was fine, Gil would take him for a drive in the woods with Nadya and Manyasha. One day towards the end of October, Lenin suddenly indicated a wish to go to Moscow. Manyasha tried to dissuade him – 'Volodya, they won't let you in. You don't have a pass for the Kremlin' – but he insisted. As they drove through the city, he began waving his cap and smiling. After taking a last look round his flat and pointing vaguely towards some books, he returned to the car.

Bukharin and a number of other leading politicians visited Gorki during November and December, but these were merely social calls. Lenin also received a delegation of workers. During the Christmas holidays, he made a brief appearance at a children's party but his health was steadily deteriorating. On the afternoon of 20 January, his eyes were examined by an ophthalmologist, Professor M. I. Averbakh (he had complained of problems with focusing). The following day, Lenin felt weaker and had no appetite. At about 6 p.m. he suddenly lost consciousness before suffering prolonged and violent convulsions. He died at 6.50 p.m. with Nadya at his bedside.

Glossary

All-Russian Extraordinary Commission for Combating Counter-Revolution and Sabotage (Cheka) Original name for Soviet secret police, formed December 1917.

Communist International (Comintern) Founded by Lenin in March 1919 as successor to defunct Socialist International.

Communist Party of the Soviet Union Official title of the Bolshevik Party (formerly Social Democrats) after March 1918.

Council of People's Commissars (Sovnarkom) Official title of first Soviet government.

Emancipation of Labour Group First organization of Russian Marxists, founded in Geneva in 1883 by Plekhanov, Axelrod, Zasulich and Deich.

International Socialist Bureau Executive of the Socialist International.

Kadets Constitutional Democrat Party.

Liquidators Right-wing Mensheviks advocating abolition of underground work after collapse of 1905 revolution.

People's Freedom (*Narodnaya Volya*) Terrorist organization which carried out the assassination of Tsar Alexander II in March 1881.

Populists (*narodniki*) Agrarian socialists opposed to wholesale capitalist development in Russia.

Russian Social Democratic Labour Party (RSDLP) First nationwide Marxist organization, founded in Minsk in 1898. Divided into Bolshevik and Menshevik factions at second Congress in 1903.

Socialist Revolutionary Party (PSR) Main Populist rival of Social Democrats, formed end of 1901.

Union of Liberation Broad liberal grouping of professional and forward-thinking members of the gentry, formed in 1903.

Union of Social Democrats Abroad Founded as propaganda adjunct to Emancipation of Labour Group (q.v.) in 1895. Later split with parent organization over Economism.

Union of Struggle for the Emancipation of the Working Class Umbrella organization of Petersburg Marxists, formed December 1895. Members included Lenin, Martov, Dan and Radchenko.

Chronology

10/22 April 1870   Vladimir Ilyich Ulyanov (Lenin) born in Simbirsk.
December 1887   Expelled from Kazan University for involvement in student demonstration.
Autumn 1891   Receives law degree.
August 1893   Moves to Petersburg; joins political circle of S. I. Radchenko while working as legal assistant to M. F. Volkenstein.
May–September 1895   First visit to Europe.
December 1895   Arrested for subversive political activity.
1897–January 1900   Exiled to Shushenskoye, Eastern Siberia.
July 1898   Marries Nadezhda Konstantinovna Krupskaya.
1899   Publication of *The Development of Capitalism in Russia*.
July 1900–November 1905   First period of European exile.
December 1900   Publication of *Iskra* No. 1.
1902   Publication of *What Is To Be Done?*
July 1903   Attends second Congress of RSDLP in Brussels, then London.
January 1905   Revolution breaks out in Russia.
April 1905   Attends third Congress of RSDLP in London.
August 1905   Publication of *Two Tactics of Social Democracy in the Democratic Revolution*.
November 1905   Returns to Russia.
April 1906   Attends fourth (Unity) Congress of RSDLP in Stockholm.
May 1907   Attends fifth Congress of RSDLP in London.
December 1907   Flees Russia to avoid arrest.
1907–April 1917   Second period of European exile.
January 1912   Attends Bolshevik Conference in Prague.
May 1912   First edition of *Pravda* published in Petersburg.
August 1914   Outbreak of World War I. Lenin arrested in Poronin, Austria-Hungary but later released and allowed to leave for Switzerland.
September 1915   Attends International Socialist Conference in Zimmerwald.
April 1916   Attends International Socialist Conference in Kienthal.
July 1916   Completes *Imperialism, the Highest Stage of Capitalism*.
March 1917   Russian Revolution begins.
April 1917   Lenin and companions leave Switzerland for Petrograd. Lenin expounds 'April Theses' to local Bolsheviks.

July 1917 Lenin accused of being German agent in wake of 'July Days' revolt. Goes into hiding.

23 October 1917 Persuades Central Committee to prepare for insurrection.

6/7 November 1917 Directs Bolshevik seizure of power in Petrograd.

January 1918 Constituent Assembly dispersed on Lenin's insistence.

March 1918 Treaty of Brest-Litovsk signed with Germany.

August 1918 Unsuccessful attempt on Lenin's life.

1918–1920 Civil War in Russia.

March 1921 Lenin introduces New Economic Policy (NEP) in the wake of Kronstadt revolt. Tenth Party Congress outlaws opposition platforms.

May 1922 Lenin suffers first stroke.

December 1922 Second stroke and effective retirement from public life.

21 January 1924 Dies at Gorki.

Notes

Prologue

1 For fuller details of the sources quoted, see the Bibliography on pp. 198–201.

2 *Russian Information and Review*, vol. 4, no. 6 (1924), p. 84.

1 The boy from the Volga

3 A. I. Ulyanova, in *Vospominaniya o V. I. Lenine* (afterwards referred to as *VVIL*), vol. 1, p. 15.

4 M. I. Ulyanova, ibid., p. 142.

5 I. Deutscher, *Lenin's Childhood*, p. 28.

6 Ibid., p. 56.

7 Payne, *The Life and Death of Lenin*, p. 70.

8 I. Deutscher, *Lenin's Childhood*, p. 57.

9 Ibid., p. 60.

10 Naimark, *Terrorists and Social Democrats*, p. 58.

11 I. Deutscher, *Lenin's Childhood*, pp. 62–3.

12 A. Elizarova-Ulyanova, in *Molodoi Lenin: povest v dokumentakh i memuarakh*, p. 250. On the foregoing, Service, *Lenin*, pp. 11–13.

2 Revolutionary apprenticeship

13 For this and other eyewitness accounts of the Kazan disturbances, see *Molodoi Lenin*, chapter 5.

14 Ibid.

15 Valentinov, *The Early Years of Lenin*, p. 133.

16 Gleson, *Road to Revolution*, p. 84.

17 Chernyshevsky, *What Is To Be Done?*, introduction.

18 Ibid., p. 46.

19 *Lenin: His Life and Work*, p. 38.

20 *Molodoi Lenin*, p. 425.

21 Trotsky, *The Young Lenin*, p. 133.

22 Krupskaya, *Reminiscences*, p. 36.

23 Trotsky, ibid., p. 154. Service, *Lenin*, pp. 44–7.

24 Trotsky, ibid., p. 163.

25 Ibid., p. 158.

26 Weber, *Lenin: Life and Works*, p. 4.

27 Trotsky, ibid., p. 173.

28 A. I. Ivanskii (ed.), *Peterburgskie gody*, p. 37.

29 Lenin, *Collected Works* (afterwards referred to as *CW*), vol. 37, pp. 65–6.

30 Krupskaya, *Reminiscences*, p. 15.

31 *CW*, vol. 37, p. 65.

32 Weber, p. 6. For the full account, *Peterburgskie gody*, pp. 133–9.

33 Krupskaya, *Reminiscences*, p. 16.

34 Ibid., p. 21.

35 A. I. Ivanskii (ed.), *Peterburgskie gody*, pp. 88–90.

36 Krupskaya, *Reminiscences*, p. 22.

37 *CW*, vol. 37, p. 72.

38 Baron, *Plekhanov*, p. 155.

39 *Perepiska G. V. Plekhanova i P. B. Akselroda*, pp. 269–70.

40 *CW*, vol. 37, p. 73.

41 *CW*, vol. 37, p. 75.

42 Loc. cit.

43 *CW*, vol. 34, pp. 20–22.

44 For the police evidence against the group, see *Peterburgskie gody*, chapters 5 and 6 *passim*.

45 *CW*, vol. 37, p. 81.

3 Prison and exile

46 Krupskaya, *Reminiscences*, p. 28.

47 Ibid., p. 29.

48 Harding (ed.), *Marxism in Russia*, p. 162.

49 Getzler, *Martov*, p. 32.
50 P. N. Lepishinsky in *VVIL*, vol. 1, p. 68.
51 *CW*, vol. 37, pp. 121–2.
52 Krupskaya, *Reminiscences*, p. 33.
53 *CW*, vol. 37, p. 97.
54 *CW*, vol. 37, p. 111.
55 *CW*, vol. 37, p. 133.
56 *CW*, vol. 37, p. 158.
57 *CW*, vol. 37, p. 196.
58 *CW*, vol. 37, p. 572.
59 Krupskaya, *Reminiscences*, p. 38.
60 Ibid., p. 42.
61 *CW*, vol. 37, p. 563.
62 *CW*, vol. 37, p. 212.
63 *CW*, vol. 34, pp. 32–7 and 262.
64 *CW*, vol. 34, pp. 219–20.
65 *CW*, vol. 37, pp. 281–2.

4   **Bolsheviks and Mensheviks**

66 Lydia Dan, in Haimson (ed.), *The Mak-
    ing of Three Russian Revolutionaries*,
    p. 116.
67 'How *Iskra* Was Nearly Extinguished',
    CW, vol. 4, pp. 333–49. Service, *Lenin*,
    pp. 80–88.
68 *CW*, vol. 36, p. 37.
69 Lydia Dan, p. 109.
70 *CW*, vol. 37, p. 323.
71 Krupskaya, *Reminiscences*, p. 50.
72 *CW*, vol. 37, pp. 603–4.
73 *CW*, vol. 37, pp. 327–8.
74 *CW*, vol. 37, pp. 334–5.
75 Krupskaya, *Reminiscences*, pp. 58–9.
76 Boris Nicolaevsky, in Haimson (ed.), *The
    Making of Three Russian Revolution-
    aries*, p. 242.
77 Krupskaya, *Reminiscences*, p. 53.
78 *CW*, vol. 34, p. 103.
79 *CW*, vol. 36, p. 112.
80 *1903 Second Congress of the Russian
    Social Democratic Labour Party*, p. 220.
    Service, *Lenin*, p. 102.
81 Getzler, *Martov*, p. 79.
82 I. Deutscher, *The Prophet Armed*, p. 90.
83 Valentinov, *Encounters with Lenin*,
    chapter 6 *passim*.

5   **Dress rehearsal**

84 *Revolyutsiya 1905–1907gg v Rossii*, vol.
    1, pp. 28–9.
85 *CW*, vol. 8, p. 71.
86 *CW*, vol. 8, pp. 143–7.
87 *CW*, vol. 9, pp. 344–6.
88 I. Deutscher, *Stalin*, p. 90.
89 *CW*, vol. 11, pp. 171–8.

90 Gorky, *Days with Lenin*, p. 21.
91 Ibid., pp. 12–13. Service, *Lenin*, pp.
    165–8.
92 *CW*, vol. 37, pp. 368–9.

6   **Return to the wilderness**

93 Krupskaya, *Reminiscences*, p. 148.
94 Kolakowski, *Main Currents of Marxism*,
    vol. 2, p. 448.
95 *CW*, vol. 34, p. 387.
96 Gorky, *Days with Lenin*, p. 13.
97 *CW*, vol. 15, pp. 358–9.
98 Weber, p. 62.
99 Lydia Dan, *The Making of Three Rus-
    sian Revolutionaries*, p. 111.
100 Weber, p. 72.
101 The minutes of the debates, thought to
    have been lost, were recently published
    in the Soviet journal, *Historical Ques-
    tions of the Communist Party of the
    Soviet Union* (*Voprosi Istorii KPSS*),
    nos. 5 and 7, May and July 1988.
102 *CW*, vol. 18, pp. 102–9.
103 I. Deutscher, *Stalin*, pp. 123–4.
104 *CW*, vol. 35, p. 56 and *passim*.
105 T. Deutscher, *Not By Politics Alone*,
    p. 62.
106 *CW*, vol. 37, pp. 479–80.
107 *CW*, vol. 34, p. 131.
108 *CW*, vol. 35, p. 112.
109 Ibid., p. 108.
110 *Pravda*, no. 164, 9 November 1912.
111 *CW*, vol. 18, pp. 163–9.
112 *CW*, vol. 35, pp. 67–8.
113 *CW*, vol. 18, pp. 449 et seq.
114 T. Deutscher, *Not By Politics Alone*,
    p. 165.
115 *CW*, vol. 37, pp. 502–3.
116 Ettinger, *Rosa Luxemburg*, p. 93.
117 *CW*, vol. 43, pp. 390–1.
118 *CW*, vol. 35, pp. 135–6.
119 *CW*, vol. 43, pp. 402–3.
120 Shub, *Lenin*, p. 152.
121 *CW*, vol. 43, pp. 409–10.
122 *CW*, vol. 43, pp. 417–20.
123 T. Deutscher, *Not By Politics Alone*,
    p. 104.
124 *CW*, vol. 43, pp. 423–5.

7   **From war to revolution**

125 Zinoviev, *N. Lénine*, p. 25.
126 Balabanov, *Impressions of Lenin*, p. 35.
127 Ibid., p. 40.
128 T. Deutscher, *Not By Politics Alone*,
    pp. 211–15.

129 Loc. cit.
130 Trotsky, *My Life*, p. 258.
131 Krupskaya, *Reminiscences*, p. 267.
132 See Krupskaya's letter to Manyasha, in *CW*, vol. 37, pp. 624–5.
133 Krupskaya, *Reminiscences*, pp. 278–9.
134 *CW*, vol. 35, pp. 259–61.
135 *CW*, vol. 23, pp. 236–53.

8 The road to power

136 *CW*, vol. 35, p. 302.
137 Krupskaya, *Reminiscences*, p. 295.
138 Payne, *Life and Death of Lenin*, pp. 310–12.
139 Loc. cit.
140 'April Theses', *CW*, vol. 24, pp. 19–26.
141 *CW*, vol. 25, pp. 15–28.
142 On the newspaper response, see Rabinowitch, *The Bolsheviks Come to Power*, pp. 17–18.
143 On Kollontai's experience, see Clements, *Bolshevik Feminist*, p. 98.
144 *Leninskii Sbornik*, no. 4, p. 319.
145 Rabinowitch, p. 109. Also Daniels, *Red October*, pp. 46–7.
146 Daniels, p. 48.
147 *CW*, vol. 26, pp. 19–22.
148 Rabinowitch, p. 193.
149 Daniels, p. 78.
150 Daniels, p. 96.
151 Reed, *Ten Days That Shook The World*, p. 82.
152 Rabinowitch, p. 265.
153 Rabinowitch, p. 272.
154 Reed, pp. 98–9.
155 Ibid., p. 100.
156 Rabinowitch, p. 196.
157 Ibid., p. 303.

9 Dictatorship of the proletariat

158 T. Deutscher, *Not By Politics Alone*, p. 203.
159 Ibid., pp. 90–2.
160 Hosking, *A History of the Soviet Union*, p. 74. On Sovdepia, Mawdsley, *The Russian Civil War*, pp. 70–85.

161 *CW*, vol. 29, pp. 146–64.
162 *CW*, vol. 44, *passim*.
163 Rigby, *Lenin's Government*, p. 68.
164 Rigby, p. 74.
165 *CW*, vol. 44 *passim*. Also vol. 29, pp. 387–91.
166 Carr, *The Bolshevik Revolution*, vol. 3, p. 116.
167 Balabanov, *Impressions of Lenin*, p. 71.
168 *CW*, vol. 44, *passim*.
169 Luckett, *The White Generals*, p. 318. On the campaigns, Mawdsley, *The Russian Civil War*, passim.
170 Tumarkin, *Lenin Lives!*, p. 100.
171 Weber, *Lenin: Life and Works*, pp. 168–9.
172 Ficher, *Lenin*, pp. 403–14.
173 Article by M. Futrell, *The Blackwell Encyclopedia of the Russian Revolution*, p. 274.
174 T. Deutscher, *Not By Politics Alone*, p. 181.
175 Ibid., pp. 174–5.
176 Ibid., pp. 178–9.
177 Weber, p. 167.
178 Tumarkin, *Lenin Lives!*, p. 106.
179 Balabanov, *Impressions of Lenin*, p. 15.
180 Weber, p. 175.
181 Carr, *The Bolshevik Revolution*, vol. 3, p. 192.
182 Hosking, *A History of the Soviet Union*, p. 101.
183 Schapiro, *The Communist Party of the Soviet Union*, p. 216.

10 *Leninu kaput*

184 Tumarkin, p. 115.
185 Weber, pp. 190–1.
186 Deutscher, *Stalin*, p. 219.
187 Lewin, *Lenin's Last Struggle*, p. 39.
188 Ibid., pp. 53–4.
189 Weber, p. 194.
190 Weber, p. 195.
191 'Better Fewer But Better', in Lewin, *Lenin's Last Struggle*, pp. 172–3.
192 Lewin, p. 101.
193 Weber, p. 197.

Bibliography

Ascher, A., *Pavel Axelrod and the Development of Menshevism*, Cambridge, Mass., Harvard University Press, 1972

Averbakh, M., 'Personal Memories of Lenin', *Labour Monthly*, 52 (4), April 1970

Babushkin, I. V., *Vospominaniya Ivana Vassilievicha Babushkina*, Moscow, 1955

Balabanov, Angelica, *Impressions of Lenin*, trans. Isotta Cesari, Ann Arbor, MI, University of Michigan Press, 1964

– *My Life as a Rebel*, London, Hamish Hamilton, 1938

Baron, Samuel H., *Plekhanov, the Father of Russian Marxism*, Stanford, Stanford University Press; London, Routledge and Kegan Paul, 1963

Baranov, I. (ed.), *The Ulyanov Family*, Moscow, 1969

Bergman, J., *Vera Zasulich: a Biography*, Stanford University Press, 1983

Biggart, J., 'Anti-Leninist Bolshevism: the Forward Group of the RSDRP', *Canadian Slavonic Papers*, no. 2, 1981

Carr, Edward Hallett, *The Bolshevik Revolution, 1917–1923*, 3 vols., London, Macmillan, 1953

Chernyshevsky, N., *What Is To Be Done?*, trans. Tucker and Turkevich, New York, Random House, 1961

Clements, B. E., *Bolshevik Feminist. The Life of Alexandra Kollontai*, University of Indiana Press, 1979

Cohen, Stephen F., *Bukharin and the Bolshevik Revolution. A Political Biography, 1888–1938*, London, Wildwood House, 1974

Crome, Dr Leonard, 'The Medical History of V. I. Lenin', *History of Medicine*, spring and summer, 1972

Daniels, R. V., *Red October*, New York, Scribners, 1967

Deutscher, Isaac, *Lenin's Childhood*, London, Oxford University Press, 1970

– *Stalin. A Political Biography*, London, Oxford University Press, 1949

– *Trotsky: The Prophet Armed*, London, Oxford University Press, 1954

Deutscher, Tamara (ed.), *Not By Politics Alone ... – The Other Lenin*, London, Allen & Unwin, 1973

Elwood, R. C., *Russian Social-Democracy in the Underground: A Study of the RSDLP in the Ukraine, 1907–1914*, Assen, 1974

– *Roman Malinovsky: A Life Without a Cause*, Newtonville, Mass., 1977

– (ed.) *All-Russian Conference of the Russian Social-Democratic Labour Party*, Kraus International

– 'Lenin's correspondence with Inessa Armand', *Slavonic and East European Review*, 65 (2), 1987

Ettinger, Elzbieta, *Rosa Luxemburg*, London, Pandora, 1988

Fischer, Louis, *The Life of Lenin*, London, Weidenfeld and Nicolson, 1965

Fitzpatrick, Sheila, *The Commissariat of Enlightenment, October 1917–1921*, Cambridge, Cambridge University Press, 1970

Frankel, Jonathan, 'Martov and Lenin', *Survey: A Journal of Soviet and East European Studies*, nos. 70, 71 (winter, spring 1969), pp. 202–6

Futrell, Michael, *Northern Underground. Episodes of Russian Revolutionary Transport and Communications through Scandinavia and Finland, 1863–1917*, London, Faber and Faber, 1963

Getzler, Israel, *Martov: A Political Biography of a Russian Social Democrat*, Cambridge, Cambridge University Press, 1967

Gleson, Abbott, *Young Russia: The Genesis of Russian Radicalism in the 1860s*, Chicago, University of Chicago Press, 1983

Gorky, Maxim, *Days With Lenin*, London, Martin Lawrence, 1932

Haimson, Leopold H., *The Russian Marxists and the Origins of Bolshevism*, Cambridge, Mass., Harvard University Press, 1955

– (ed.) *The Making of Three Russian Revolutionaries*, Cambridge, Cambridge University Press, 1987

Harding, Neil, *Lenin's Political Thought*, vols.1 and 2, London, Macmillan, 1977–81

– (ed.) *Marxism in Russia. Key Documents, 1879–1906*, London, Macmillan, 1982

Haupt, Georges and Marie, Jean-Jacques, *Makers of the Russian Revolution, Biographies of Bolshevik Leaders*, London, Allen & Unwin, 1974

Hill, Christopher, *Lenin and the Russian Revolution*, London, Hodder and Stoughton, 1947

Hill, Elizabeth and Mudie, Doris (eds.), *The Letters of Lenin*, London, Chapman and Hall, 1937

Hosking, Geoffrey, *A History of the Soviet Union*, London, Fontana/Collins, 1985

Katkov, George and Shukman, Harold, *Lenin's Path to Power: Bolshevism and the Destiny of Russia*, London, Macdonald; New York, American Heritage Press, 1971

Keep, J. L. H., *The Rise of Social Democracy in Russia*, Oxford, Oxford University Press, 1963

Kennan, George F., *Russia and the West under Lenin and Stalin*, London, Hutchinson, 1961

– *Soviet-American Relations, 1917–1920*, 2 vols., London, Faber and Faber, 1958

Kolakowski, L., *Main Currents of Marxism*, 3 vols., Oxford, Clarendon Press, 1978

Koltzov, M., 'The Last Journey', *Russian Information and Review*, vol. 4, no. 6, 9 February 1924

Krupskaya, Nadezhda K., *Reminiscences of Lenin*, London, Lawrence & Wishart, 1960

– *Vospominaniya o Lenine*, 2nd edition, Moscow, 1968

– *Lenin Through the Eyes of Lunacharsky*, Moscow, 1981

Lenin, V. I., *Polnoe sobranie sochinenii*, ed. I. Ya. Gladkov *et al.*, vols. 1–55, Moscow, 1958–65

– *Vladimir Ilich Lenin. Biogreficheskaya khronika*, ed. G. N. Golikov *et al.*, vols. 1–12, 1970–82

– *Collected Works*, 45 vols, Moscow, 1960–70; London, Lawrence & Wishart

Leninskii Sbornik, vol. 1 et seq., Moscow-Leningrad, starting 1924

Lewin, Moshe, *Lenin's Last Struggle*, trans. A. M. Sheridan Smith, London, Faber and Faber, 1969

Luckett, Richard, *The White Generals*, London and New York, Routledge & Kegan Paul, 1971

McCauley, Martin, *The Soviet Union since 1917*, London and New York, Longman, 1981

McNeal, Robert H., *Bride of the Revolution: Krupskaya and Lenin*, London, Gollancz, 1973

Mawdsley, Evan, *The Russian Civil War*, Boston, Allen & Unwin, 1987

Mendelsohn, E., *Class Struggle in the Pale: the Formative Years of the Jewish Workers' Movement in Tsarist Russia*, Cambridge, Cambridge University Press, 1970

Modern Encyclopedia of Russian and Soviet History, ed. J. L. Wieczynski, Gulf Breeze, Florida, Academic International Press

Molodoi Lenin: povest v dokumentakh i memuarakh, ed. A. I. Ivanskii, Moscow, 1964

Morgan, M. C., *Lenin*, London, Edward Arnold, 1971

Moscow Institute of Marxism-Leninism, *Reminiscences of Lenin by his Relatives*, Moscow, 1956

Muravyova, L. and Sivolap-Kaftanova, I., *Lenin in London*, Moscow, 1983

Naimark, N. M., *Terrorists and Social Democrats: The Russian Revolutionary Movement Under Alexander III*, Cambridge, Mass., Harvard University Press, 1983

1903 Second Congress of the Russian Social Democratic Labour Party, trans. Brian Pearce, London, New Park Publications, 1978

Payne, R., *The Life and Death of Lenin*, London, W. H. Allen, 1978

Pearson, Michael, *The Sealed Train*, London, Macmillan, 1975; New York, Putnam, 1975

Perepiska G.V. Plekhanova i P.B. Akselroda, vols. 1 and 2, Berlin, 1925

Pethybridge, Roger, *The Spread of the Russian Revolution. Essays on 1917*, London, Macmillan, 1972

Pipes, Richard, *Social Democracy and the St Petersburg Labor Movement, 1885–1897*, Cambridge, Mass., Harvard University Press, 1963

– *Struve: Liberal on the Left, 1870–1905*, Cambridge, Mass., Harvard University Press, 1970

'Protokoly VI (Prazhskoi) Vserossiiskoi Konferentsii RSDRP', *Voprosy istorii KPSS*, nos. 5, 7 (May and July, 1988)

Rabinowitch, Alexander, *The Bolsheviks Come to Power*, London, NLB, 1979

Reed, John, *Ten Days That Shook The World*, London, Penguin, 1977

Rigby, T. H., *Lenin's Government: Sovnarkom 1917–1922*, Cambridge, Cambridge University Press, 1979

Rogger, H., *Russia in the Age of Modernisation and Revolution, 1881–1917*, London and New York, Longman, 1984

Rothstein, A., *A House on Clerkenwell Green*, London, Lawrence & Wishart, 1966

Sablinsky, W., *The Road to Bloody Sunday. The Role of Father Gapon and the Assembly of Russian Factory Workers in the Petersburg Massacre of 1905*, Princeton, NJ, Princeton University Press, 1976

Schapiro, Leonard, *The Communist Party of the Soviet Union*, London, Eyre and Spottiswoode, 1970

– and Reddaway, Peter (eds.), *Lenin, the Man, the Theorist, the Leader, A Reappraisal*, London, Pall Mall Press, 1967

Schneidermann, J., *Sergei Zubatov and Revolutionary Marxism: the Struggle for the Working Class in Tsarist Russia*, Ithaca and London, Ithaca Press, 1976

Schorske, C. E., *German Social Democracy, 1905–1917*, New York, Harper Torchbooks, 1972

Senn, Alfred Erich, *The Russian Revolution in Switzerland, 1914–1917*, Madison, Milwaukee and London, University of Wisconsin Press, 1971

Service, R., *The Bolshevik Party in Revolution, 1917–1923*, London, Macmillan, 1979
– *Lenin: A Political Life*, vol. 1, London, Macmillan, 1985

Shub, D., *Lenin*, London, Penguin, 1966

Shwartz, S., *The Russian Revolution of 1905: the Workers' Movement and the Formation of Bolshevism and Menshevism*, Chicago University Press, 1967

Shukman, Harold, *Lenin and the Russian Revolution*, London, Batsford, 1966
– (ed.), *Blackwell Encyclopedia of the Russian Revolution*, Oxford, Blackwell, 1988

Solzhenitsyn, Alexander, *Lenin in Zurich*, London, The Bodley Head, 1966

Sukhanov, N. N., *The Russian Revolution 1917. A Personal Record*, ed. and trans. Joel Carmichael, London, Oxford University Press, 1955

Swain, G., *Russian Social Democracy in the Legal Labour Movement, 1906–14*, London, Macmillan, 1983

Szamuely, Tibor, *The Russian Tradition*, ed. Robert Conquest, London, Secker and Warburg, 1974

Theen, Rolf H. W., *Lenin*, Princeton, NJ, Princeton University Press, 1980
– *Lenin. Genesis and Development of a Revolutionary*, Princeton, NJ, Princeton University Press, 1979

Trotsky, Leon, *The History of the Russian Revolution*, trans. Max Eastman, 3 vols., London, Gollancz, 1932–3
– *My Life: An Attempt at an Autobiography*, London, Penguin, 1975
– *The Young Lenin*, trans. Max Eastman, ed. Maurice Friedberg, Newton Abbot, David and Charles, 1972

Tumarkin, Nina, *Lenin Lives! The Lenin Cult in Soviet Russia*, Cambridge, Mass., and London, Harvard University Press, 1983

Ulam, Adam B., *The Bolsheviks*, London, Collier Macmillan; New York, Macmillan, 1965

Valentinov, Nikolai (N. V. Volski), *The Early Years of Lenin*, trans. and ed. Rolf H. W. Theen, Ann Arbor, MI, University of Michigan Press, 1969
– *Encounters with Lenin*, trans. Paul Rosta and Brian Pearce, Oxford, Oxford University Press, 1968

Venturi, F., *The Roots of Revolution*, London, Weidenfeld & Nicolson, 1960

Vospominaniya o V. I. Lenine, vols. 1–5, Moscow, 1968–9

Walicki, A., *The Controversy Over Capitalism: Studies in the Social Philosophy of Russian Populism*, Oxford, Oxford University Press, 1969

Weber, Gerda and Hermann, *Lenin: Life and Works*, ed. and trans. Martin McCauley, London, Macmillan Chronology Series, 1980

Wildman, A. K., *The Making of a Workers' Revolution: Russian Social-Democracy, 1891–1903*, Chicago, 1967

Wolfe, Bertram D., *Three Who Made a Revolution. A Biographical History*, Boston, Beacon Press, 1955

Zeman, Z. A. B. and Scarlau, W. B., *The Merchant of Revolution: The Life of Alexander Israel Helphand (Parvus), 1867–1924*, Oxford, Oxford University Press, 1965

Zetkin, Clara, *Reminiscences of Lenin*, London, Modern Books, 1929

Zinoviev, G., *N. Lénine*, Paris, Librairie de l'Humanité, 1924

Index